Business Architecture

Collecting, Connecting, and Correcting the Dots

Roger Burlton, P.Eng., CMC

Technics Publications

TECHNICS PUBLICATIONS

TECHNOLOGY / LEADERSHIP

115 Linda Vista
Sedona, AZ 86336 USA
https://www.TechnicsPub.com

Edited by Jamie Hoberman
Cover design by Lorena Molinari

ISBN, print ed.   9781634629706
ISBN, Kindle ed. 9781634629713
ISBN, ePub ed.   9781634629720
ISBN, PDF ed.   9781634629737

Library of Congress Control Number: 2021947337

To Sasha Aganova, my business partner in Process Renewal Group, who for the past ten years has diligently worked with me to enhance our methods, challenged me to continue to grow, inspired me to keep innovating, and supported me every step of the way. We have come a long way together and there is more to come.

Contents

About the Author

Roger T. Burlton, P.Eng. and CMC, is the founder of Process Renewal Group, a consulting and training organization he founded in 1993. He is an industry pioneer in Business Process Management (BPM) and Business Architecture, having established many industry methods and techniques now commonly found in practice in organizations worldwide. In addition, Roger is a respected thought leader, practitioner, and coach, helping companies and governments with strategic methods for improving business performance.

Roger has been instrumental in advancing the maturity of hundreds of organizations in a wide variety of industries. His successes cover pioneering contributions to Enterprise BPM (1991), Knowledge Management (1997), Stakeholder Relationship Management (1994), Strategic Alignment (1993), People-centric Project Management (1980), and Prototyping and Rapid Systems Development (1984). In addition, he has recently become a leading global figure in Cross-Functional Business Architecture (2009).

Roger has conceived and continues to be chair of several globally leading industry events, including Enterprise Architecture and BPM Europe (for over 15 years), Building Business Capability (for over ten years), and others in

Scandinavia, Europe, the Middle East, Australia, and China. He has also taught over three hundred and fifty hands-on sessions for tens of thousands of practitioners and managers globally. Roger, moreover, is a seasoned practitioner, having worked with more than two hundred clients.

Roger authored the industry bestseller, *Business Process Management: Profiting from Process,* in 2001. His work appeared in several other industry journals and books, including the *Handbook on Business Process Management,* and his monthly column on Business Architecture at BPTrends.com. He was the leader of the global effort that produced the *Business Process Manifesto*—now in 14 languages. He was also a co-author of the *Business Agility Manifesto* with John Zachman and Ronald Ross and *Self-Management Principles* with Sasha Aganova and Doug Kirkpatrick.

He graduated with B.A.Sc. in Industrial Engineering from the University of Toronto and is a certified Professional Engineer. Recently, Roger has returned to his alma mater to teach new Industrial Engineers to apply business architecture and improvement methods in an uncertain and real business world so they can connect the dots themselves.

Acknowledgments

The approaches and ideas reflected within this book result from evolution built upon the great work of others.

First of all, I have had the honor and pleasure of working closely with Paul Harmon, the Executive Editor of BPTrends. Paul and I have had many discussions over the years, and several of the diagrams in this book are to his credit. Paul constantly challenged me, and together we have created refined ways of tackling some tough issues.

I also wish to thank others who have been continuing collaborators in the journey, providing critical feedback and innovative insights that have found their way into many of our practices. Gilles Morin, Alex Aganov, Alex Mello, Brent Sabean, Adriana Debska-Gil, Sandra Foster, Li Yang, and Tim Evans have not been reluctant to make the methods better based on their application of the approaches in practice. Alex Sharp, Roger Tregear, Louise Harris, Ron Ross, and John Zachman have all been strong influencers on my thinking from the perspective of professional practices related to Business Architecture in ways that have enriched the framework.

I must also acknowledge my clients, who have been a significant source of knowledge, bringing various methods and a grounding in reality to ensure what this book is promoting is practical and valuable. The trust they have placed in this way of working has been a welcome validation of the advice I am advocating.

Lastly, I would like to acknowledge Angie Burlton and the rest of my family for their understanding, support, and patience over the years to make it possible to pursue my passion, which has led to getting this book produced.

Introduction

Business architect mindset

In 2001, I wrote a book entitled *Business Process Management: Profiting from Process*. It sold well and helped many organizations and professionals (so they have told me) to grasp the professional aspects of managing value-creating business processes from an enterprise-wide perspective. It introduced new concepts such as process architecture, process enablers and guides, and the perpetual active management of processes beyond simple process improvement. It helped put the M in BPM.

In my professional consulting practice since then, I have conducted hundreds of projects in a wide range of industries and countries based on the principles and practices of the approaches that the original book espouses. Along the way, with the constant application of the methods, new ideas have emerged and have proven themselves. This evolution in approach has seen incorporating additional domains of interest when dealing with business design. Business decisions and rules, information/data management, organization design, and business capabilities are all nowadays spoken about when discussing processes to make for a more holistic view of what makes a business tick. In addition, other professional practices have emerged that have made our professional practices richer, emphasizing various concerns such as customer journeys, personas and experience, business risk and regulatory compliance, and business agility.

As architects, we have had to be adaptable enough to remain relevant to the numerous changing interests under new business scenarios, morphing stakeholders' needs, and outside business drivers. This has led most process architects to incorporate other business domains into their practice, and many have become complete business architects offering a wide range of interrelated services.

In parallel with the maturing of business process architecture, a broadening view of the perspectives of Enterprise Architecture (EA) has occurred. Originally very focused on the IT concerns of application system functionality, databases, networks, and IT infrastructure, EA practitioners have realized that without a strong alignment to measurable business value, the business will never view them as strategic partners. They will be under constant pressure to justify what they do. This pressure has led many enterprise architects to look upstream and search for evidence of strategic traceability and business justification for their models they build. Consequently, EA models have gradually incorporated business and operational perspectives in addition to IT ones.

While all of this has been happening, executives have been wondering why it is that more than half the time, their apparently great strategic planning has not yielded the promised return on investment made in business cases. Despite spending fortunes on new business models, major transformation programs, customer experience roadmaps, and digital solutions, outcomes remain disappointing. This is especially painful for business leadership teams since external business threats and opportunities are arriving fast with potentially devastating effects if they are not addressed quickly and effectively, sometimes risking the survival of the leaders and even the enterprise itself.

Those responsible in each of these camps are now striving to paint a more complete picture. Many use the term 'Business Architecture' to describe what they are trying to do to 'connect the dots.' The challenge is that each comes with a different mindset and is often unknowingly constrained in perspective and positioning. For example, business architects from IT-centric EA backgrounds see things differently than strategic planners from the business. Business process-centric business architects will typically focus on the operational work of the business and its performance because that is what, traditionally, they have had to design, measure, and manage. IT-centric EAs may focus on shared technical capabilities because they have to build them.

Over these last years, many peers and clients encouraged me to articulate how all this comes together. I can assure you that this has not been easy. There have been several tribal battles over varying perspectives, with each methodological camp standing its ground. Harmonizing these was not easy, but I have not been deterred and feel that the time is right for a more encompassing point of view. My experience has been that an appropriate mix of all viewpoints is needed, tailored to each challenge at hand. That is what I see as *Business Architecture* and what I will cover in this book.

Target audience

Every organization has some degree of architectural practice underway. Their starting point and their recipes will vary somewhat. All also have a number of common philosophies and artifacts that I will address. Some domains of primary interest will differ from one to another. That means that this book should be of interest to a range of professionals, such as:

- Business process architects wanting to broaden their point of view and be able to assure that processes execution is aligned to the strategic intent of the business and traceable to external stakeholder value creation. They will need to be able to articulate the many-to-many relationships among business processes, business information, and business capabilities—especially for the reuse of capabilities across multiple processes.

- Enterprise architects that want to enable true business effectiveness and not just focus on the artifacts or models for the building of systems and IT infrastructure usage. They wish to associate IT solutions (applications and microservices/APIs) to the processes that need to use them. Also, they need to be able to connect IT solutions back to the business problems they are intended to solve or business opportunities they can exploit.

- Current business architects that want to better connect all the domains that they are tackling and finding the interrelatedness among them including value streams, business capabilities, business information, and the like, and be better able to recommend a traceable portfolio of change initiatives that delivers business value cross-functionally and best utilizes the set of scarce resources (human and financial) available to implement change.

- Business analysts (BAs) responsible for holistic Business Design seeking to step up their career to take on a wider set of business issues in analyzing more broadly scoped programs. This is a natural progression towards becoming a senior BA with greater knowledge of the business overall and competency in a number of additional BA techniques that they can apply to scale up to enterprise-wide challenges.

- Enterprise leaders who wish to discover how to lead the journey of transformation to a more responsive and agile business in the face of never-ending pressure and the constant need for change.

Point of view

My perspective will be somewhat wider than many conducting this type of work. I include more than a set of models for information, processes (value streams), and capabilities in a business architecture discipline. I also include strategy issues, including ecosystem assessment and external stakeholder analysis. For me, a business architecture must also deal with performance and the performance structure of the enterprise or value chains in scope. A business architecture is so much more than a set of capabilities that IT professionals must build. As Figure I-1 shows, IT must enable and deliver new abilities and ways of working to keep the enterprise relevant and sustain its success operationally in all aspects of change and not just technology.

Business Strategy **(Aim)**   Business Information **(Know)**   Business Performance **(Optimize)**

Business Processes **(Do)**   Business Capabilities **(Build)**

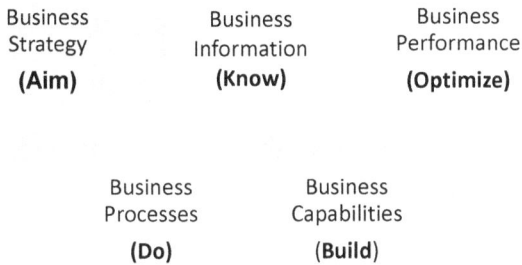

Figure I-1. IT must adapt.

There are clearly many things we need to understand to be useful business architects. Some time ago, I was sitting outside on a beautiful day at a conference venue for an event that I was chairing overlooking Darling Harbour in Sydney, Australia. In discussion with other conference speakers—and after several beers—we discussed what makes a good business architecture. The consensus was that 'connecting the dots' was critical due to needing to understand the impact of a potential change in any item on everything else in play. I commented that to 'connect the dots,' we would have to 'collect the dots' first or we just have a blank page, and no useful drawing could be established or shared. It would be like developing the solution without knowing the need. That launched a search for similar words—remember it was a group of nerds after several drinks—but we could only come up with one more, and that was 'correct the dots.'

We were very proud of ourselves, so we ordered another round of drinks. That was the source of the credo I have used ever since and how the book got its name. Each of these practices will show up as I tackle the various domains of business architecture in the following chapters. Sometimes we will collect all then connect. Sometimes we can work in a defined scope and connect as we go in an agile and iterative learning cycle.

We will always try to correct once we have enough knowledge to proceed. All three phases will be discussed along the way in a logical order, although that order is fluid based on the need at hand. I will talk about the reason for business architecture first. A business architecture will be inevitable for organizations to survive as pressures to respond to real-world conditions accelerate.

Topics

The book will follow the structure described below.

In the first section, I will deal with the foundational issues upon which business architecture depends. Chapter 1 will get us started by looking at the pressures facing our businesses today and those that we may anticipate seeing in the future. These are mostly from the external world—our ecosystem. These certainties and uncertainties force us to be constantly vigilant and ready to change and drive the need for business architecture. Chapter 2 will examine the heritage of business architecture methods and practices since most aspects have been around in some form or fashion for some time. It is useful to know their perspective – some would say their bias. It will also introduce our business architecture landscape that assembles the various points of view. This framework structure is the focus of the remainder of the book. Chapter 3 will help you establish the scope of your architecture and identify the lines of business that you will take on. In doing so, it will introduce the concept of value chains within which our value streams will be found.

The second section will focus on gathering the critical knowledge needed—Collecting the Dots. Chapter 4 will examine the ecosystem of the organization and value chains in scope. Chapter 5 will enable you to derive the guidance and decision criteria needed from the business strategy to make later investment and design choices. Through establishing a business concept model, Chapter 6 will help you develop the semantic baseline to assure a common language going forward. Chapter 7 will introduce the techniques required to establish your process architecture, including connecting your value chains with value streams, stages, and business processes. Chapter 8 will help you to establish your business capability map. These chapters gather and validate the building blocks of a sound architectural framework.

The third section will show you how to identify the interconnections we have collected—Connecting the Dots. Chapter 9 will include establishing a robust Business Performance Measurement structure. In Chapter 10, we will connect and align the architectural domains collected earlier.

In the last section, we start the journey of Correcting the Dots by prioritizing change in Chapter 11 and building the change portfolio in Chapter 12. In the last chapter, I will present examples of the need for tackling Business Architecture from a pragmatic point of view that emphasizes needed variability in how the dots get connected. We have to be relevant and solve real problems and in Chapter 13, I present the case and thinking needed.

CHAPTER 1

Pressures on Businesses

When I wrote my original book in 2001,[1] I described the pressures organizations were facing and the rationale for taking change seriously. In going back to read that chapter, I was amazed to see that there were many of the same challenges then as now. There are new ones that have emerged, of course, and some pressures have not changed much in nature but have in intensity. That has led me to conclude that many of these ecosystem drivers are maybe with us perpetually. They have become a fundamental characteristic of the new era of fast-paced constant change in the market. The difference seems to be in their concentration and the accelerated need to tackle them in very short order as they pop up.

One of the companies that I wrote about in 2001 had just successfully navigated the pressure of successfully implementing cross-functional operations with a better

---

[1] Burlton, Roger (2001). Business Process Management: Profiting From Process (1st ed.). Sam's Publishing.

connection to its external stakeholders due to well-connected thinking and establishing knowledge of all the moving parts to step up to a new level of performance. Since then, they have had to do it two more times due to marketplace and strategic choice, each time successfully, but each time building on their retained baseline of aligned knowledge and leveraging a culture that understands that nothing is permanent.

Each time, they faced challenges of the marketplace and competitive change, new products into the market, new ways of reaching customers, competitor acquisition, and integration. Each time, within five years, they doubled their business from the previous level of performance while also generating profit and cash to pay for the acquisitions and transformation. Their ability to repeatedly carry out integration and transformation is now a core competency of the enterprise, making them hard to catch.

This current chapter examines some of the most pressing of today's business drivers—old and new. I will show that managing your processes and capabilities constantly to stay connected to your strategy—and not just when there is a problem—is a key factor in navigating the difficult transitions that arise.

Your enterprise's specific responses to these drivers will vary depending on its mission, value proposition, and current situation in the marketplace. However, your enterprise cannot ignore these pressures for change. Change is not an option—you will change whether you like it or not, for better or worse.

Your business architecture will become an essential asset to make sound decisions on reconfiguring your path forward.

Return on Investment (ROI)

Repeating the message from my book, *Business Process Management: Profiting from Process*, enterprises expect to receive a fair return on their investments when they commit to change. These investments pay off in terms of business performance results as shown in Figure 1-1.

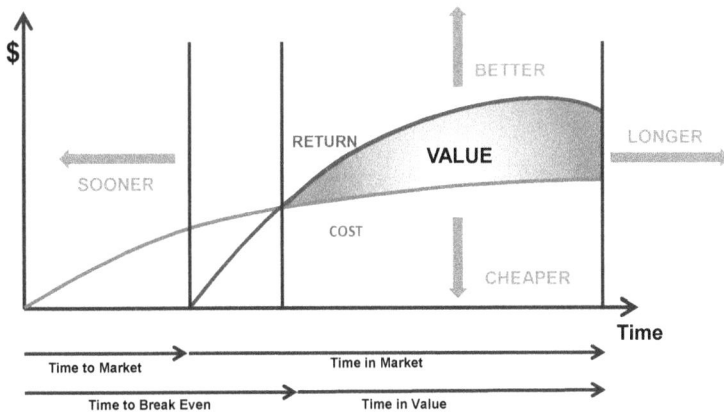

Figure 1-1. The challenge for executives everywhere, independent of organization type (pro-profit, non-for-profit, or public) and industry.

A change leads to a new organizational capability. This can be in the form of new products and services that allow the organization to better meet its mandate. After spending time and money and utilizing other resources, the capability is ready for use—this time is called *time to market*. The organization then realizes the benefits of its investments and, at some point, hopefully, reaches the break-even point, when the accumulated investments and operating costs are exceeded by the contribution made through the availability of the product, service, or capability. I will refer to this point as the *time to ROI (Return on Investment)*.

The enterprise then continues to reap the rewards until the product reaches the end of its useful life and is retired or renewed. The positive return occurs unless it never gets to market, or the contribution does not catch up to the investment and cost line when products miss the mark or projects fail.

Competition and external (and possibly also internal) factors make it more difficult to achieve the ROI expected for several reasons. Traditionally we would have tried to reduce cost (be cheaper). This choice was widespread in the last century but is not as prevalent now as time to market becomes a bigger factor due to the shrinking of market time, robbing the organization of sufficient opportunity to recover investments that took too long and cost too much. Better products, services, and capabilities will deliver more uptake on the top line (be better), but not if competitors beat you to market.

The problem in this chart is that if everything we do is fast but not designed for reuse or ease of change, then the time to market will always be slower as the pressure grows to deliver sooner because there is nothing to reuse or leverage. If business designs and capability delivery are not well-architected, the obsolescence date will arrive too early. If well-architected, the business solution can stay relevant (stay in the market longer).

A traditional response by organizations has been to conduct weak strategic planning by doing analyses like SWOT (strengths, weaknesses, opportunities, and threats). With this approach, organizations typically proceed directly from a weakness and start up an isolated project to strengthen it or, from an opportunity, build a specific, sometimes disconnected, capability to exploit it. These types of approaches are reactive and devoid of real aligned strategy formulation from an enterprise perspective. Historically, many organizations have attained the terrible legacy of multiple databases with the same data types in them but with no integrity, and disparate websites with conflicting or confusing styles and messages. Today, these approaches are insufficient because they miss the reuse of capabilities defined by a sound business architecture. The dots are not connected, so the impact of change is unknown until unintended consequences show up later.

A business architecture that identifies changes in the business model, stakeholders, processes, capabilities, and organizations, and links them to the products and services of the organization are now very much the starting focus. Many organizations align these elements to their IT architectures. Ideally, organizations will close the loop through a never-ending learning cycle that feeds back to strategic planning and architecture in near real-time.

Monitoring progress against planned program initiatives and measuring business performance on an ongoing basis allows organizations to reset priorities periodically and realistically.

Designing for agility

There was less intense competition in the industrial era, so a longer time to market was not as much an issue as nowadays. In Figure 1-2, in the bottom left, we had standard products with standard work methods and operating procedures and standard jobs that did not change much over time. This scenario also witnessed a hierarchical command and control organizational structure and did not require many workers to think, create, and problem-solve—just to do.

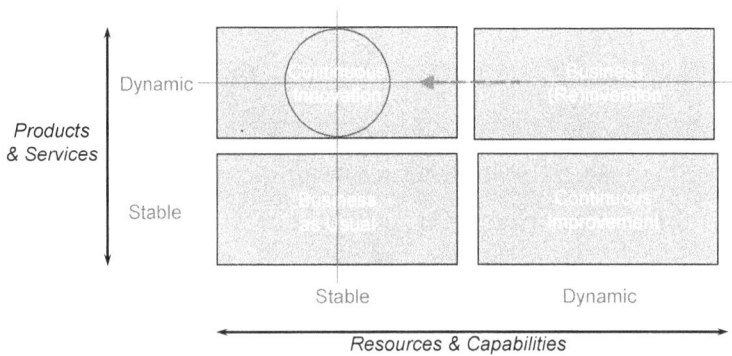

Figure 1-2. The classic approach was to build products and
   capabilities concurrently in the top right corner and throw them
   over to the bottom left once a new idea was ready.

With the advent of quality management and the likes of
Deming[2] and Crosby[3] the drive was towards better, faster,
and cheaper, as shown in the bottom right corner. This
approach did not challenge the assumption that the
products and services needed to be swapped out or retired
quickly as intentions changed. Working in this quadrant,
at its best, would not naturally lead to dynamic products
and services getting to market. Clearly, the payoff for
today's businesses is to make the right changes fast and
keep things easy. For that, it is essential to build the

---

[2] Deming, W. Edwards (2012). The Essential Deming: Leadership
   Principles from the Father of Quality (1st ed.). McGraw-Hill Education.

[3] Crosby, Philip B. (1979). Quality Is Free: The Art of Making Quality
   Certain: How to Manage Quality - So That It Becomes A Source of
   Profit for Your Business (1st ed.). McGraw-Hill Education.

business, its products, services, and capabilities, to be inherently adaptable, and to do so without having to tear apart previous designs and start over each time. In other words, design for continuous fundamental change beyond continuous improvement. The goal should be to live in the top left quadrant. This does not happen by accident.

It requires careful consideration of how we can restructure what we build as soon as it has to be reconfigured.

For me, this is the real payoff from business architecture. By doing so, we can identify configurable components (collect the dots) and trace the impact of a suggested change of any one of them on all the others (connect the dots) and thus avoid surprises later.

Drivers

Today, we must be ready for several critical drivers:

- Intensified competition
- Individualization at scale
- Commoditization of products and services
- Digitalization and omnichannel
- Industry concentration and scale
- Collaborations and extended value chains
- Customer focus

Intensified competition

Competition is more aggressive, comes from surprising and nontraditional industries, from those big and small, from inside and outside your industry, and from far and near. The tearing down of barriers allows new entrants into traditional markets more easily and plays havoc with the old rules. However, there is not a sole pattern to copy. Innovation comes from everyone and everywhere.

It can come from big players who have the resources to experiment, fail, and try something new and morph into another market. Amazon's start in books quickly became all consumer products, branched into delivery services, now threatening their own suppliers who have to compete with Amazon in their own markets. They now generate significant revenue through Amazon Web Services (AWS), their cloud services business. They became very good in cloud services for themselves, and then recognized a market opportunity due to this strength.

National retailers will typically focus on products from the top national brands. So, the large suppliers get better access to markets than the small players. An example is Mars, Inc.'s acquisition of Wrigley, giving them a stronger presence with supermarkets and more bargaining power. Acquisition is a common strategy for suppliers to try to build scale. Scalability is also apparent at the consumer front line, as seen by Amazon's acquisition of Whole

Foods. Few people saw that coming, but now the integration and synergies of each are threatening incumbent local grocers who are unsure what's next for them.

Larger competitors, such as Amazon, who know what they are doing, are playing harder than ever before. Many players are broadening their position in the economy and taking over a larger and larger share of markets. Many are driving out unresponsive incumbents who are too slow to adapt to consumer expectations of simple and easy experiences.

This does not mean that small players cannot win. The economy is full of examples where an upstart disrupted the marketplace and wounded the big players with better products and services and customer experience, gradually draining the life out of the previous winners. Digital upstarts can gain market share when the incumbent does not have the vision and guts to disrupt themselves quickly enough or cannot make a difficult large-scale transformation in time.

Opportunity still exists if you can be nimble enough or offer unique products and experiences. If local knowledge is critical and differentiation is valued, locals can win. Being able to move fast as a local can have distinct advantages. The explosion of micro-breweries as a local phenomenon has dug deeply into the international breweries business due to their ability to have variety, specialization, freshness, seasonal menus, appeal of environmental sustainability, weekly features, and match with local chefs' new food choices or a specialized food truck outside. This is not your traditional national pub chain or restaurant. No one micro-brewery had the ability do it alone but together they can. In Vancouver, Canada, where I live, there are currently 70 such establishments listed as making their own, often innovative and interesting brews. The incumbents don't stand a chance unless they acquire their more nimble upstarts.

Competition can also come from afar, and incumbents often do not see it coming. By the time it shows up, it's a powerful tsunami that is impossible to hold off. An example is a strong service in some geographies but relatively unknown elsewhere. Many of us are very familiar with What's App (from Facebook) and use it often to have simple asynchronous encrypted communication with our friends, families, and confidants. In China, the monster-sized equivalent with over 1 billion users (at the time of writing) is 'WeChat' from Tencent. This app is now showing up around the world, and one of its components, 'WePay' digital wallet service, can be seen in cities worldwide. What is the future of this new (to the western world) service versus other social platforms and payment systems markets for incumbents like Apple, Google, and the like, who are already disrupting traditional credit card companies, payment services, and banking organizations? We can be sure that we will import a lot more disruption. Potentially a company could also export and be the disruptors. For sure, it will be different, but how?

Individualization at scale

As discussed earlier, products and services don't remain constant for very long anymore. In the 20th century, it wasn't unusual to expect a new product or service to remain fairly consistent for many years. Since the nineteen nineties especially, the in-market time, or product life, has continued to shrink. Products and services can now last for months, not for years. The Industrial Revolution model of invest, invent, and mass produce for a long time is no longer valid.

At the extreme, it means that every instance of a service or product configuration can potentially be unique, whereby customers receive tailored, individualized treatment. Strangely enough, in looking at this extreme, the need arises for some sort of higher-level stability because it's clear that we can't reconfigure our work methods every time a customer places an order at scale unless we have built for that. The trick is to design, develop, and implement innately adaptable and scalable capabilities, whereby variations are called upon at each transaction level.

Facilities, technologies, and people must deliver results, each of which might be different every time out. Looking at Mars-Wrigley again, M&Ms contained defined colors and pack sizes and configurations for a long time. Now I can go to mms.com and order specific colors, images, and words for what I want in and on an M&M and have my unique order shipped the next day to my home. Nike does the same for sports shoes. In both cases, the capability was built to deliver any configuration that the customer would choose. It is hard for a small-scale organization to replicate this without significant order lead time and cost.

This evolution strongly impacts how we set up our organizations and build our capabilities. Some of the requirements are:

- To adopt a customer and process focus, not a product specification one, because the product will vary

- To design products and services as basic, customizable modules that can evolve and change independently

- To use adaptable technologies whose rules and workflows can be changed declaratively and instantly by customers or business people without programmers getting involved

- To focus on the continuous enhancement of the knowledge of workers

- To build flexible, responsive processes

Commoditization of products and services

In many industries, products and services look much alike. It's hard for individuals and organizations to pick and choose among them because their features are similar.

Most organizations have learned from one another and have incorporated the best features of others into their offerings.

In addition, many products work well enough for most customers, and added features seem to contribute marginally in terms of differentiation of value to most of them. Over time, there is less and less significance of new concepts or capabilities as many of these products mature. As a result, there is little to choose regarding demand accounts, loans, and mortgages from financial institutions. The difference seems to be in the level of trust, convenience, and the experience in transacting and less in the products themselves. Businesses that become commodity providers must make available relevant knowledge about their products and services to make it easy for customers to buy and use them with confidence.

Having painted an apartment during the initial COVID lockdown, I was appreciative of the instructions and tips from the paint manufacturer on how best to apply that type of paint, given that I am not a painting expert. I am sure that their paint was similar in quality to others', but their ability to help me get it right the first time through access to written instructions, pictures, and their YouTube channel was a good reason I got it done. I would trust them again.

Digitalization and omnichannel

Electronic delivery of products, services, and other customer interactions has an enormous effect on all organizations today. Service is available and business is transacted anywhere at any time. Nowadays, we expect organizations to be accessible everywhere all the time. As a marketplace supplier and customer, you can be in an electronic relationship with all of your stakeholders. Many businesses now conduct a high percentage of their transactions without human-to-human interaction. Some airlines only allow digital reservations, for example.

Digital business solutions can be more easily scaled upward to accommodate growth. Clearly, this type of interface is faster and cheaper than traditional "bricks and mortar" retailing, and many customers like it better because it is more convenient. However, digital technologies in and of themselves may not prove to be sufficient for all products, services, markets, and situations outside of a happy path.

The implications of digital business for organizations are significant. It means that processes must be cross-functional and work incredibly well since few human intermediaries can sort out all the variations outside the standard or happy path. Traditionally, an order placed by mail might take weeks to deliver. An order captured by an agent in a customer contact center will be faster. However, a digital order confirmation could be instantaneous. It always amazes me when ordering a product online on a weekend morning results in a same day knock on the front door – job done. Disconnected processes will be apparent right away in terms of failed performance, resulting in loss of customer loyalty. Seamless value streams are mandatory regardless of the organizational structure. This factor alone should be sufficient to convince an enterprise to organize and manage around processes that deliver direct value.

Digital alone is not necessarily the answer. There are many situations where a human can provide input or make a decision, and the customer may have to navigate several channels to complete their expectations. Hence, we see a great interest in an Omnichannel ability to provide extra value extending digital to greater possibilities and finding the opportunity to go beyond pure online services. This is not to be confused with multi-channel where the customer can choose which path to take and stick with one or another of digital online, mobile, customer contact center, voice response, or physical visit in an office. Instead, it is the ability to start in any channel and navigate through another in one seamless and consistent experience. For example, recently, I started a transaction online, hit a snag, and went to the call center to help me out, and we had to start all over again since there was no visibility to my online data. This is an example of multi- and not omnichannel.

Omnichannel always knows where you are or where you left off in the process and picks up from there. If I start work on my mobile device and get interrupted and later go to my online browser and keep going and find that I need to discuss with a live agent through a chat option, I can seamlessly. Mixing channels to the best effect is very valuable to many customers and knowing you can, if you need to switch, is a strong retention motivator. An omnichannel ability needs processes to be well understood and specific capabilities to be developed to assure that the steps along the way have integrity.

Digital and omnichannel require high data quality. Since customer and company data are created and used throughout the experience journey, design for single capture, common access, and security is essential. In addition, data must be the same throughout the digital experience and across omnichannel components of the service. This requires an architectural view of data and the processes, rules, and capabilities needed for end-to-end synchronization.

Industry concentration and scale

There is a clear trend within organizations that reflects the belief that bigger is better. The largest players often gobble up competition to gain efficiencies and cost advantages. Some do so to restrict competition and market access and get monopolistic price advantages. Others do so to access market share with customers that only wish to deal with the large suppliers. Regardless, the ability to do this globally can bring distinct benefits. Many management gurus have claimed that companies will need to choose to become truly global or just be a smaller focused niche player. They claim that there will be little in between.

As more organizations try to manage globally, they require their suppliers to do the same. For example, one of my clients is a significant supplier to Wal-Mart. The supplier's operations in different countries each had responsibility for its own national sales in the past. However, Wal-Mart Germany discovered that it could buy more cheaply from another European country operation and demanded the same pricing and terms from its supplier in Germany. This quickly escalated into treating Wal-Mart as one organization with a set of global terms. It also meant that the supplier organization's processes for sales and service had to change significantly from country-based to global customer-based. The supplier soon realized that, although it already was an international company with sales, manufacturing, and distribution all over the world, that didn't qualify it as a global supply entity. Working globally was quite different. The transition to truly behaving globally was even more difficult as they had to overcome constraining and misaligned homegrown systems and practices as well as incentives and cultures.

Likewise, a large bank with operations in more than 70 countries discovered that its clients wanted to be treated as one entity globally for many services. Although different central bank regulations governed every one of their country operations, customers wanted one deal globally. So instead of selling to the local country customer, a relationship was formed under the direction of a global relationship manager. This led to the philosophy of one global balance, one global credit limit, and one set of terms operating globally for real-time decision-making on decisions around credit worthiness and risk. The impact on processes was and still is widespread.

The changes in processing locations from country centers to global centers are having a large impact on staff and country power. The technological upheaval is significant. Despite the cultural implications, it must be done if the bank wants to compete against the other handful of banks that could succeed in treating global customers with a truly global service.

Consistent with these challenges is the need to have a set of capabilities that themselves are globally shared and a common set of value streams and, in many cases, the use of a common and often, one single instance of large technology ERP implementation. This architectural challenge is off the charts concerning complexity, risk, and change management globally. Globalization can be both a threat and an opportunity. After recognizing it, the biggest risk is to not go far enough in reconfiguring your internal capabilities because of compromises and internal power struggles.

Tied in with this trend is the seemingly unstoppable tidal wave of consolidations, mergers, and acquisitions. Of course, it's possible to win in acquisitions, but there must be a focus on integrating processes, data, and culture more than anything else. In addition, acquisition requires consolidation of work and assets, which require a business architecture blueprint to drive the transformation.

Collaborations and extended value chains

Closely related to the restructuring of business models associated with mergers and acquisitions and to the wave of digitalization of business is the significant number of new collaborations among parties serving the same market. Organizations have found that they can't meet higher customer expectations if they try to do everything on their own. Market leverage can only be attained by working together. It's an opportunity for incumbents to stay fresh through hot upstarts or innovative partners. For the upstart, it's a way to become exposed to a wider market. They couldn't scale to higher business volume levels if there were too much to build reach and capacity. For many, it's simply a matter of avoiding the risk of something new or unproven.

In any case, every organization must anticipate or respond to business events affecting customers and meet their expectations when they do.

Collaboration is required across internal and external corporate boundaries from the customer triggering event to their closing outcome. Processes must work on behalf of the end to end process customer regardless of internal or partnership structure. Information technology and device brands often don't make all or any of their own computers—they work with contract manufacturers. Most sellers of consumer goods do not tackle all outbound logistics themselves. They call upon FedEx or their local postal service. Many mutual-fund and insurance companies do not sell directly—they equip and train independent financial advisors and agents.

I recently worked with a transit service covering a province in Canada, whereby the transformation and supporting business architecture covered the scope of the corporation and local municipalities responsible for schedules, routes, and also with contracted bus operating companies. This had to be the case since a more effective citizen transit service would have to seamlessly integrate all three types of entities. Tackling each separately would have led to sub-optimization in the very best case and far worse in the worst case.

To do this effectively, organizations have to ask themselves what business they are really in. What is their value proposition to their customers and their customers' customers? What can they be good at, and what should they have others do on their behalf?

Some people might wonder what the difference is between real partnerships and traditional outsourcing. I believe that many well-conceived and executed outsourcing arrangements have all the hallmarks of true partnerships. The main one is that of trust among all the partners. In a partnership arrangement, all parties involved must have a shared interest and incentive in attaining the outcome of value to the ultimate customer. The business processes and architectural design to make this happen are shared as one.

Customer focus

Customers are getting smarter and perhaps less loyal more quickly. It is not possible to fool them anymore. They keep informed of products and the status of services. They know more about how to use your products and the nature of your business than ever before and will make choices based on that knowledge. They learn more quickly, so you must do the same to stay ahead. If you miss a market trend that they see and expect you to do business that way or provide new products you do not have yet, you will lose them. Your difficulty in staying with your customers' growing awareness is exacerbated by the shortening of business cycles that make it hard to stay relevant.

Along with customers' greater awareness has come a greater demand for responsiveness and a higher intolerance of lack of performance. Most customers want more choice and flexibility. Each customer wants service when he wants and in his own way, which might change from time to time. Many of these changes will require the supplier to take on responsibilities that it would not have done before. Inventory management, direct shipment, and customer support are examples of these responsibilities. Mass customization or individualization programs are expected. Many customers feel that they do not need an intermediary to initiate or provide service—they would prefer to help themselves directly with you.

Often, customers become caught in the time crunch where faster service is mandatory for their own customers and hence for them. Twenty-four-hour-a-day access is required because business never stops globally. Therefore, both physical and virtual access channels must be convenient.

Automating as much of the process as possible provides time savings for the participants in the business process. In addition, it allows fewer people to do the existing work or the same people to do more work.

For the reasons mentioned here, segmentation of customers and consumers is critical to understand each one better, serve them well, and assign staff with the right set of matched skills. It will save them and you time. Time is their scarcest resource and one that they can never get back. It's also yours, so be prepared to consider getting rid of those customers that don't warrant your effort. You can understand their end-to-end journey based on a set of representative personas described as user stories and ultimately a compendium of scenarios or epics. This is a useful way to make design decisions.

I had a client in Europe that manufactured drinks and drink machines. After careful segmentation, this company concluded that the top tiers of customers were those who bought the most repeatedly. They chose to continue to provide personal service to that top tier. However, the bottom tier contained many small customers who bought very little and required a lot of support to manage orders and deliver small amounts of supplies. They decided that the cost of supporting these customers was prohibitive relative to their bottom line contribution. Instead, it was recommended that individually licensed franchisees service this segment managing a defined local territory. The company would serve the franchisees with volumes consistent with their top segment customers.

Some customers demand that the organization take complete ownership of their entire set of needs and deal with all actions to deliver a consolidated result. Again, this will save time and worry. For example, travel services and websites that allow travelers to book all aspects of a trip are more valuable than those that separately or only handle car or limousine rental, hotel, or air travel. This total response is in the best interest of many customers, who do not want to deal with many people or technologies. One-stop shopping is in demand.

Customers' and consumers' needs are becoming more complex. These stakeholders are also less loyal when their needs are not met.

Summary

This chapter described some of the major pressures facing enterprises today. It looked at hyper-competition, growing organization complexity and reach, rising external stakeholder power, and digital technology. Each of these is changing the face of how business is transacted globally. There are many other considerations that an organization has to navigate, such as the need for agility in business, the scarcity of experienced resources, a number of social factors such as cancel culture, racial and gender challenges, environmental expectations of tackling climate change, and even politicization of sensitive issues and, of course, pandemics.

No organization is immune from these driving forces' changes, and your issues will likely be an interesting combination of such pressures. Regardless of what is most relevant and important, your business will be faced with anticipating and responding effectively and rapidly. Business architecture will be essential in all industry segments to anticipate and respond. Would it not be nice to know that your response will be based on understanding impacts on your ways of working and your capabilities before you act?

CHAPTER 2

Business Architecture Landscape

B usiness architecture is a meeting point for many perspectives of what an organization or some set of value-creating activities need to know to design, build, sustain, change, and optimally operate its business. When done well, it accommodates and aligns diverse interests. However, the reality is that there are many narrowly focused camps, each with its own view of what a business architecture should address. As discussed in the opening chapter, there are many opinions from specific types of professionals with a particular need at their core. The different professional backgrounds of their members bring different perspectives and biases.

My personal predisposition is a business one, not focusing on specific topics such as digital technologies in isolation of the other domains essential for alignment. For me, a business architecture is represented by a set of models, perhaps the most complex ones we could imagine, since together these should cover all relevant aspects of the whole business, including how it operates and what we need to design and change to keep it relevant.

Joe H. Ward and Earl Jennings, citing Russel Ackoff, said in 1973 that *'models are idealized in the sense that they are less complicated than reality and hence easier to use'*.[4] This is certainly true, but our business architectures comprise many interdependent parts that are still quite complex despite their abstract nature. Their many interacting components influence one another in mysterious ways that the architect must somehow unravel, interrogate, and communicate. It is an impossible journey for those who crave perfection and are not comfortable until they have indisputable detail.

In 1987, George Box said, "All models are wrong, but some are useful," and that is where I will strive to focus the chapters that follow. I will aim to be comprehensive and yet as pragmatic as possible, bringing useful experiences and insights gained from working on over 100 business-oriented efforts that have provided some key learnings about business design and architecture.

---

[4] Joe H. Ward, Earl Jennings (1973). Introduction to Linear Models. Prentice Hall.

Idea behind the architectural framework

Several years ago, I developed a simple two-by-two matrix of the challenges we face as architects. I called it the **Burlton NICE model** shown in Figure 2-1. It keeps me focused when I take on any new venture.

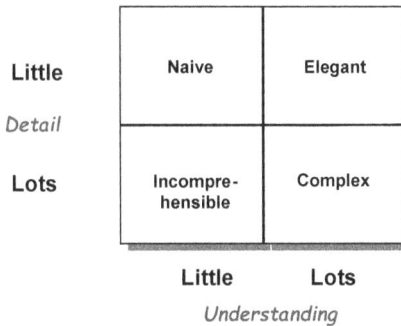

Figure 2-1. The Burlton NICE model.

We all usually start an initiative in the *Naïve* state where we do not have much detail about the effort (in this case, business architecture discovery). Still, we are characteristically delusional or optimistic at the beginning. The challenge does not seem all that difficult since everything makes so much sense logically, but we do not know what we do not know, so we must be cautious. Unfortunately, many executives seem to stay in this quadrant throughout and do not appreciate the challenge of sorting out the uncertainty and difficulty of the effort.

As architects and analysts, we typically tend to enthusiastically delve to the next level below, where we can easily end up with incredible amounts of detail but remain baffled by what we are tackling. We can quickly become overwhelmed knowing that we still do not know enough. It seems *Incomprehensible* and therefore impossible to communicate easily to others. We still have a low level of understanding despite a lot of work and documentation. Symptomatic of this level are the presence of many detailed and separate diagrams that are missing interconnections and contain confusing semantics. It is easy for architecture efforts to die here due to the perception that the work is of little business value by those still in a state of naivety.

If we are diligent, survive long enough, and work even harder, we will start to make sense of the mess and realize that what we have now is naturally *Complex,* but we mostly understand it. We may not explain it very well yet, but we are confident in our understanding what is happening. As Isaac Newton is once purported to have said, "I can describe Gravity to you. I just can't explain it."

To be truly successful, we have to move upward to the top right in the grid by simplifying our deep knowledge and learning how to articulate it straightforwardly. As my grade 12 math teacher often said, "Your work proves the theorem as requested, Mr. Burlton. Now take it away and make it **Elegant**." To me, that meant it should be simple yet powerful. Newton's Law of Universal Gravitation and Einstein's mass-energy relation exemplify elegance with incredible power derived by each brilliant scientist but only after a lifetime of searching.

This highlights the challenge we face as business architects. We want to have sufficient knowledge but cannot go as deep as desirable due to time, cost, and expectations.

We have to be comfortable with a level of uncertainty and obscurity and not be seduced into going too far before coming back for socialization and validation. Adopting the philosophy of agile, learning, and validation through iteration is the way to go. We must learn how to see through the mess and abstract some key insights more readily, gaining feedback and consensus in a timeboxed way as we go and then keep cycling through and adding critical knowledge of value a part at a time. We have to be comfortable knowing we can build greater detail and understanding iteratively over time. Remember George Box's words, "All models are wrong, but some are useful."[5] We aim to be useful, knowing we will not get it perfect. Perhaps that dictates against some professionals becoming an architect, but this book will strive to help.

---

[5] Box, G. E. P. (1976), "Science and Statistics" (PDF), Journal of the American Statistical Association, 71 (356): 791–799, doi:10.1080/01621459.1976.10480949.

Business architecture landscape principles

I will lay out a set of principles for business architecture and examine some popular architectural approaches. In the upcoming chapters, I will reveal and then delve into an approach that honors these in a way that I hope you will find both elegant and useful.

Business architecture principles

Most of the business architecture paradigms in the subsequent sections are valuable to business executives and change agents. I believe that as a foundation, the following big rules are critical in evaluating which methodologies will be best suited for you:

- **Clear business scope:** The business that will be the subject of your architecture efforts can be large or small. Anything from a set of enterprises working together across a common value chain and mission for the same marketplace or simply a distinct part of a company are good candidates for business architecture. Within a specific legal entity and across several are both suitable choices. Regardless, the scope of what's in and out must be well-defined and commonly understood to establish appropriate boundaries and avoid scope creep.

- **An abstraction:** The business architecture is, by nature, a conceptual simplification of reality, and we will need to make compromises to make the architecture useful and easier to communicate (remember the George Box observation earlier).

- **Contextually driven:** The business architecture must be purpose-driven, serve and be served by stakeholders outside the chosen scope, be strategically traceable, and be business performance motivated.

- **Multiple domains (subject areas):** Although we do not need to develop all subject areas at the start, we should at least cover a core set of stakeholders, processes, and performance indicators. The architectural value will come from knowing which items in one area, if changed, will impact other areas. Associations among items in disparate areas are as important as the domain items themselves. A shared business architecture should have multiple beneficiaries.

- **Traceability.** Relationships among items of a particular domain, such as business capabilities, will have a composition/decomposition structure. All component items within a level of decomposition in a domain should be traceable to the items in the level above within which they are a subcomponent.

- **Elegant models:** Business architecture models should be simple yet powerful and not overly complex (see the Burlton NICE model earlier). Remember Einstein's famous quote, "Everything should be made as simple as possible, but no simpler."[6] This will be harder than you think.

- **Associate do not integrate:** Relationships among architectural domains are not hierarchies but associations. The Capabilities, Business Processes, and Business Rules, for example, are potentially linked through many-to-many associations, not as subcomponents of any one within the other.

- **Organization structure is just a domain:** Items within business subject areas (Domains) serve the enterprise or value chain stakeholders for which they are relevant. They should not be built to solely support a specific organizational unit model per se. Organizations will surely change their form, but the value creation of value chains and streams should not change nearly as fast. The organization of people is one of the choices to be made to support value creation. Building around organizations will lead to irrelevance and obsolescence very quickly.

---

[6] https://bit.ly/3EpVEuq.

- **Notation agnostic:** Business architecture is not about driving a particular standard notation. Specification and implementation notations are rarely suitable for architectural concepts. The detailed level of BPMN2.0, for example, is not suitable for a process architecture depiction. However, it may be required at the specification level much later in the journey when we strive to 'correct' the business. Traceability among levels is still essential regardless of the shape of the boxes or rules about lines.

- **Semantically consistent:** Every term used should be defined once, not redundantly or inconsistently. Describe each individual domain object using a consistent semantic structure appropriate for its area of specialization. For example, processes should follow a verb-noun structure and data objects follow a noun structure. In addition, the associations connecting domains must have similar consistent semantic rigor.

- **Journey not a destination:** There is no architectural destination that indicates completion. It's a never-ending journey (a lifestyle change, not a crash diet). Get going with just enough architecture, iterate, and learn how to evolve over time. Do not simply treat it as a project. It has to be sustainable and sustained.

Business architecture model

> *The purpose of any business (or any organization) is to deliver the right mix of outcomes of value for all of the main stakeholders of the business.*

The Business Architecture has to strive to more than satisfy just one type of product or service recipient, the owners, the staff, and even society. It has to truly understand the blend of essential needs and provide a superior experience across multiple channels. It has to do this while keeping a healthy relationship with all other external stakeholders like various suppliers, regulatory bodies, and communities, to name a few.

The business is first and foremost defined by its success in its relationships with external parties. All work inside the organization should aim to achieve the desired outcomes at the interface between your organization and those in your business ecosystem. Getting everything right to make this happen is a monumental task with many moving parts that must come together to form a total result. Some of the business architecture components or concepts to consider in having a comprehensive view of what needs to be optimized and aligned to required outcomes appear in this table:

Business Context	• Opportunities and threats • Stakeholder needs and expectations
Business Strategy	• Business strategic intent • Business products and services • Business strategy • North Star
Business Processes	• Value chains • Value streams • Business processes
Business Decisions and Rules	• Regulations and business policies • Business decisions • Business rules
Business Performance	• KPIs / PIs • KPI/PI objectives
Business Concepts, Semantics, and Information	• Business concepts • Business semantics • Business information
Business Capabilities (IT and Physical Resources)	• Business capabilities • Software services/applications • Physical assets
Business Capabilities (Human)	• Human competencies and behavior • Organization structure and culture • Incentives
Business Transformation	• Change prioritization • Change portfolio • Change roadmap
Business Sustainability	• Business performance accountabilities • Governance of change • Support services • Continuous improvement

Clearly, it would be extremely difficult to tackle all of these in one go, and perhaps you may only need a subset. A plan to build them up from a critical core starter set will take a lot of time to deliver, but that's part of the journey. Paraphrasing John Zachman, *'One day when you're going to wish you had all of this.'* The only practical way is selecting the essential aspects to start with and rolling out the remainder over time. Use this list to evaluate business architecture requirements for your organization and the required methodologies when you are making that choice.

Popular models

For those who have been in and around architecture debates for some time, I will now survey some of the more popular methods that organizations may be familiar with to establish a business architecture baseline. Each of those that follow has a particular perspective. Not all aspects of the myriad of possible concepts are covered in each, begging the question, "What do you need from a business architecture?" Many methods and models have a heritage in the information technology domain. Therefore, business related concepts are traditionally included because they are needed to attain a specific IT goal, such as building or acquiring the right software capability.

It is not unusual to see a particular approach with a limited choice of domains chosen if, for example, the architectural leaders are striving to establish a Service Oriented Architecture for IT service reuse versus buying an enterprise platform or making a culture shift in the enterprise. Concepts perceived as unnecessary for a particular purpose often do not make their way in because the advocates do not feel they are of interest. I am not trying to pick on IT groups here. IT is often who puts a high value on a more comprehensive approach.

Governance, Risk, Compliance, and other supporting programs should also be based on an architectural foundation. We must be cautious when labeling narrowly focused programs or exercises with a specifically defined outcome as business architecture. When this occurs, it should be no surprise if those responsible for some other perspective, such as Process Improvement, do not find what they are looking for in the architecture.

The Business Model Canvas is not typically seen as a business architecture framework. However, for those who are striving to rethink the direction, strategy, and business model of the organization, it contains many architectural components that describe both strategic intent (Vision, Goals, and Objectives as defined by OMG's Business Motivation Model[7]) as well as strategy itself (Value Proposition, Mission, Strategies, and Tactics). It also covers

---

[7] https://www.omg.org/spec/BMM/1.3/About-BMM/.

some prime Stakeholders, Activities, and Resources, all of which are key aspects of any robust business architecture that is striving to enable a different way of running the business.

Osterwalder's Business Model Canvas

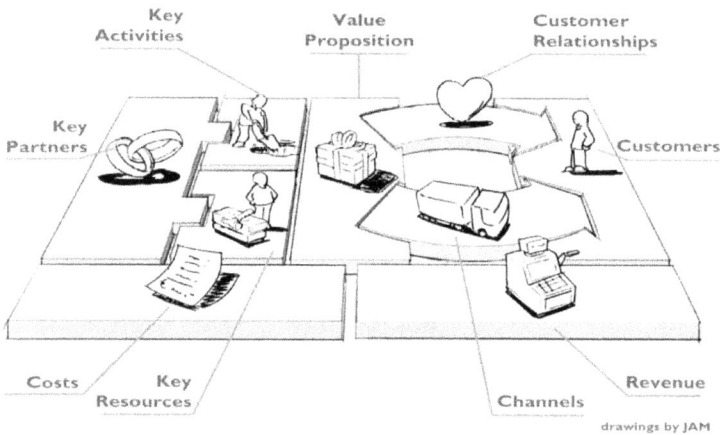

Figure 2-2. Alex Osterwalder's Business Model Canvas.[8]

This canvas does not deal with all of the knowledge ultimately required for a comprehensive business architecture. It certainly does not deal with the connection with IT architecture, although its answers should be essential to make the right IT decisions and architectural

---

[8] Osterwalder, Alex. Business Model Generation: A Handbook for Visionaries, Game Changers, and Challengers. John Wiley and Sons; 1st edition (July 13, 2010).

choices. Its strength is that it engages business executives and provides a good architectural start and, in that regard, serves the purpose of its planning and executive constituency while enabling traceability with the detailed architectural components.

Zachman's Enterprise Ontology

	What? (Data)	How? (Function)	Where? (Location)	Who? (People)	When? (Time)	Why? (Motivation)
Business Concept Planner	Inventory Identification	Process Identification	Distribution Identification	Responsibility Identification	Timing Identification	Motivation Identification
Business Concept Owner	Inventory Definition	Process Definition	Distribution Definition	Responsibility Definition	Timing Definition	Motivation Definition
Business Logic Designer	Inventory Representation	Process Representation	Distribution Representation	Responsibility Representation	Timing Representation	Motivation Representation
Business Physics Builder	Inventory Specification	Process Specification	Distribution Specification	Responsibility Specification	Timing Specification	Motivation Specification
Business Component Implementer	Inventory Configuration	Process Configuration	Distribution Configuration	Responsibility Configuration	Timing Configuration	Motivation Configuration
User	Inventory Instantiations	Process Instantiations	Distribution Instantiations	Responsibility Instantiations	Timing Instantiations	Motivation Instantiations

Figure 2-3. The Zachman Enterprise Framework.

A useful way of thinking about the complex multi-domain and multi-perspective nature of organizations is to consider the John Zachman's Enterprise Framework[9] Figure 2-3 shows the thinking model, which can be traced back to the mid-eighties from John's pioneering work at

---

[9] https://www.zachman.com/about-the-zachman-framework.

IBM. Enterprises have a set of areas of interest (domains) defined as a set of 'primitives.' When considered together, they can be composed into useful 'composite' business capabilities.

Each column answers a fundamentally different question about the enterprise, and we cannot build a functioning business or run one without each aspect being somehow covered off. The classic six interrogatives (what, how, where, who, when and why) are the basis for this domain categorization. So, the question is, "What primitive domain models do we need in order to design and run a business?" The answer is, of course, "All of them!"

One challenge is that even these distinct domains may be seen differently by different parties with different responsibilities, backgrounds, points of view, interests, and personal motivation. These domains also may be represented differently depending on the roles that deal with them, as shown in the rows of the framework. For example, strategists are not necessarily architects, engineers, technicians, or workers/performers. All have their architectural needs based on their particular responsibilities.

When we put together the vertical and horizontal axes, we can understand that each cell has two locators on the grid: its domain (column) and its role (row).

Each cell in the framework identifies a unique perspective. In reality, architects need to understand how these connect with one another. Models that show the connections or combinations are referred to as composites. The components from each cell in the row are interrelated with one another in a 'where used' type of structure describing a holistic perspective for enterprises or complete business designs. To build anything of a complete nature, all rows must be connected to higher and lower-level views in the column. Each column must also make sense with one another in each row (my view of alignment is integrity across a row). In addition, to building anything that works operationally, we need all components in all rows for a column to trace to one another as we transform views from top to bottom (my definition of traceability is integrity up and down the views in a column).

TOGAF

TOGAF is an architectural framework supported by The Open Group. It has the set of optimized requirements for Information and IT assets and capability management as its main perspective. It is very popular with IT-oriented enterprise architects, many of whom have gained formal certification in its practices and standards. As can be seen in the diagram that depicts its main themes, it does have a specific component that tackles business architecture as the basis for IT Architectures as its ultimate raison détre. Its view on business architecture is one that strives to capture the necessary business knowledge for making the right IT design decisions. It is not strongly focused on processes or stakeholder value creation explicitly, but rather on internal capabilities required to ensure delivery of internal assets to enable that goal.

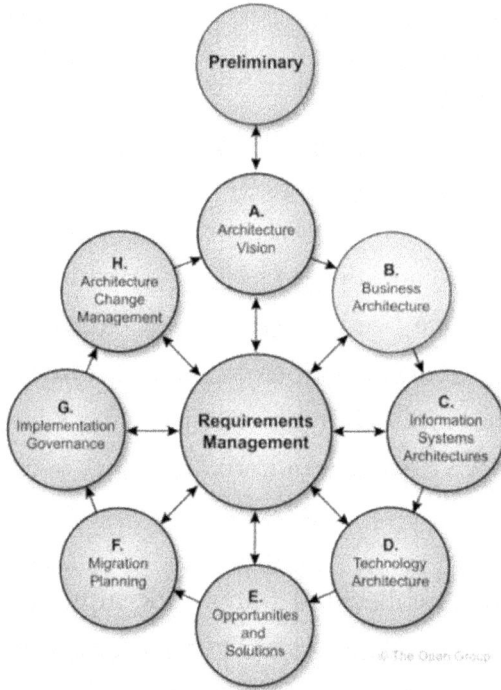

Figure 2-4. TOGAF.[10]

---

[10] https://www.opengroup.org/togaf.

Business Architecture Guild BIZBOK

Figure 2-5. The Business Architecture Guild's BIZBOK.[11]

The BIZBOK provides a rich body of knowledge concerning many aspects of internal capability for businesses. However, it is not as strong in external stakeholder analysis and external drivers as some other approaches. It emphasizes business capabilities as the primary organizer of what's needed to make the business work. Recently, it has come to grips with strengthening the association of business processes with a view on value streams and capabilities and how all three are connected.

After many years of intense debate, this difficult reconciliation recognizes the treatment of business processes as a concept of the first order and not a

---

[11] https://www.businessarchitectureguild.org/.

subcomponent of a capability as implied in prior versions of the body of knowledge.

In my opinion, as one of the main authors of the Guild white paper that tries to articulate how the ideas can be associated,[12] it still struggles with the absence of top down process architecture. Thus, it is missing some aspects of a full process architecture connected to the business's operational accountabilities and management system and an aligned motivation to deliver stakeholder results by executives and managers in the operating model. I am confident that this disconnect will resolve itself over time.

There will be complete integrity and traceability for process management as an operational management discipline and for outside stakeholder value creation reasons. That said, the body of knowledge has an EA heritage and distinct IT flavor and is not as business outcome-oriented as I would like. Nonetheless, it is a rich source of knowledge in many areas, and I recommend it as a useful resource for business architects.

---

[12] https://cdn.ymaws.com/www.businessarchitectureguild.org/resource/resmgr/public_resources/bpm_paper_final_dec2019.pdf.

Burlton Hexagon

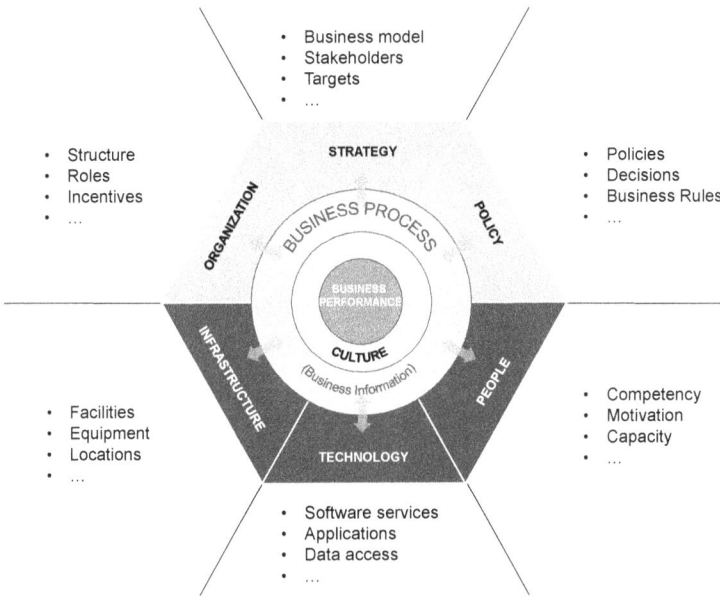

- Business model
- Stakeholders
- Targets
- ...

- Structure
- Roles
- Incentives
- ...

STRATEGY

ORGANIZATION

BUSINESS PROCESS

POLICY

- Policies
- Decisions
- Business Rules
- ...

BUSINESS PERFORMANCE

INFRASTRUCTURE

CULTURE
(Business Information)

PEOPLE

- Facilities
- Equipment
- Locations
- ...

TECHNOLOGY

- Competency
- Motivation
- Capacity
- ...

- Software services
- Applications
- Data access
- ...

Figure 2-6. The Burlton Hexagon.[13]

20 years ago, I developed the Burlton Hexagon to encapsulate what is required to define a complete set of aligned attributes required for a business process. The various perspectives apply at any level of decomposition from value chain through each sub-level of process decomposition. It intends to define the components to question and then link them together instead of developing disparate aspects of business solutions that

---

[13] https://www.bptrends.com/business-architecture-essentials-the-business-architecture-landscape/.

potentially will not work as one. We use this model to examine what works well and what does not. It is the basis of root cause analysis categories and the establishment of an integrated program of change as well as the estimation of what it will take to deliver it.

The focus of the hexagon is on attaining business performance goals shown in the bull's-eye using processes and business information as the measurable organizing/synchronizing elements.

The information asset and the knowledge needed and available in the surrounding ring are key aspects of the processes that consume and create both of them. It evaluates the Strategic Intent and Strategy of the business and the processes that make it up. It reflects the philosophy that processes are the value creators of the organization and the natural aligners of work and resources of various types needed to accomplish the purpose of the work. It addresses the Policies and Business Rules to assure the optimum decisions are made in those processes and to change the sub-optimal ones. It examines and changes the Organization Structure and the incentives of the positions and position holders to find changes needed to provide the appropriate aims of each organization unit traceable to the outcomes of the processes that pass through the various parts of the organization. Finally, it examines the Physical

Infrastructure, which, for many organizations that are capital intensive, can be a source of critical capability that is often skipped in typical business architecture approaches even when capital assets are a large investment.

Given that today there is a strong trend to blending both physical and virtual work, this domain will sustain its relevance for many organizations. The Enabling Technology domain is a critical capability in its own right. Still, it is better when we see it as a part of the overall enablement of the process in capturing and provisioning the required information for the process to function and the navigation of the workflow to execute, monitor, and manage the work itself.

We often overlook the next segment in business design and business architecture. The People requirements define key attributes of the employees and business partner side of capability. If ignored or neglected, they will surely come back to bite us in unforeseen ways. Otherwise, the capability will be incomplete. Having the required competency in our staff and partners is essential, especially if the plan is to scale the business or the learning curve for new staff is long. Having human resources with a shared motivation with that of the process outcomes (the bull's-eye) as opposed to conflicting objectives in the organization chart is critical. People with the appropriate behavior needed for the process individually and how they work in groups will define the culture required and any gaps we may encounter.

The strength of the hexagon is its ability to establish aligned composite models to get the right work done with the right results for the right people in the right way.

Many advocates use the components of the Burlton hexagon to articulate the various resources and investments that have to be made to bring a business capability to life. I will come back to the hexagon in later chapters where we can put it into action.

The approaches shown above have all added something valuable to the discussion of business architecture. In the next section, I will take what we have learned and consolidate it into an overarching framework to guide your efforts.

Process Renewal Group (PRG) Business Architecture Landscape

Framework methodology

The Process Renewal Group framework was originally formulated in the mid-nineties and has undergone continuing evolution for over twenty-five years to remain a pragmatic way of designing a business. It incorporates the best modern approaches combined with ideas that have stood the test of time. It has been subject to ongoing updates based on practice in many initiatives. This comprehensive business architecture framework and foundational methodology shows the main logic of the discovery and design process, and appears in Figure 2-7.

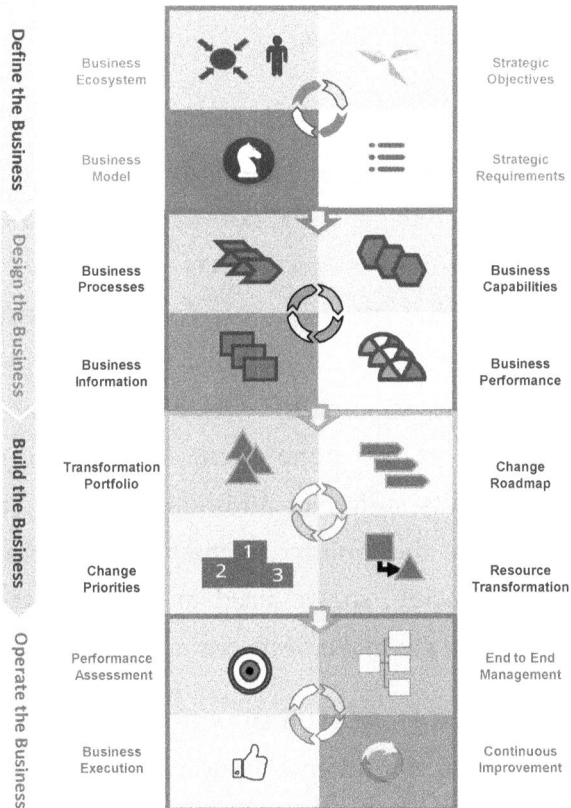

Figure 2-7. Comprehensive business architecture framework and foundational methodology.

In reality, the four major phases and the four sections within each happen every day in an organization with an ongoing business architecture practice. There is a logic, nonetheless. As is shown in the central circles in each of the four phases, there is a cycle of learning about the business that builds the knowledge up over time, 'correcting' as we go. We will deal with each of these aspects in what I believe to be a logical order, understanding that each organization should decide on its own starting point and focus.

Operate the business phase

Working with the end in mind, the overall approach simply implies that you cannot properly '*Operate the Business*' day-to-day if you have not carefully and effectively built the processes, capabilities, systems, and human competencies to do so. Most organizations suffer from the poor provisioning of ways of working and tools to enable jobs to be done well. When this occurs, operational results suffer. In addition, effective business results requires the ability to measure and monitor performance quickly, so we need appropriate access to measurement data to make decisions and adjustments.

To stay connected to operational performance, there must be some form of end-to-end accountability for strategic and operational results, in addition to the functional management of departments and divisions. There is also the need to continue quickly and effectively to improve on the mechanisms utilized to conduct work and to question the value of what we are doing given then-current operational circumstances. As indicated by the center circular arrows in each part of the Framework diagram, all of these should be acting in an agile way with all in play every day and adapting together.

Build the business phase

Moving from bottom to top, we still need to be sure that when we '*Build the Business,*' we build the right things as defined by the previous design work. That means we must prioritize all the possible things that may need to change to populate the transformation portfolio with the right projects to tackle changes in all required aspects of the Burlton Hexagon. These have to be agreed upon, estimated, and subsequently resourced to schedule a commonly agreed roadmap. All types of resources are committed and available when required to pull off the actual changes as defined by project plans. Then, the actual execution of projects can be conducted and controlled by project teams dealing with various hexagon components in play, such as process articulation, technology development, and training production, among others. The rollout of changes can also be accomplished to allow operations using new capabilities to start up and keep going.

Design the business phase

To 'Design the Business,' we need to be sure that we are solving the right problems and establishing the ability to fulfill the strategic intentions from the top of the Framework diagram. Presuming there is a clear set of criteria to know what is important to focus on, this section will let us know what abilities need to be identified and resourced. This section covers many domains and aspects that are typically involved in business architecture efforts. It will provide the scaffolding of most of the architecture and a place to connect everything of interest.

It is possible to start in any of the four sections since none can achieve a significant degree of completion without the others getting to a similar level of accomplishment. However, the cycle starting from the bottom left and progressing clockwise in each phase makes the most sense. Defining business information is a good place to start since it provides the business concepts and how they relate to one another. These definitions are necessary for the processes that create and update the information.

The semantics established will be critical to be sure we know the relevant processes.

The processes will establish the work needed to deliver stakeholder value and provide the structure for the performance indicators. The capabilities provide the reusable resources needed by the processes. Many of these will be used by more than one process, and the interrelationships will tell us the impact of changing any one item on all the others.

We build our capabilities around the structure of the information concepts, which must therefore be reliably described. The Key Performance Indicators (KPIs) will follow the structure of the process hierarchy to establish scorecards for management and operations. The domains in this section are highly interrelated, and an iterative agile approach is called for to avoid missing insights or unintended impacts.

Define the business phase

To *'Define the Business,'* the strategic intent and strategy of the organization are central. This phase will not necessarily create the strategy. At the very least it must interpret it and synthesize it into a form suitable to assist in establishing the process architecture and especially inform the prioritization of processes and capabilities for change later. The work here assumes a good definition of the nature of the business—its business model. If this is about to change, it will significantly impact the architectural models defined here.

Given an established business model, attention should turn to the ecosystem of the business, understanding possible external pressures and drivers that may, now and in the future, affect our business or even our entire industry. The external stakeholders' expectations will tell us what's most important as well as the beginning and end of the processes that need to turn out results for them. From this, we can define our elegant North Star to later help us know the most impactful business processes and business capabilities. It will also provide traceability for the performance indicators we use to assess operations.

In combination, the strategic capabilities—critical success factors—based on the strategic intent will help position what the processes must deal with, and which business capabilities we must be able to realize later. This section requires significant senior leadership input and consensus for the structural aspects of the architecture to be designed.

Framework concepts

Another way to view the PRG Framework is through a model of key concepts representing the knowledge areas that are in play for the first two phases. Whereas the previous Framework diagram shows the general methodology to follow, this next diagram represents the types of knowledge to be captured regardless of how it is attained.

Consequently, the image in Figure 2-8 is not to be read from left to right necessarily but to be read from one concept box to another by reading the box name and then the connecting box one at a time following the arrow. This shows the fundamental nature of understanding the knowledge needed and the logical connections among the pieces. So, the information in boxes is needed regardless of method, and the connections between each shown pair are established. This diagram should be helpful in examining potential repository tools to store information that you have collected and connected, and to search for important associations.

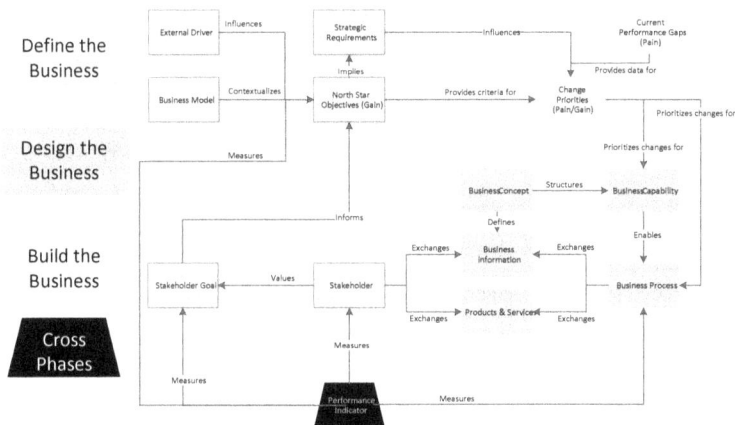

Figure 2-8. Key concepts representing knowledge areas.

The rectangles are generally introduced in the 'Define the Business phase,' the rectangles with rounded corners in the 'Design the Business phase,' the parallelogram in the 'Build the Business phase,' and the Performance Indicators can be connected to any phase. However, information about any concept can be picked up and enhanced at any point. We will delve into concept modeling for the business itself in a later chapter.

Up next

The following chapters in this book will deconstruct the components to be collected and connected and delve more deeply into various domains. They will also address related descriptors, which are part of each of the domains shown. A set of techniques will supplement these to enable the methodology that we have found useful in numerous efforts to make each domain easier to make work. I will reinforce the business architectural principles as we go. Finally, the whole approach will be dissected and put back together again to accommodate the complex nature of the real world and provide an elegant way of describing business design to optimize it.

CHAPTER 3

Architecture Scope and Value Chains

In the previous chapter, I discussed the current interest in business architecture and several frameworks that professionals use for guidance and inspiration. That chapter provided an overview of the field. It introduced an overarching set of business areas that we successfully documented to classify and categorize issues of interest.

As noted earlier , the Process Renewal Group Landscape model was originally formulated in the mid-nineties and has undergone continuing evolution for twenty-five years to remain a modern way of designing a business. It incorporates the best practice of several approaches combined with other ideas that have stood the test of time as well as some of our own innovations. Figure 3-1 introduced in the last chapter repeats the main logic of the discovery and design process.

In the following chapters, I will examine all of these areas and some others not apparent in the diagram. Still, before I get specific on any one of them, we have to look at the scope of the application of business architecture itself in an organization. This is not an easy question to answer.

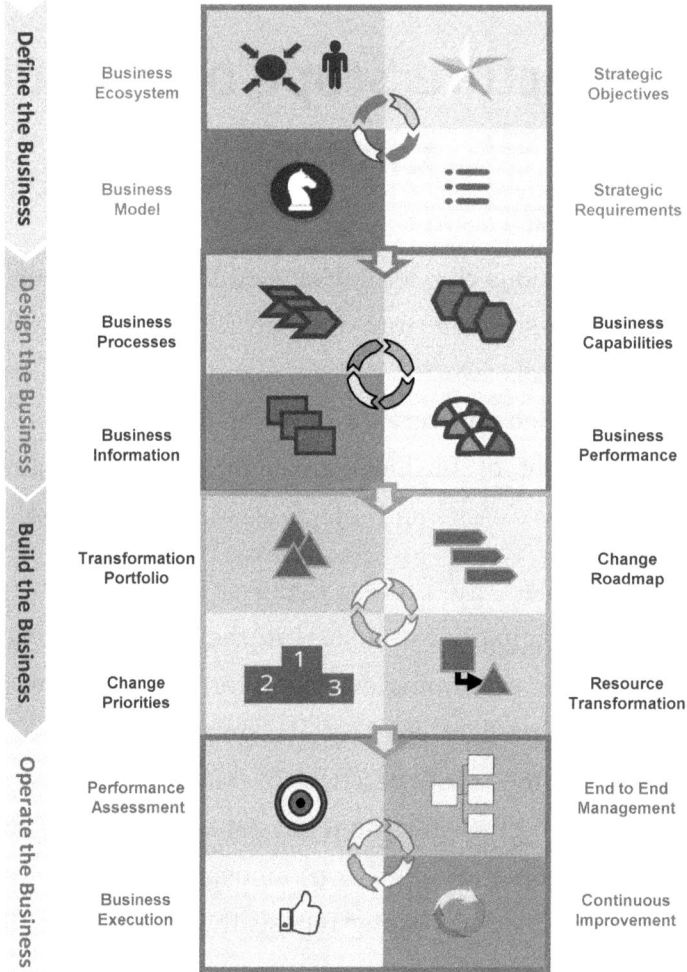

Figure 3-1. Comprehensive business architecture framework and foundational methodology.

Will we include an entire large corporation or a whole government? That sounds daunting. Will we only look at a small and focused organizational unit or group? That sounds limiting. Will we go outside the bounds of our organization to include others? That sounds attractive but possibly political and slow. Everyone must agree on the scope of inclusion and the line of exclusion of the effort and be clear on the knowledge to be captured and sustained. If scoping is not tackled upfront, the effort is ripe for confusion, argument, and probably paralysis. What about a line of business (value chain) approach rather than an organizational structure one? If so, which lines or value chains are in or out if there is more than one? There are also many ways to look at value chains that we must agree on. We will sort through all of these thorny choices in this chapter.

Organizational question

An organization sits within an environmental context outside its direct control, sometimes called its ecosystem. An organization may have many component organizations—divisions, departments, and site locations—each typically managing its own work. Thus, one choice of the business architecture scope of inclusion is an organizational structural one. If we choose this approach, the question is, "What is the scope of organization in play?"

The Business Process Manifesto, developed in 2012, defines an organization as "an entity that pursues collective goals, exercises control over its own performance, has a boundary separating it from its environment, and includes all defined entities participating."

The first question is whether or not all branches of the organization chart will be included in the architectural coverage or the change program, as shown in Figure 3-2.

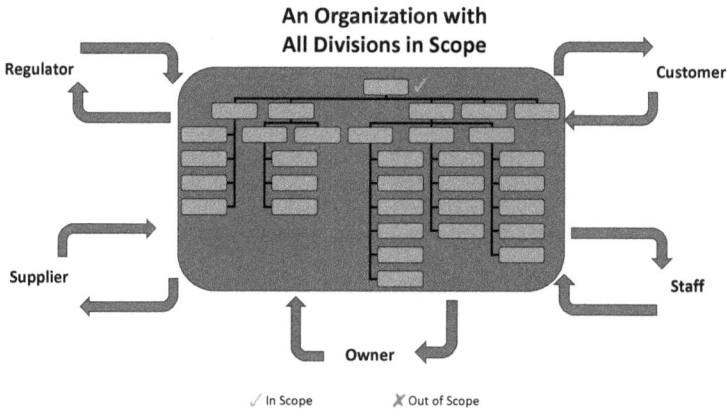

An Organization with All Divisions in Scope

Regulator

Customer

Supplier

Staff

Owner

√ In Scope   ✗ Out of Scope

Figure 3-2. Are all branches of the organization chart included in the architectural coverage or the change program?

Is it possible to take on a whole corporation, or should some parts be excluded? Perhaps only some divisions or departments will participate. For example, we could architect the core business units but not the IT department.

Alternately, we could do the inverse, focusing only on the IT department. The rest of the business is seen as a set of customers, suppliers, and other 'external' stakeholders as far as IT is concerned. We have conducted several such efforts for an IT department to get its act together to better serve the rest of the company. We have also taken on the Real Estate division of a major bank since its issues were well-defined, had clear boundaries, and was a shared service to all other bank lines of business. So, structural partitioning is one possibility. See Figure 3-3.

The department then inspired the rest of the business once its performance picked up and its credibility was established.

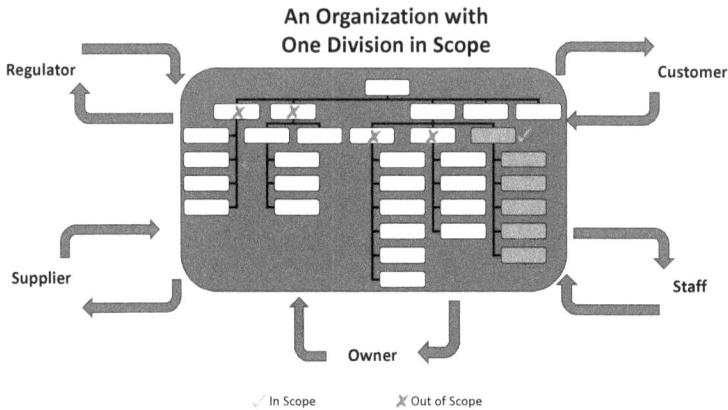

Figure 3-3. Organizational structural partitioning.

However, the risk with this approach is that we may easily miss the mark by architecting and designing aspects of the business that are integral with other units in value creation. The true end-to-end connection to the outside world may not be optimized. The challenge is that the more fine-grained the organizational scoping choice, the more likely it is to sub-optimize and create siloed solutions that do not serve the overall value proposition of the larger organization.

The result is that the less granular and broadly covered is the scope, the more complex, time-consuming, and political the architecture and business design may become. In this scenario, conflicts easily arise around the required political control and cultural changes associated with managing ways of designing the business. This can easily sink the effort politically if we are not careful. We can mitigate this by taking a cross-functional business line baseline from a value chain point of view as described in the remainder of this chapter.

Finding the right balance can be tricky.

Line of business – Value chain argument

Another way to segment and partition the architecture is an outside-in value creation that tackles each of the organization's main lines of business, also known as value chains. This view strives to ensure that everything done is focused on the ultimate value created for specific lines in defined customer markets regardless of your internal organizational structure. As a matter of fact, the organizational structure itself may be on the table since if we change it perhaps we can improve the value creation abilities of the lines of business in scope. So it may not make sense to start with a functional organization structure in an ideal world.

This market-centric approach is outcome-of-value focused and requires a strong end-to-end orientation.

From experience, I know that organizations will struggle even to define a value chain. Some want to use geographical factors such as regions of the world or countries as the basis for differentiating value chains.

The argument from each geographic area is typically that, "We are different." Each may desire to hang onto as much local control as possible. Regions and countries fear losing the self-determination that they feel is important to them, overlooking the benefits of having as much sharing of approach as possible. Other organizations will choose different value chains based on the channels to market that they use. They will often see the direct business relationship with customers as quite different from relationships intermediated by partners and distributors who will get to the customers directly. Web channels are seen quite differently from in-store or branch office ways of working. Size of customer can also often result in different treatments following the classic Pareto principle whereby 20%, or even less, of your customers, provide 80% of your revenue, and so organizations consider them a separate value chain.

Many organizations are still trapped in the quagmire of seeing each product line as its own value chain, resulting in overlapping relationship managers, thus creating issues from each product. In addition, there is a tendency to hang onto products and services long after they are no longer of optimum value to the customer since the existing product manager wants to keep it. As a result, products themselves are slow to change or even terminate themselves when their time is up. Large banks and insurance organizations have historically been guilty of this and, in many places today, have not solved the inertia and cultural problem because of it.

Our preference is to take a value creation approach based on the chosen aggregate line of business encompassing multiple products and services in the markets that the business is pursuing. So rather than having mortgages products separate from personal account services from personal investments, we would prefer to see one value chain for the consumer banking line of business and possibly another for the business banking line. Each could have a different value proposition and be measured somewhat differently.

One company—one value chain for its one line of business

Although multiple value chains exist in many large corporations or government agencies, we'll start with the simplest scenario, as shown in Figure 3-4. That is the case when the entire business has one clear market with a focused and defined set of products and services for that market.

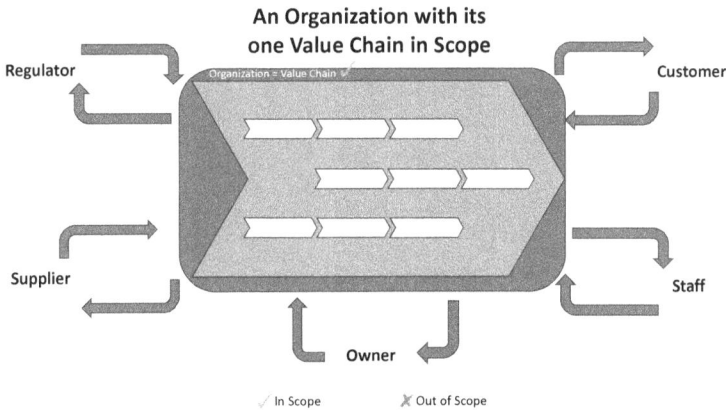

An Organization with its one Value Chain in Scope

Regulator Customer

Organization = Value Chain ✓

Supplier Staff

Owner

✓ In Scope ✗ Out of Scope

Figure 3-4. One clear market with a defined set of products and services for that market.

Imagine a local Thai restaurant that makes and serves Thai dishes in response to on-site dining for individuals, groups, or families. It also delivers food to addresses within a defined delivery territory. Therefore, we would classify the value chain 'Serve Diners' as the only value chain that the restaurant has despite having two means of getting meals to customers. This value chain would comprise everything the restaurant does, including purchasing raw materials, creating recipes, hiring staff, and establishing weekly plans to name a few things. Thus, the organization is represented wholly by its only business line (value chain), which has a clear value proposition for its customers in its market.

One company—multiple distinct value chains

Let's expand our thinking to an organization with multiple diversified business lines, as shown in Figure 3-5.

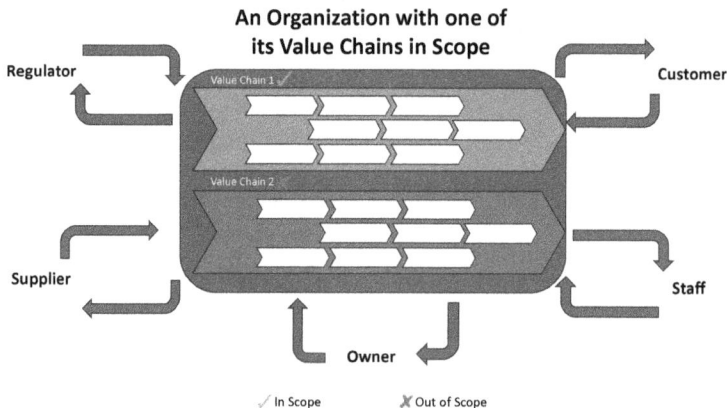

Figure 3-5. An organization with multiple diversified business lines

A compelling example is Michelin Group which has several separate lines of business under its purview. It makes tires, produces restaurant and hotel guides, has a digital mapping business, and other active ventures. Clearly, each of these provides a different suite of products and services for a different market than the others, and each represents a different value chain from the others.

It is possible, of course, for individuals to participate in more than one of these markets, each with a different value proposition. In this case, different divisions most likely operate each line within the corporate organization chart. The 'Produce Tires' value chain is remarkably different from the 'Produce Guides' one. This is easy to appreciate and having one business architecture at the core covering both is unrealistic, so two separate architectures are more appealing. There may be some internal shared services, but I will come to that a bit later.

One company—multiple interacting value chains

What about a company that develops and sells software products and provides business consulting services? On the one hand, it is tempting to go with two value chains, but it is also true that there may be one sales strategy and team that will call on the same client and even sell both in the same proposal. It is a bit more complex because we may want the two business lines to apply their own unique practices but avoid conflicts between the two teams in optimizing the customer relationship overall. Therefore, our preference would be to have two value chains, but with one core shared sales value stream serving the best combination of business lines for the best long-term interest of supporting the customer and its own corporate strategy, as illustrated by Figure 3-6.

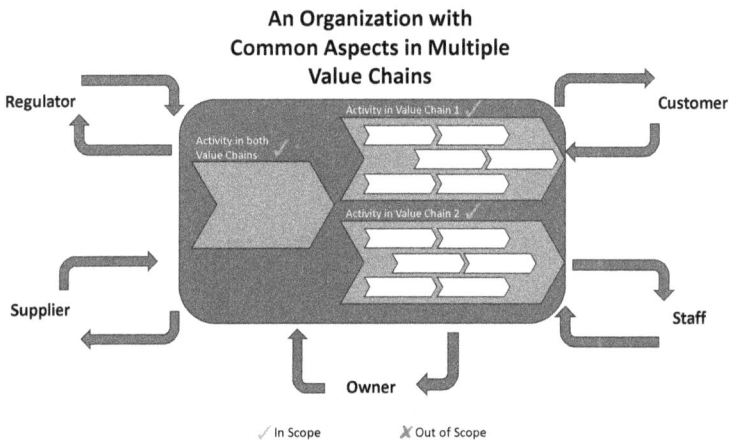

Figure 3-6. Two value chains with one core shared sales value stream.

If the professional services are closely tied to the software itself, choosing one chain is appealing. However, we would expect two chains if they are not much related, and we are essentially selling and delivering consulting unrelated to the software. It depends!

A good example of this is one of the world's largest air travel technology services providers. It has a distinct value chain for taking airline, hotel, and train capacity data, seat by seat and room by room, and making it available to its over six hundred customer airlines, hotels, and travel agencies. Its services are for booking spaces and maintaining real-time updates to customers making such bookings. In addition, it also operates an IT outsourcing service for many of the same airlines acting as their 'outsourced' IT department. These are distinct value chains even though they may have the same airline as customers for both lines of business.

One company—internal value chains

As mentioned earlier regarding organization units that could be excluded from the architectural scope, there are often one or more value-creating activities that almost stand alone and focus solely on their internal customers. They operate as a shared service. This is true of services such as 'Provide IT Services,' 'Support HR Needs,' or 'Engineer Facilities and Equipment,' as illustrated in Figure 3-7.

Often these services correlate closely to the organization units that are the internal lead players in specific professional services, and they support multiple other internal processes. This provides professional management of the resources and professional practices (i.e., processes and capabilities) required to assure that all core external facing business value chains remain most effective. Their customers are internal within the organization. This can work well so long as these supporting value chains (shared services) see their line of business as serving their internal company customers, who, in turn, have their own external business customers. So, their job is to make their internal customers' external customers successful.

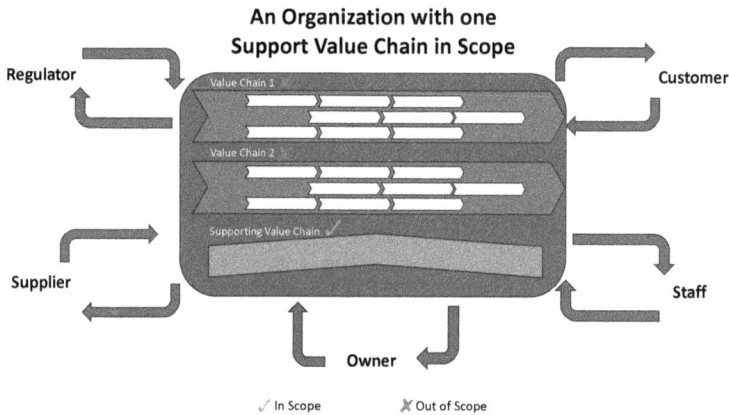

Figure 3-7. Value-creating activities that stand alone and are focused on their internal customers and operate as a shared service.

The supporting value chain incumbents must resist the temptation of becoming too internally focused on their own professional work and becoming dogmatic in their ways of working due to having a perceived monopoly internally. It is useful to think about each of these shared service groups responsible for the supporting value chain as a company in its own right that manages itself as a business with a full set of stakeholders, many of which are internal to the larger entity and, therefore, just like a value chain but serving the rest of the company.

A good example of this type of support value chain could be 'Acquire Goods and Services,' which would cover all of the activities required from first identifying needs to the end result of the right goods or services in place for a fair cost. This could be confused with the organizational view of the Purchasing department architecture. The difference is that the value chain view will include more than what is occurring just in the Purchasing organization view and include all activity needed from purchase to pay.

Multiple companies—one value chain

We are starting to see many innovative business model examples whereby companies collaborate to provide new and exciting offerings to the marketplace by extending their value chains into and across work performed by multiple independent legal entities. This can deliver a value-added service not possible by any individual entity alone, as shown by Figure 3-8.

There are many good examples of exploiting an opportunity for new services not available previously, as shown by organizations such as Uber, Open Table, and Airbnb where the value chain involves several collaborating stakeholders as part of service delivery and whereby the one value proposition as seen by customers requires an architecture for multiple players working together in one logical set of activities.

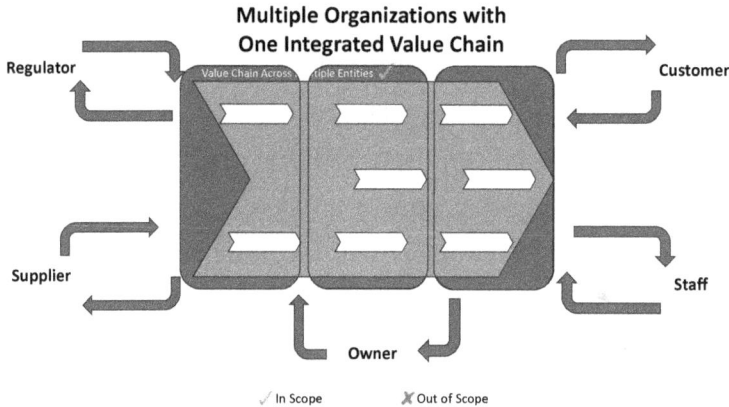

Figure 3-8. Extending value chains into and across work performed by multiple independent legal entities.

Process Renewal Group has been involved with the design and architecture of end-to-end value chains that span multiple government agencies across more than one level of government, sometimes in combination with the private sector. All parties must be involved in the architecture work if it is to be effective for the citizens and other participants in the ecosystem of the jurisdiction. So we consider the combination and collaboration to be one value chain.

For example, in one of the Canadian provinces, the cross-organization value chain involved a transit agency, municipalities, and transit operating companies to optimize transit experience and increase transit ridership. Optimization by each entity separately would not have served the riders of transit. In another, numerous stakeholders from insurance companies, police agencies, the justice ministry, various cities, and special interest groups got together to take on the focused mandate of architecting the capability to improve road safety in the province, something not possible alone.

A tricky yet critical choice

Sometimes the choice you make of the value chains to be in scope of the architecture work is fairly obvious and can be settled very quickly. Sometimes it can be tricky and possibly require a political negotiation to ensure readiness to go wider together. You must have a good idea of what you are trying to do for the external stakeholders so you can choose. What is your vision? Selecting something too small may not be sufficient to achieve your aims. Sometimes taking too big a challenge may be premature for the organization's culture and readiness.

There are many pros and cons associated with each choice, and careful discussion and gaining commitment with leadership for the choice is essential. No matter what you decide, this part of the architecture effort needs to happen early to get everyone on the same page and to be able to negotiate and commit the time and appropriate resources for the needed effort. In our experience, many critical issues get raised even this early, and their resolution upfront will guide the rest of the architecture work you will do. By addressing them here, you will avoid messy re-negotiation later when you are knee-deep in details, and it is more difficult, costly, emotional, and political.

Up next

The next chapter will start to deconstruct the components of the landscape model and delve into the first domain, Ecosystem and Stakeholder Analysis.

CHAPTER 4

Analyzing your Ecosystem and Understanding External Stakeholders

In the previous chapters, I discussed the current interest in business architecture and some frameworks that professionals have been looking at for guidance and inspiration. The business architecture landscape was introduced, which contains an overarching set of domains that we in the Process Renewal Group have successfully used to classify and categorize issues of concern. Our reference will be the Landscape shown in Figure 4-1. The diagram shows the main logic of the discovery and design work that we have to do.

Given that in an architectural initiative, we should have gained agreement on the scope of inclusion of the value chain(s) to be addressed, we can now understand the requirements of the grouping we have called, 'Define the Business.' Within this grouping, we have four component domains. This grouping and all of those that follow should be read from the bottom left and considered in a clockwise manner. But in reality, the four components cannot be completed one at a time—each will iterate with the others as learning and feedback occur.

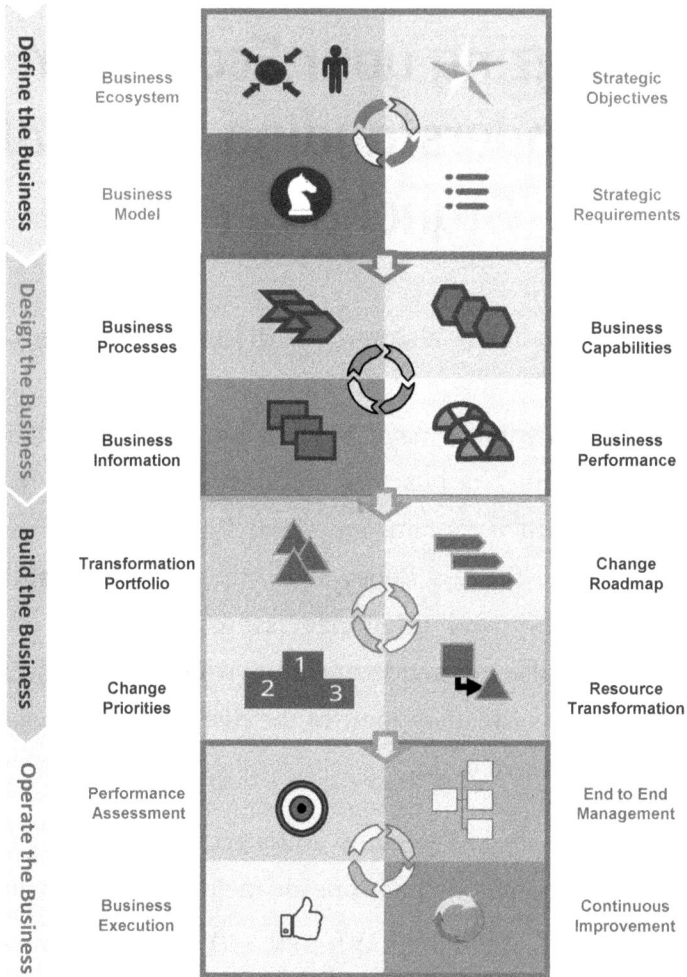

Figure 4-1. Comprehensive business architecture framework and foundational methodology.

In this grouping, we must quickly review the enterprise's business model for the value chain in scope. Then, external drivers and the external stakeholders, who care about what we do and what is important for relationship and business success, will be addressed.

In this analysis, we continue to view the enterprise-in-focus as a black box and work at the edges, for now, to ensure we know what the value expectations are for all of those external entities that we serve or that serve us. We are trying to keep the end in mind by defining what the desired ends are and looking at how well we and the stakeholders are performing. The premise is that stakeholders give things into the value chain and get things from it. External stakeholders have expectations of us in terms of satisfying their needs and having an easy experience. We have the same requirements from them if the relationship is to remain a healthy one over time.

Business model

A business model describes the rationale of how an organization creates, delivers, and captures value, in economic, social, cultural, or other contexts. It describes how you plan to make money or how you plan to deliver according to your mission and achieve your vision. As we saw in previous chapters, some models can describe this, such as the Alexander Osterwalder view of the Business Model Canvas shown again in Figure 4-2.

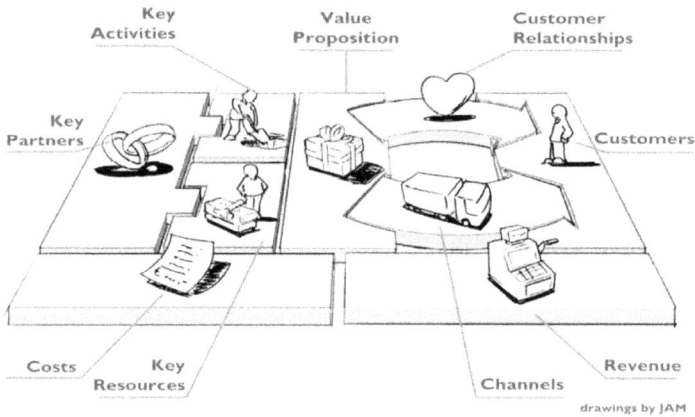

Figure 4-2. Business Model Canvas. [14]

We do not necessarily expect business architects to invent the contents of the business model. Still, they must derive it from senior leaders, understand it intimately, and potentially influence and document it since it will supply critical direction for later models to be connected to it. The Business Model is mostly directional and gives us a head start on defining some of the domains that constitute a useful architecture. The big and risky issues should come out early as opposed to later. Customers, Key Partners, and our relationships with them begin our stakeholder analysis. Value Proposition of the Value Chain(s) in scope

---

[14] https://en.wikipedia.org/wiki/Business_Model_Canvas.

helps us with the value we bring to the stakeholder relationships. Key Activities start to bring to light the value streams/business processes needed. Key Resources will help us with defining our business capabilities. Costs and Revenues tell us how we will measure what we do and stay in business and prosper.

Business ecosystem external pressures

Along with understanding our external stakeholders, which we will tackle in this chapter, we must also gain a common view of the business's current and anticipated external realities of the chosen value chain. Most of these contextual factors are beyond our control and possibly our influence. They are often not considered thoughtfully or are optimistically willed away as if they do not exist. However, some will impact us for a long time and cannot be ignored. We must accommodate them in our planning and design for adaptability.

There are several categories of pressures and several schemes to consider. I like the STEEPL structure: Social, Technological, Economic, Environmental, Political, and Legal. Depending on the industry and the timing, some types will be more relevant than others. Some will impact more negatively over time, and some will offer great opportunities for a while or even go away. Guessing the severity and vector of each can be a hazardous proposition, but if you are not ready to be agile when one pops up, consequences may occur. Considering what each means to us is essential for business design agility.

Social

Social pressures happening in the world or even in a defined market are not under our control and, once underway, hard to resist. Examples include:

- The age distribution of the North American and European populations versus new world countries
- The unacceptability of smoking or recognition of the need for masks in buildings during a pandemic
- The demand for privacy versus transparency of personal data
- The rise of the millennials and generation Z's expectations of work-life balance and corporate hierarchy abhorrence
- The expectations of social responsibility, environmental sustainability, and plant-based food momentum

Technological

There can be no denying the impact of technology on markets, stakeholders, and companies. The fundamental expectations of an easy customer experience come from digitalization and information sharing. Examples include:

- The universal adoption of smart mobile devices
- Cybercrime, electronic spying, and cyber-attacks
- Information sharing across multiple channels, omnichannel, and devices enabled by cloud-based infrastructures
- The ubiquitous accessibility of wireless services
- The continuing predominance of ERP software in businesses and 'an app for that'

Economic

The economy is constantly changing and the position of various interest groups within it does not rest. The current scenario will continue to morph with changes such as:

- Extreme swings in currency valuations—forced or market-based
- The availability and price of particular commodities
- Tax schemes such as global minimum taxes for corporations
- Interest rates and lending stress tests
- Stimulus programs to incentivize behaviors
- New forms of payment options such as cryptocurrencies

Environmental

In the past few years, extreme weather events are increasing in frequency and severity. Many factors will grow in importance:

- Weather events and climate change such as fire and floods that threaten entire communities and supply chains
- Global pandemics and lockdowns
- Food safety
- Worker safety
- Carbon footprint/pricing
- Water/air quality

Political

Like rust (thanks to Neil Young), we know that politics never sleeps and can bring dramatic changes. The following examples continue to happen:

- Government changes
- Government political pressures and change gridlock
- Trade pacts, wars and protectionism
- Border protection and refugee crises
- International and domestic terrorism (real and cyber)

Legal

Laws and regulations are being rewritten due to political or environmental pressures. Some types of challenges are:

- Tax changes
- International treaties creation or decommissioning
- Regulatory reporting and compliance for industries or consumer protection
- (De)regulation
- Worker rights and the gig economy

These are but a few potentially relevant factors that may affect your organization or value chain proposition. Depending on your situation, each of these may provide an opportunity to be exploited, become a threat, or be irrelevant. It all depends on your strengths and weaknesses of each relative to your competitors. Identifying the risks and opportunities and selecting the ones to be ready for and how to do so will be a foundation for your strategic scenario analysis and planned responses embedded in your business design.

Natural uncertainty will mean that you must design your business to be agile in the knowledge economy.

Stakeholder value

Who cares and about what?

Knowledge documented regarding outside stakeholders provides the context (start and end) of the processes we conduct, defines the ultimate capabilities we need to have to be able to attain results for them, and helps us formulate the right balance in our strategic intent reconciling external perspectives that may otherwise conflict with one another. The business scope chosen for our architecture sets the context of the stakeholder analysis activity, as shown in Figure 4-3.

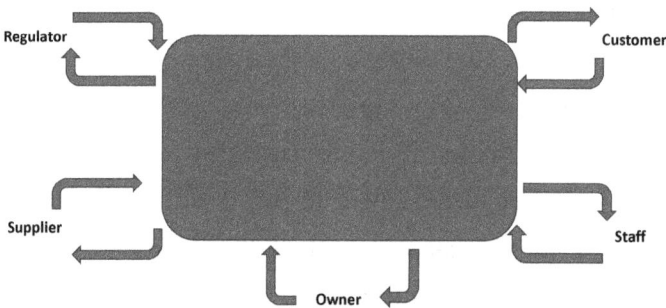

Figure 4-3. Context of the stakeholder analysis activity.

We must gather knowledge or infer insights regarding:

- Who are the stakeholders of note? Who cares and what do they and we care about?
- What tangible or virtual items do we exchange with them?

- What expectations of value do we have of them and them of us? What experience is expected by each party?
- What measurement indicators can we evaluate? relationship performance and what are the gaps between the current state and future objectives?
- What aspects of the relationship are unhealthy?
- What are the required capabilities for relationship success?

Who are the stakeholders of note?

The first questions to be answered regarding external connections are, "Who do we care about?" and "Who cares about us?" Some stakeholders interact with us regularly and often exchange things with us. Some stakeholders may not interact or transact with us frequently but certainly affect what we do or are affected by what we do, perhaps indirectly. Others may be interested but are not as involved as these first two groups. We need to care about all of them and get them to care about us in the way we want.

Once we understand our stakeholders, we can decide what we need to do to optimize our part in the ecosystem within which we all participate.

It all starts with gaining agreement on classifying the various types of stakeholders that we wish to see. Be aware that how we segment can be a source of major semantic, cultural, and political dissonance. It is also easy to get lost in segmentation and sub-categorization without usefulness in the detailing.

We first need to structure the stakeholder types which we serve. We tackle this by looking at customer segmentation, markets, products or service types, business volume, the nature of how direct or indirect the relationship is, or other considerations that may be unique to the business or common in the industry. This can be as much art as science and reflects thoughts on strategic intentions regarding markets and trends. In negotiating the mix, some people tend to lump into groups and others to split into subgroups. It will be a challenge to gain consensus on segmentation, but this is the time to have that debate. Once we have a good handle on the customer segmentation, we can look at other stakeholder types and sub types. The highest levels of stakeholder types are:

- **Customers and Consumers (those we are in business to serve).** This category is often not as simple as it may seem since there may be direct customers with segmentation such as large and small, intermediaries or channels to market such as distributors or resellers, consumers of our offerings sold through other organizations, recipients of specific types of products and services in differing geographies or different markets, and various roles played by buyers, brokers, influencers, users, and end consumers. We have to catch and describe them all since our processes must optimally deliver to or through each.

- **Suppliers (those who provide products, services and resources to us)**. Suppliers may be considered a generic type of stakeholder or be differentiated according to what they supply. For example, buying office supplies may be handled quite differently than purchasing software or agreeing to and executing an outsourced operation. Since we often consider some of these essential to what we do, we may consider them partners if they share the same interest in our customers.

- **Staff (those who work on serving and supporting the enterprise value chain and its stakeholders)**. Staff is an external stakeholder type since members join the enterprise voluntarily and will thus need to be personally attracted and subsequently assume internal roles once hired. They must also remain satisfied to be retained and motivated to do their best. They can also leave if they choose. There may be several types of staff based on the longevity of their tenure, if they are part-time or full-time, or even their association with collective bargaining units. There are often names for this category, such as associate, colleague, and employee, so use the term that is common in your organization.

- **Owners (those who invest in or direct our activity).** This category includes all the investors, boards of directors, and possibly top-level executives. Again, there will likely be sub-types depending on the degree of control of each owner. The picture will be different for different types of industries: public sector organizations, public versus privately held organizations, and different countries' legal governance requirements. Shareholders may also be considered a category perhaps represented by a board.

- **Community (those who govern, guide, or influence what and how we do what we do).** This very broad category may have many segments since those who provide regulatory and compliance requirements and certification will differ from those who may be simply influencers on us or for us. This can include geographic-based, professional-based, or industry-based relationships. At Process Renewal Group, we consider environmentally motivated influencers as a stakeholder type. It is not unusual for us to list 'the planet' as a stakeholder in its own right.

- **Competitors (those who fight in our markets for our customers and/or their budgets).** Competitors may be targets for our capacity enhancement by acquiring them or they us. They may also be partners or collaborators under certain conditions. At the very least, we should know what they are up to and how they are doing.

- **Enterprise (the enterprise itself).** This category is somewhat esoteric in that it considers the enterprise to be a different stakeholder from its staff, owners, or customers. Its perspective is one of sustainability beyond the short term management team and its mandate is to act in the best interest of the organization's longer-term health. This perspective does not actually exchange anything, but it assures we consider business agility as something required to emerge over time while staying young and relevant.

- **Overlaps and Oddballs (those which may play conflicting roles).** There will always be other types that do not fit neatly into the customary categories. There will also be those who play multiple roles, such as customers or suppliers that compete with you or competitors that own part of your company.

In structuring the stakeholder categories, take a role-based point of view since certain entities will play more than one role. Stay focused on the value by role and let the consolidation deal with finding the right balance.

These categories are all decomposable into sub types, often articulated through personas, which are modeled representations of who service recipients are, what they are trying to accomplish, what goals drive their behavior, how they think, how they buy, and why they make buying decisions. Examples may be senior citizens with privileges versus recent college graduates, customers with high buying power versus the occasional buyer, and high loyalty users versus opportunistic bargain hunters.

There is a practical limit to over-refining categories beyond the point of usefulness for enterprise-level work. Each type can also be weighted so that some will be considered more heavily when influencing strategic choices and capability design decisions. For example, should the five customers that account for seventy-five percent of your business volume be given equal weight as the thousands who make up the remaining twenty-five percent? If you choose not to weigh them, then you are actually weighing them by making them all equally important. Is that what you believe or want?

Our business aims to create maximum possible value, as defined by our intentions for our stakeholders, and ourselves.

Finding the balance among all stakeholders can be very tricky and tenuous. Not paying attention to customers is suicide these days, even though companies sometimes arrogantly do not realize it. Doing everything to satisfy consumer demands while failing regulatory compliance can find you shut down or result in serious reputational problems afterward. Pushing your workforce beyond their capacity can lead to high turnover and a poor customer experience.

So, let's look at what creates value. I have found that as architects and analysts, we should look for three things to capture, model, and document. Value will come from the combination and not simply one of them (Figure 4-4).

The first and easiest is to find the actual items *exchanged*— what we give and what we get. For example, we provide our name when we get to a hotel and in return gain access to our room based on our reservation. The next is what *expectation* of benefit we attain from successfully exchanging the item if we do it right. For example, after arriving from a long trip, the nap and shower we can take before going out to dinner may be considered essential. The last is the ease of the *experience* that occurred while providing or receiving the item or service. For example, how long did it take to access the room, did the key work, how helpful and friendly was the check-in person, or how easy to use was the check-in app? We examine each of these three perspectives next.

Stakeholder Value = E^3

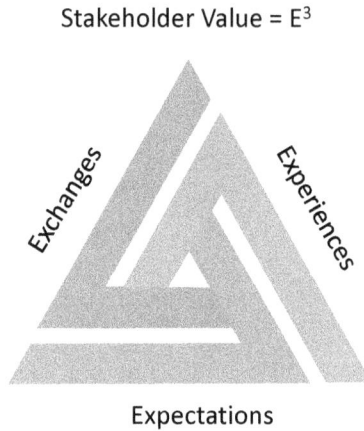

Figure 4-4. Elements of stakeholder value.

What tangible or virtual exchanges do we have with business stakeholders?

A great way to start understanding the peculiarities of outside stakeholders and determine what we must do and be good at is to build a value chain context diagram, as shown in Figure 4-5.

This exercise is the least politically challenging of all the stakeholder work. Such a diagram is essentially a model of stakeholder interactions and exchanges, represented by drawing a simple diagram of the actual and planned exchanges delivered to and received from each stakeholder type using our "Value Chain in Focus."

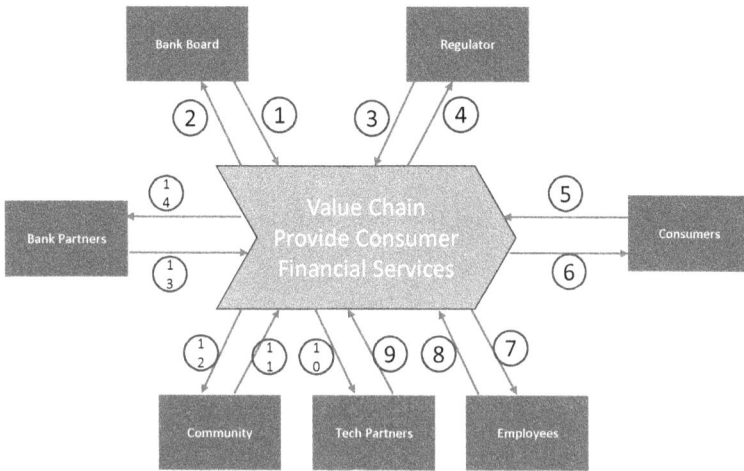

Stakeholder Value Item Exchanges

1. Capital, Targets, Board Decisions
2. Board Reports, Requests for Decisions
3. Regulatory Requirements, Certification Requests
4. Reports, Regulation Change Requests
5. Requests for Services, Fee Payments
6. Financial Services, Charges
7. Contracts, Requests for Supplies and Services
8. Contracts, Supplies, Services
9. Skills, Labor, Employment Commitment
10. Compensation, Employment Commitment
11. Community Concerns and Requests
12. Community Programs, Sponsorships
13. Service Agreements, Services for customers, Revenue share
14. Service Agreements, Customer lists

Figure 4-5. Value chain context diagram.

Clearly, many activities must somehow come together inside the box to deal with what comes in and make what goes out become a reality. This starting point of analysis is the only real way to find your end-to-end business processes from a value and integrity point of view. These exchanges will happen to start, continue, or end your high-end business processes (aka value streams). Like it or not, they are quite agnostic to the departments and individuals that do the work or the tools you use. Sometimes the exchanges are or need to be of high quality, and sometimes not so much. We are all familiar with what happens when we have incorrect or delayed input data. We can show all exchanges, including:

- Products delivered and received
- Services provided and received
- Information exchanged
- The results of decisions made
- Know-how
- Commitments (formal and informal) made and received
- State changes of various assets or relationships
- Resources of all types

When building a context model, we expect to find that an incoming item will often be paired with one or more outgoing exchange items. For example, a request for a credit card may come in, and a rejection or acceptance (the result of a decision) may go out in response, along with instructions on what to do next to safely initiate the card (know how). An illustration of a context model for a hypothetical bank appears in Figure 4-6. Paul Harmon and I developed this model and many other banking illustrations in the book when creating a training course for BPTrends Associates clients when we were both active there.

What expectations do we have of the benefit of the exchange or interaction?

A useful technique for sorting out the ideal stakeholder benefit is called Time Machine Visioning. In this 'back to the future' scenario, the architect and strategist imagine arriving at the future they would like to see at the end of the planning horizon when all results are in place and the processes are all performing as desired (the ideal world). Statements are postulated to reflect the *expectations* of each stakeholder type's value needs. It then becomes the designer of the value chain's role to do everything necessary to make the statements come true by building the appropriate architecture artifacts (to come later). These will become our aspirational goals for the relationship.

The *expectations* of value should keep everyone aimed squarely towards the purpose of any necessary changes you are planning to make. These design criteria must be used as the main guideline when making business design decisions or choosing among several design options.

What was the experience while going through the interaction?

This aspect of value will assume that the right items were delivered. Maybe you got into your hotel room eventually. It also presumes that you could get the benefit that the item enabled you to do. You got showered and out the door in time for dinner. Now the question is, "How easy was it compared to what you expected?"

If your room was unavailable because the hotel overbooked and sent you away, it does not matter if the check-in clerk was friendly, or the app was easy to navigate. You are probably not coming back. However, if all the hotels you could have booked provide the same items and services and you realize the same benefit, you are more likely to stay with the one that treated you in the best way and made it easy for you.

Experience is important but not relevant if you do not get the satisfactory delivery of the product or service. When all competitors equally exchange similar items and can deliver the same results of value, the industry is essentially commoditized. In commoditized businesses the *experience* becomes a differentiator. *Experience* is emotional. It's how people feel. Accessibility, usability, simplicity, sense of trust and safety, and consistency over time and across channels are all *experience* factors that can be important. I know all banks have similar mortgage interest rates and risk rules, but the experience of getting approved for a loan can vary widely. Faster decisions, less of my time in the deal-making, and helpful people are what I want.

How can we assess value?

The stakeholder *exchanges, expectations, and experiences* are the basis for determining the performance indicators required to monitor the success of stakeholder relationships and progress towards targets. These goals and measures will now be used to derive Key Performance Indicators (KPIs) to contribute towards the strategic intent statements and should be directly linked to the assessment of them. They measure value creation from the perspective of the stakeholder as well as the value chain itself. Both sides must realize value from the relationship to attain and sustain benefits.

There should be a combination of effectiveness such as net promoter score, efficiency such as cost per transaction, quality such as % of transactions in compliance to standards, and agility such as success rate in handling special requests. To avoid sub-optimization, one KPI typically will not cover all perspectives. Some combination of these points of view is more realistic, even if some are potentially conflicting. The value statements, dealing with items exchanged, perceived benefit realized, and interaction experience, are also the basis for establishing the measurable relationship objectives.

These objectives, by definition, are the target values of the KPIs for the organization or value chain. They will be set for the same timeframe as the time machine planning horizon. They may also be established for interim points in time as milestones to be achieved along the way. These stakeholder KPIs and targets can now become part of a scorecard connecting to traceable process measures derived from process architecture (discussed in and upcoming chapter).

What aspects of the relationship are unhealthy?

Once we know the stakeholder value and operational drivers, we can perform a triage-like assessment of the exchanges into good (green), bad (red), and in-between (yellow) health of each, comparing today's state versus what we strive to attain in the future. See Figure 4-6.

This will give us a good start on understanding likely relationship issues and opportunities. Taken together, it becomes obvious which relationships are in good health overall and which need serious attention in terms of the processes that support them or are supported by them. We may produce a strategic Ishikawa (Fishbone) diagram to find out. Still, the real value of the exercise lies in the common insights gained across a typically diverse and siloed group of internal decision-makers discussing the situation from a range of perspectives and arriving at a shared consensus of where the largest issues rest.

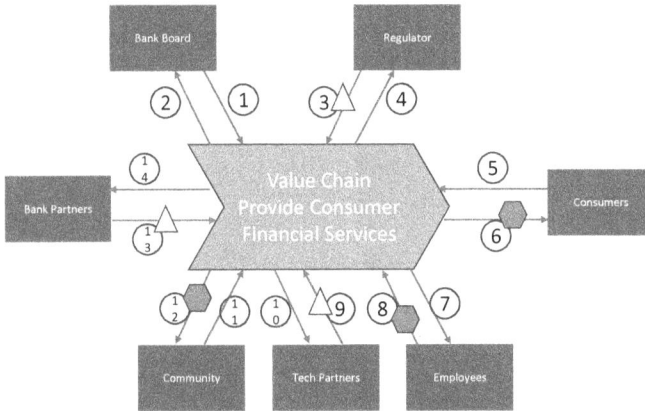

Stakeholder Value Item Exchanges

1. Capital, Targets, Board Decisions
2. Board Reports, Requests for Decisions
3. Regulatory Requirements, Certification Requests
4. Reports, Regulation Change Requests
5. Requests for Services, Fee Payments
6. Financial Services, Charges
7. Contracts, Requests for Supplies and Services
8. Contracts, Supplies, Services
9. Skills, Labor, Employment Commitment
10. Compensation, Employment Commitment
11. Community Concerns and Requests
12. Community Programs, Sponsorships
13. Service Agreements, Services for customers, Revenue share
14. Service Agreements, Customer lists

Figure 4-6. Triage-like assessment.

Stakeholder Analysis Worksheet

We can obtain stakeholder knowledge through modeling tools if they have the data fields to capture all of the critical knowledge we have illustrated. Use a simple matrix if you do not have access to a suitable software repository toolkit. Figure 4-7 illustrates this for our banking situation.

Stakeholder Analysis Worksheet

Organization-in-Scope: BPT Bank

Value Chain or process-in-Scope: Provide Consumer Banking Service

Stakeholder Relationship	Perspective (receives)	Exchange to stakeholder or from stakeholder	Expectation of Benefit	Experience	KPIs	Target KPI Objective
Consumer	Consumer	Financial Services, Charges	No errors in transactions and statements	Easy way of to transact	Error rate %	<3% this year
	Consumer	Access to banking app'	Full suite of smart phone banking	Easy user interface	No of new app's available this year	3 new services this year
	Bank	Requests for Services, Fee Payments	High volume of product and service sales	Readiness to interact online	Revenue growth per consumer	Revenue growth per consumer increase by 4%
Bank Regulators	Bank Regulators	Regulatory Requirements, Certification Requests	Timely daily reporting on relevant suspicious transactions	Submitted electronically	Submission rate (%) on time	100% submitted by cut off daily
	Bank	Reports, Regulation Change Requests	Stay in compliance	Easy to report	Audit failure rate (%)	0% within 18 months
Bank Management / Board	Bank Management / Board	Board Reports, Requests for Decisions	Sufficient income from consumer banking	Forecasts and projection accuracy	Income from all lines of consumer bank business	Increase by 7% this year
	Bank	Capital, Targets, Board Decisions	Clear strategies and targets	Commitment to strategies	Strategy changes during the year	0 Changes

Figure 4-7. Banking stakeholder analysis example.

Up next

The stakeholder analysis results will provide additional strategies and criteria for later decision making and provide the beginning of the design of the process architecture, which will touch each stakeholder type. There will be conflicts among stakeholder perspectives that will have to be sorted out and balanced. These tensions must be addressed and resolved as part of our strategy formulation, which will be covered next, rather than later when inconsistencies pop up in process analysis and capability development.

CHAPTER 5

Deriving your Strategy

T he framework, shown in Figure 5-1, provides an overarching set of concepts that we in Process Renewal Group have successfully used to classify and categorize business architecture work. Earlier, we tackled the challenge of scoping your architecture and the usefulness of selecting what's in and out based on value chains reflecting lines of business rather than organization charts reflecting internal functions. In the last chapter, we tackled the challenge of defining the value expected by the external stakeholders of such value chains.

Now we strive to gain acceptance of the criteria for design and decision-making, especially the determination of a consolidated set of strategic statements needed to guide many architectural choices to come. Connecting the architectural design components to this strategy is essential for everything that follows.

I will continue to view the organization or value chain as a black box, for now, to ensure we gain the essential knowledge of the overall drivers, goals, and objectives that inform what we have to do inside. How we use the criteria to make decisions among competing choices for change prioritization and capability investment will come later.

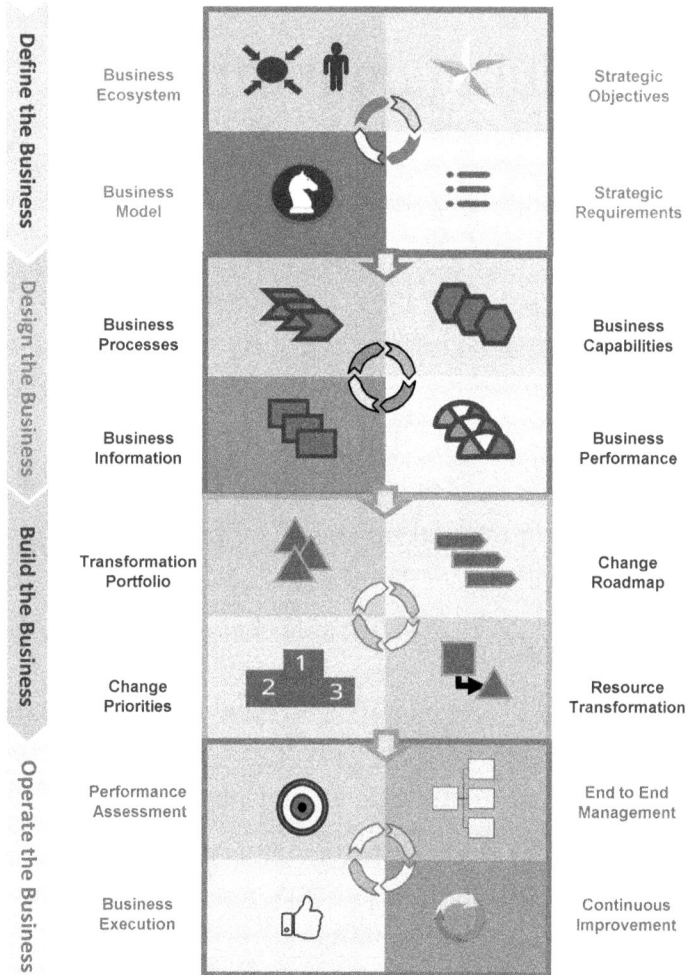

Figure 5-1. Comprehensive business architecture framework and foundational methodology.

All external perspectives must be balanced to arrive at an unequivocal guiding North Star intention that will be commonly shared as our guide rather than arguing from the perspective of internally conflicting departmental or personal interests.

What makes up strategic guidance?

The knowledge we documented on stakeholders' expectations of value and experience provides a critical set of considerations to define and assess the processes we conduct. It defines the ultimate strategic capabilities we will need to have in order to attain results and formulate the right balance in our strategic intent. To do so may require reconciling perspectives that may otherwise compete with one another.

Sound strategic guidance also requires broad analysis of the business environment within which the organization or value chain exists, also covered in the previous chapter. Our scope for this chapter includes examining favorable and unfavorable factors that will affect strategic and architectural choices. Once we understand these issues, we can craft a thoughtful strategy.

Business context scenario analysis

In a world of increasing VUCA (volatility, uncertainty, complexity, ambiguity), the potential variations in those STEEPL factors of greatest relevance to your circumstances must be assessed to determine the ones that bring most potential variations, good and bad, and therefore, risk or opportunity to the business should they occur. These scenarios are an opportunity to plan for an uncertain future. This was best articulated in the book, *The Art of the Long View*, made famous during the OPEC oil embargo of 1973 when Shell Oil rose to prominence in an otherwise pessimistic scenario for the oil industry. It shows there may be opportunities even if the industry is facing threats.

There is no better example of big winners and losers when businesses face a crisis than became apparent during the Covid-19 pandemic. This was not a good time to be in the travel industry, but wine and beer consumption jumped by approximately 50% in some places. So, with the world having to change quickly, any business design must work for a range of possible future business scenarios, not just for one set that is assumed based on today's assumptions. The relative certainty/uncertainty of future events must be a major consideration in defining requirements for process and capability adaptability. Your business design must account for key variables affecting the future for which our business and technology solutions must be planned to be agile and resilient enough to reduce or mitigate operational and business risks. Smart organizations and governments will have thought through such scenarios, have scripted crisis management plans, and will not be reluctant to follow them immediately when the situation calls for it.

The subset of the planning elements from the STEEPL assessment from an earlier chapter (products, regulation, price, competitors, etc.), which have the highest potential impacts and greatest uncertainty, should be examined for a range of possible responses. We should look at each factor to determine if the direction each could take is inevitable, strongly possible, or simply possible. For each of these, you will have to sort out whether or not the assessment for ourselves is optimistic, neutral, or pessimistic. These combinations can then be synthesized into a small set of representative alternative scenarios and validated as low to high risk. Some of these may be positive for the organization if it is ready to change quickly or if business designs chosen are inherently versatile. Some of these will be negative and represent real threats if the value chain is brittle and cannot bring sufficient strengths to weather the storm.

We will pick a small set of scenarios from this assessment to test any business models and architectures for robustness and flexibility. Figure 5-2 illustrates the range of possibilities. From these we would derive approximately five to seven combinations for business architecture and business design testing.

Scenario	Planning Element 1	Planning Element 2	Planning Element 3	...	External Opportunity or Threat	Internal Strength or Weakness	Strategic Response
A	Optimistic	Optimistic	Optimistic	...	...	...	...
B	Optimistic	Optimistic	Expected	...	...	...	...
C	Optimistic	Optimistic	Pessimistic	...	...	...	...
...							
Z	Pessimistic	Pessimistic	Pessimistic	...	...	...	...

Figure 5-2. Range of possibilities.

Defining strategy

There are many ways of defining a strategy for an organization or value chain. However, we tend to follow the Business Motivation Model (BMM), originally conceived by the Business Rules Group and formally adopted by the Object Management Group.[15]

The main message from this standard shown in Figure 5-3 is that there needs to be a clear distinction between the ends we strive for and how we attain them.

---

[15] https://www.omg.org/spec/BMM/1.3/About-BMM/.

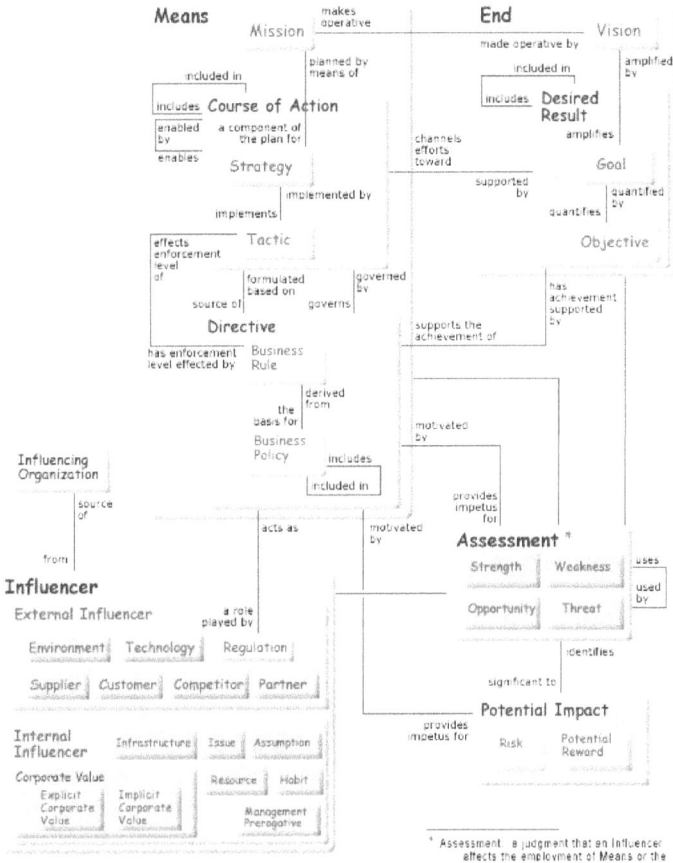

Figure 5-3. The ends we strive for and the means to attain them.

Business Motivation Model

'Ends' are results of the end-to-end process work performed to benefit the recipient stakeholders as we discussed in Chapter 3. 'Means' are the actions we take and the mechanisms we employ to realize them. Ends are what we aim to achieve. Means are what we need to do and have to achieve the ends. The misunderstanding of the difference is frequently a key source of confusion for those defining strategic intent and the strategy itself (these are different).

In this regard, it is not unusual to see organizations mix up Mission and Vision. A 'Mission' is what the organization or value chain is mandated or chooses to do to create value for those it serves. Unless the business changes, the Mission statement does not vary substantially over time. On the other hand, the 'Vision' is what we (the business) are trying to achieve by some defined point in time (a planning horizon). Our Vision should be measurable with clear comparable units of measure against which we can get accurate data. The Vision may change from planning period to planning period. It should reflect the result or outcome of what we will do if we do the right things right in the right way. Being strong at actioning great Means (methods and tools) is in and of itself no guarantee of achieving the Ends if they are not aligned. Some guidelines for statements of strategic intent appear in Figure 5-4.

Delivering outputs according to quality standards does not assure that your business outcomes will be achieved. Being efficient with resources does not mean you have satisfied recipients' needs or been effective in their eyes. We always start with the Ends and determine the courses of action required to achieve them. Otherwise, we easily get caught up in building what we think are great processes and capabilities that do not match a purpose or enable business results.

> Statements of strategic intent often include:
>
> - A planning horizon
> - A mission statement (what we do for those we serve reflecting the value proposition)
> - A vision statement (what we aim to achieve and how we will be recognized for it)
> - A statement of key goals or strategic outcomes (what we want to achieve based on needs and expectations)
> - A set of KPIs
> - A set of objectives (target measures for the KPIs by some specific date

Figure 5-4. Strategic intent guidelines.

We figure out what the right things are—this is the role of executives—and then determine the right way to accomplish them—this is the role of managers and professionals. To support the Mission, we will have to define the right courses of action. To support the Vision, we will have to establish several strategic goals (general statements of intention) and a set of strategic objectives (target measures of goals with crisp performance indicators by a defined timeframe).

Goals are not Objectives. BMM makes that clear. All of the key Ends and Means choices are influenced by the outside stakeholder goals and objectives and the outside pressures as documented in our STEEPL analysis and Business Scenarios. Clearly, there is a tricky balancing act to gain agreement on these choices among executive team members.

Value proposition

Another useful discussion to delve into is that of the Customer Value Proposition. A Customer Value Proposition is a business or marketing statement describing why a customer would buy a product or use a service from the supplying company. It reflects a philosophy, real or aspirational, that should be apparent to everyone in an organization in terms of the focus and behavior needed by the company and all its staff. It is operational and cultural. It is specifically targeted towards customers more than other external stakeholders such as employees, owners, or regulatory bodies.

Made popular in their book, *The Discipline of Market Leaders,* Treacy and Wiersema advocated that organizations should initially excel in one discipline and retain a base level of sufficiency in the others and not try to be leaders in all three at the same time. They argue that this will lead to a lack of shared focus and potentially miss the opportunity for differentiation and building trust in the market. The typical three classic propositions or styles are Product Leadership, Customer Intimacy, and Operational Excellence.

Product leadership

In Product Leadership oriented organizations, there is a focus on innovation and turning insights into breakthrough technologies, products, and services, not just once but on a continuing basis. World-class processes and capabilities will be found in the research and, product, and service lifecycle areas. Time-to-market is a major performance driver. An example of this proposition would be Apple, innovating with new products continuously. Another is Dyson, with its creative vacuums and air movement product lines. Often prices are higher, but a large proportion of the market will pay the uplift happily to have the latest and the best.

Customer intimacy

In Customer Intimacy, the focus is on continuing specialized and personalized customer service and a unique relationship with each customer beyond a single transaction. In this proposition, the customer relationship is more valued than any particular product at any a point in time. It has a strong service orientation. An incredibly strong sense of trust is established in more of a partnership style with customers. World-class processes and capabilities exist in and around customer relationship management and the creation and sustainment of loyalty.

Share-of-spend, which means more business from each customer, is a major performance driver in the relevant market categories.

Perhaps the most renowned long-term example of this proposition is Nordstrom, the high-end retailer of fashion and lifestyle products in the US and Canada with a very strong following of customers who buy a lot of their clothing through a personal shopper relationship. The Nordstrom personal shopper will always have their eyes open for suitable items that may be held for the customer to come in and try.

Another one, perhaps surprisingly, is Amazon which is always striving to offer the most appropriate products but doing so by using its powerful knowledge of the customer, its data analytics capability and delivery promise through Amazon Prime. Amazon is always experimenting and putting together proposals that are not mass offers but individually tailored ones. It knows a lot about its customers' buying habits. Once hooked, it is hard for many to shop any other way due to established trust.

Operational excellence

In Operational Excellence, the focus is on the efficiency of day-to-day operations and the price and simplicity of buying products and services. This is the domain of traditional Lean and Six Sigma improvement programs whereby reliability, waste reduction, and quality consistency are a prime focus. Unit costs and price competitiveness are major performance drivers. An example of Operational Excellence is Walmart or Costco. These organizations feature price as a differentiator and extremely efficient supply chain management and overall operations. This may go to the point that when a supplier finds an efficiency in its own operations, the distributor to the consumer market (Walmart or Costco) may demand a share of their suppliers saving in the price to them and on to consumers.

Value propositions and markets

Although there may be a predominant proposition particularly prevalent in a particular market, there is often room for different companies with different value propositions in many markets. Not everyone will purchase a $350 Dyson hair dryer, but some will have a house full of Dyson paraphernalia. These choices may not be tied to a particular income segment. There is typically not one for an industry that all players have to adopt. It is a matter of strategic choice. It is not unusual to find a scenario whereby a consumer exhibits all three propositions by driving to Nordstrom in her Tesla to buy a fashionable coat but dropping into Costco to buy inexpensive paper towels and getting a five-dollar coffee at Starbucks on the way home.

> *Whatever your strategic choice may be, once made, the proposition must be reflected in the design of your processes and capabilities and the organization's culture as witnessed by consistently aligned motivations and behaviors in all staff and reflected in management decisions that support the proposition's intent.*

North Star

At Process Renewal Group, we synthesize the factors mentioned so far into a simplified set of statements that make it easier to communicate direction and align the business aspects of architecture. By melding the conclusions from the external pressures and business scenarios, the strategic discussion of ends and means and the stakeholder expectations of value and experience, along with the value proposition, we can arrive at a set of unequivocal decision criteria that balances interests that may otherwise compete with one another and pull us in different directions depending on which executive is asked.

Especially useful in this synthesis are the stakeholder value expectations. This is the set of results that we must ideally deliver to satisfy the needs and experiences of our stakeholders to sustain healthy relationships and deliver on the value proposition. This will be much easier if we have done the expectations work described in Chapter 3 and know the expected results, experiences, and measures of value. In that case, we can inform process improvement and architecture guidance, thus arming decision makers with shared decision-making criteria. We will later be able to derive the specific outcomes for particular processes and projects if we decide to improve them.

From an architectural point of view, we can now synthesize a set of four to seven directional guiding statements. We call this the North Star. You may name it the Southern Cross if you are south of the equator. The implication is to establish a fixed point for all to refer to in charting the course of the remaining architecture work independent of political pressures internally. Our experience is that it is better to surface any differences of opinion or strategic misunderstanding at this early point rather than later. We want different points of view to come up here and not remain underground and later become potentially political, fractious and paralyzing.

Establishing this set of statements is not an exact science, even with the great work we will have done and the insights gained up to this point. The discussion to arrive at the list is perhaps as valuable as the list itself, surfacing joint insights not initially apparent to all participants. The statements should try to be consistent with several proven principles:

- Be targeted towards an agreed planning horizon
- Ideally have four to seven statements
- Each should have a vector (increase, decrease, sustain, or equivalent words) to reflect the intention of action
- Amplify shared expectations among our external stakeholders identified in our value analysis
- Balance inherent conflicts among stakeholder outcomes, considering more than one perspective
- Weight the contribution value of each factor out of 100% for later consideration—criteria for a strategic choice
- Ensure all statements are measurable with clear KPIs and aspirational performance targets

Figure 5-5 illustrates a North Star for our own consulting company, Process Renewal Group. Remember, the percentages are how important each outcome statement is relative to one another, given our mission and vision. The higher percentages are where we want to focus our efforts in our upcoming planning period. All items are important, or they would not be on the star, but not all will have the same emphasis for action. When we look at prioritization later, this will become invaluable.

In looking at all the knowledge gained so far in our journey, first of all, look for desired outcomes that are of shared value to multiple stakeholders such as customers, suppliers, and staff, if possible. These will likely be the highest rated in weighting percentages. Next, determine those uniquely critical to the customers and other downstream stakeholders. Next, find statements that make it easier for employees since they are on the front lines with customers. Now examine results for owners/shareholders/governing boards. Subsequently, find essential ones for suppliers and compliance bodies if not already covered by the prior ones. Examine these to ensure that any other important factors are considered, and the choices reflect the essence of where you want the organization to end up. Next, add the vector to be attained, such as increase, decrease, sustain. Determine the KPI. Gain agreement from the executives.

Figure 5-5. North Star for PRG.

Now you can negotiate the weightings. This is often difficult to get done because it is an exercise that no one willingly wants to do in front of others, all of whom may have a different motivation. Do not do it solely from the executives' personal motivations, but from the stakeholders and overall business intentions. However, make sure you have the executives' shared acceptance. They have to own it and use it later. Also, do not willingly allow them the choice of not choosing a weighting factor. When they decide not to differentiate and they say all points are equal. Ask, "Is everything truly equally important to the organization at this point in time?"

Having this discussion and making the choice is essential to business architecture and investment in processes and capabilities, since it allows us to rationally recommend what to do with the design of models and where change should occur. It may be helpful to document the outcome of this exercise as a template, as illustrated in Figure 5-6.

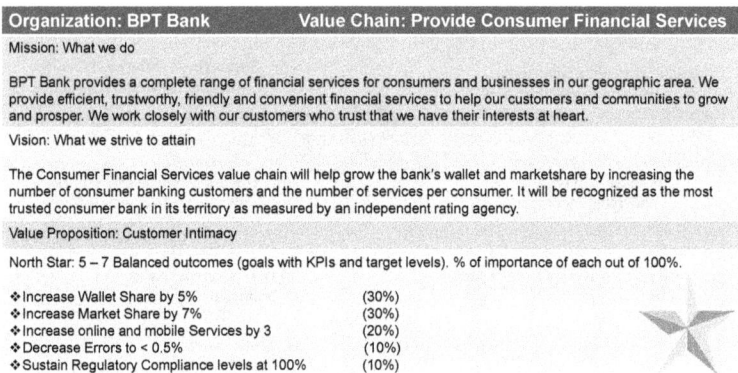

Organization: BPT Bank	Value Chain: Provide Consumer Financial Services

Mission: What we do

BPT Bank provides a complete range of financial services for consumers and businesses in our geographic area. We provide efficient, trustworthy, friendly and convenient financial services to help our customers and communities to grow and prosper. We work closely with our customers who trust that we have their interests at heart.

Vision: What we strive to attain

The Consumer Financial Services value chain will help grow the bank's wallet and marketshare by increasing the number of consumer banking customers and the number of services per consumer. It will be recognized as the most trusted consumer bank in its territory as measured by an independent rating agency.

Value Proposition: Customer Intimacy

North Star: 5 – 7 Balanced outcomes (goals with KPIs and target levels). % of importance of each out of 100%.

❖ Increase Wallet Share by 5%   (30%)
❖ Increase Market Share by 7%   (30%)
❖ Increase online and mobile Services by 3   (20%)
❖ Decrease Errors to < 0.5%   (10%)
❖ Sustain Regulatory Compliance levels at 100% (10%)

Figure 5-6. North Star for BPT Bank.

The North Star should be a constant in all presentations and meetings to assure a common focus on the end game. It is a constant reminder to stay focused.

Strategic capabilities

As we will see again later on, the term 'capability' can mean different things to different people, which can be a source of dissonance among professionals and executives. For example, business architects often think about the word related to the ability to deliver certain specific outcomes of particular work that we have to perform. On the other hand, strategic planners have used the term for decades to reflect the more macro issues that the strategic intent (such as the North Star goals) will require us to deal with if we are ever going to accomplish our aims.

The strategy community often alludes to these needs as Strategic Capabilities. An example of Strategic Capabilities can be seen in a product manufacturer/distributor that we worked with whose intention was to double revenue and profits in five years in market categories, only growing naturally at 2% per year. Clearly, organic growth would not suffice. The company recognized that they had to become very good at bringing new products to market much faster and also that they had to acquire competition to have the products and capacity to scale sufficiently.

These are specific Strategic Capabilities to be recognized early on, not to be confused with the comprehensive map of specific Functional Business Capabilities such as 'onboarding a customer' and 'claims management' that will be needed to support value streams and business processes. Unlike Strategic Capabilities, Functional Capabilities do not require the attention of executives this early. We will describe them in later chapters.

We tackle strategic capabilities as part of strategy work because we have to quickly figure out what programs we may need to get in place immediately to deal with these tough challenges in sufficient time. We have to start acting soon.

The heritage of this approach can be traced back to Dr. John Rockart at MIT's Sloan School of Management and his advocacy for an approach named 'Critical Success Factors' (CSFs). John stated that, "Critical success factors thus are, for any business, the limited number of areas in which results, if they are satisfactory, will ensure successful competitive performance for the organization."[16]

---

[16] Rockart, John F. *Chief Executives Define Their Own Data Needs.* Harvard Business Review, March 1979.

These are the few key factors that businesses should focus on to be successful; what is central to its future and achievement of that future. The favorite technique that I learned from John early in my career is to simply ask managers to complete the statement:

"In order to achieve the strategy and meet our strategic performance objectives, it is critical that we are able to ...."

It is remarkable how quickly and assuredly that senior leaders can answer the question if they all agree on the North Star.

Some of the factors may have larger gaps than others. The gap in current versus target goals and objectives will indicate the extent of the changes needed. We can expect a large potential performance gap to imply a large effort to close it.

One approach to help will be to examine some macro drivers from your STEEPL analysis that may be pushing some CSFs your way. Consider:

- **Environmental CSFs** from economic or technological changes whether you like them or not

- **Industry CSFs** resulting from specific industry characteristics; relevant to the whole industry, which will leave you behind if you do not get ahead of them or get you ahead if you do.

- **Strategy CSFs** resulting from your chosen competitive strategy (North Star and Value Proposition) of the business and your position in the industry

- **Temporal CSFs** resulting from current unavoidable internal needs and changes

The Burlton Hexagon segment analysis shown again in Figure 5-7 may also be helpful to derive your response.

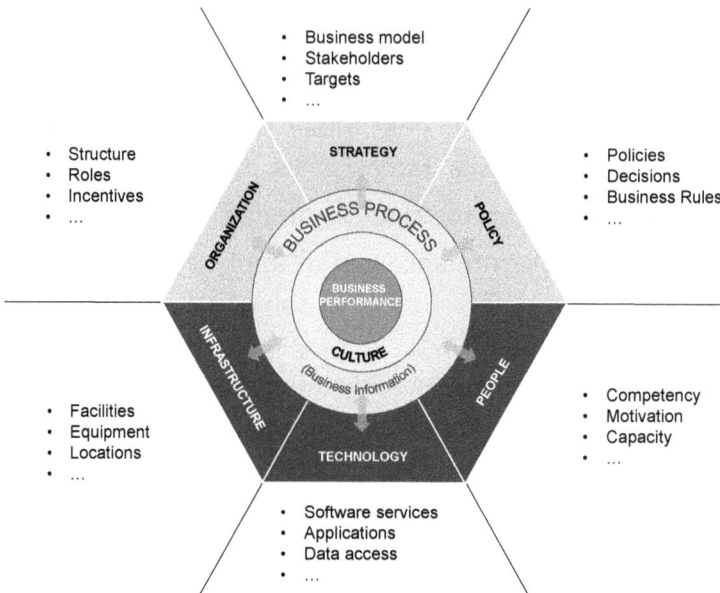

Figure 5-7. The Burlton Hexagon.

The types of factors represented by each section are critical if they must be achieved to attain the North Star. Otherwise, the stakeholder goals and performance objectives will absolutely not be achievable without its realization. Figure 5-8 shows a hypothetical illustration for our consumer banking example. Not all of these will be critical, but some will rise to the top. The hexagon is a useful tool to structure your thinking.

Category	Strategic Requirement
Business Performance	Have near real time access to performance data
Business Process	Get the customer journey supported by a set of lean processes that proactively provide the opportunity to gain wallet share at the right time
Business Information	Establish one integrated source of all business master data always current and without redundancies
Culture	Establish a full service culture focused on customer. Must establish a program to train managers to continually observe behavior and coach staff
Strategy	Share it broadly and deeply
Policy	Implement a lower risk profile in our lending and servicing decisions while satisfying the regulator.
Organization	Restructure around our value chains not our products or functions
People	Train our workers to be knowledgeable on all products and how to sell the best mix for the customer's true needs
Technology	Get the mobile and web business together and become omni-channel capable
Infrastructure	Establish new branches and bullet proof networks

Figure 5-8. Strategic requirements for BPT Bank.

Focus on identifying strategic capabilities needed to meet the CSFs. This is the time to do it - not in the middle of change when inconsistencies are typically discovered.

Up next

The knowledge gained here is more than a box to be ticked or an artifact stored. The insight gained by the participants and the agreement by management will pay off. If you do not do this, I guarantee that later you will wish you did because the arguments about it will surely arise but in a hurried, unstructured, and political manner. The architecture team will better relate to the business and talk their language through these mechanisms. The structural information, process, and capability models in the next few chapters will have a reason for being and a direction for changing. Everything will connect to value creation. The performance management system will connect to these top levels of the scorecard.

CHAPTER 6

Developing Concept and Information Models

I have seen various business-oriented models in many industries and in many types of organizations. Some models were well-formed and some not. Typically, there is a tacit presumption—sometimes misplaced—that we have a good grip on what we need to understand and how we can communicate what we know. Architectures built will reflect the presumptions that everyone knows the business and how to talk about it using consistent definitions and terms . When this is not true – most of the time – major disagreements can arise and roadblock arise.

In my experience, these are dangerous assumptions. Poor communications and diverse terminology understanding among business members get us into difficulties regularly. The longer the semantic gulf exists, the greater are the consequences. It is not unusual for employees in companies to use the same words for different things and different words for the same thing, and it is not unusual to find that there is no agreed structured vocabulary to clear this up.

Working recently with two corporate acquisitions and integration efforts drove this challenge home to me. In each case, it was critical to establish a common understanding of what the words mean early on in order to merge operations and organizations into one way of doing things supported by data and IT infrastructure integration, comparable performance indicators, and information across locations and lines of business. These integrations were successful because we solved the semantic differences long before dealing with processes and other architectural concerns. It was important to get on the same page because of cultural differences tied to naming things and the desire to establish a shared corporate identity.

The importance of a common semantic framework cannot be overemphasized—although it sometimes is. It is essential if we are to develop other architectural models that are part of a business architecture practice. More and more, it is becoming clear that the formal structuring of a business concept model as the foundation of several other types of domain models is essential. It is the foundation of the 'Design the Business' section of the Process Renewal Group (PRG) architectural framework, as shown in Figure 6-1.

Based on the business concept model, we will see that the business information model will establish the foundation for the business processes needed to act on those concepts.

Business capabilities must realize the ability to make the concepts work. Key performance indicators start with quantifying concepts to assess the business's performance.

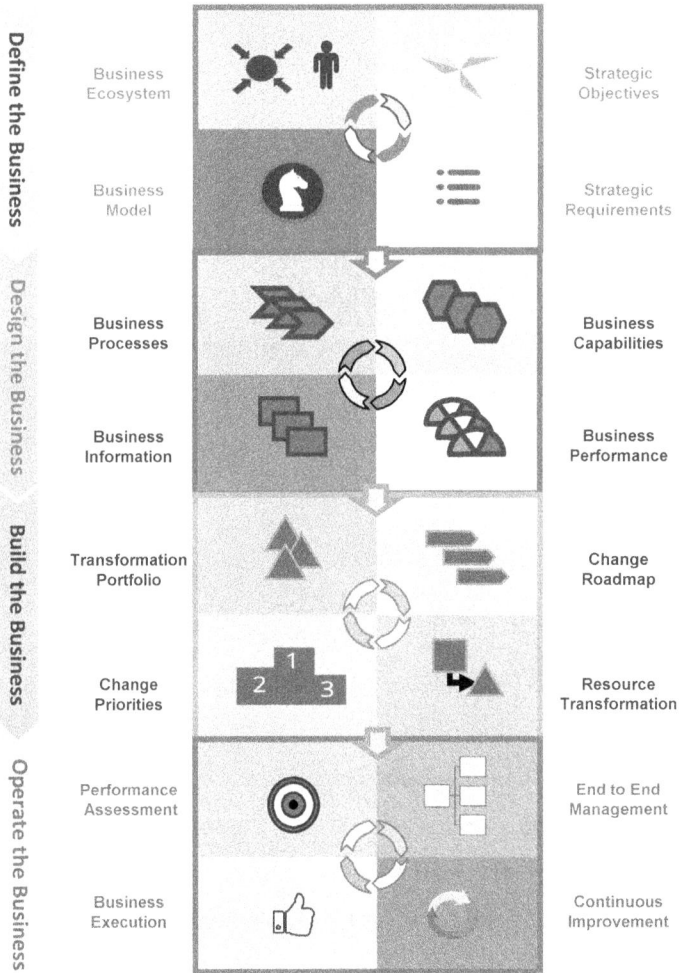

Figure 6-1. Comprehensive business architecture framework and foundational methodology.

The concept model will directly translate into what we need to know about—the information—to keep the organization alive and healthy. In addition to these critical architectural building blocks, the concept model provides a rigorous foundation for structuring business rules to be used in making business decisions that are made in our processes.

I will describe the essential elements of the concept model in this chapter and show how it provides the basis for an information model. In later chapters, I will deal with the other domains and how each can leverage the concept model to allow ease of defining each one's models and the changes critical for sustaining business agility.

About the concept model

I would like to thank Ron Ross of Business Rules Solutions for providing some of the information for this section. His latest book, *Business Knowledge Blueprints: Enabling Your Data to Speak the Language of Business*, contains the foundation for much of what is contained in this chapter. Figure 6-2 shows some definitions that we will use to ensure clarity in this chapter.

The concept model is a semantic model and not a data model per se. It is indispensable when you develop or derive a data model later. There is an Object Management

Group (OMG) standard that establishes the structure of the model to guide practitioners. This standard is named Semantics of Business Vocabulary and Business Rules (SBVR for short).[17] It helps us figure out how to define the business meanings of concepts and the words used. It contains terms (nouns), term definitions, and term associations (verbs). Associations are how the terms are related to one another. The model is non-procedural, so sequencing is not relevant here.

- **Concept**. Something conceived in the mind. (Webster's Dictionary)
- **Business Concept**. An abstraction of things in the real world: anything in the business you must know about and manage. (Roger T. Burlton)
- **Concept Model**. A set of business concepts as represented by standard terms and business definitions along with the logical connections among the concepts. (Ronald G. Ross)

Figure 6-2. Important concept modeling definitions.

Noun concepts

For the nouns, we typically come across words that represent real things in the real world, such as 'car', or a word that represents something less tangible, yet important to the business, such as 'trip.' A well-formed

---

[17] https://en.wikipedia.org/wiki/Semantics_of_Business_Vocabulary_and_Business_Rules.

business concept defines something fundamental to the business operation and its management. It is anything that we must know about and make decisions about. Its definition is independent of any organization structure, process, or technology that deals with it. If it can be counted or otherwise quantified, it is probably a viable concept to be modeled. One classic approach to getting this modeling started is searching for nouns in key documents.

One set of nouns describes the stakeholders with whom we have relationships. We should have already identified these in our ecosystem analysis. We have to know about them to execute the business. We will have to have information about each of these relationships since these parties will be involved with our business operations or affect the management and support of the core business. Stakeholders for our ongoing banking example appear in Figure 6-3.

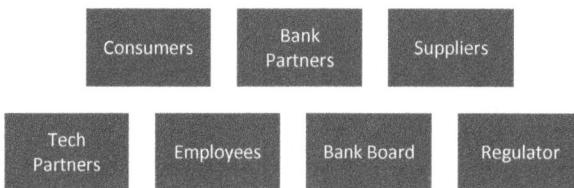

Figure 6-3. Stakeholders.

Some of these will be involved in day-to-day business operations, and others will guide our actions or provide enabling capabilities. There are also a set of big things that affect the whole enterprise. Many of these are similar across companies in like industries. For example, in financial services, we would expect to find, among others, concepts such as shown in Figure 6-4.

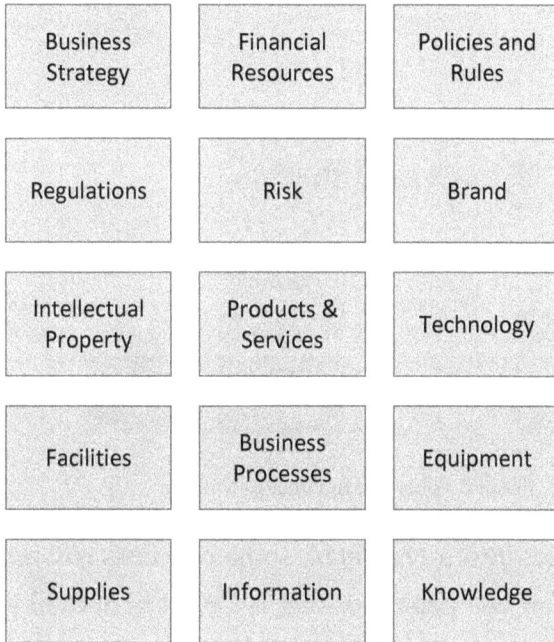

Business Strategy	Financial Resources	Policies and Rules
Regulations	Risk	Brand
Intellectual Property	Products & Services	Technology
Facilities	Business Processes	Equipment
Supplies	Information	Knowledge

Figure 6-4. Some Concepts.

If we organize these into Guiding, Core, and Enabling bands, we see the beginning of the value chain concept model. These appear in Figure 6-5. This is clearly a macro set at a high level of abstraction to start with. It is not practical to try to show all concepts at once and certainly not to show all concepts and relationships graphically on one page, so split them up into areas of similar focus.

Guiding

Business Strategy	Brand	Regulator	Regulations
Risk	Intellectual Property	Policies and Rules	Bank Board	Financial Resources

Core

Products & Services	Bank Partners	Consumers

Enabling

Business Processes	Information	Employees	Knowledge	Facilities
Equipment	Technology	Tech Partners	Suppliers	Supplies

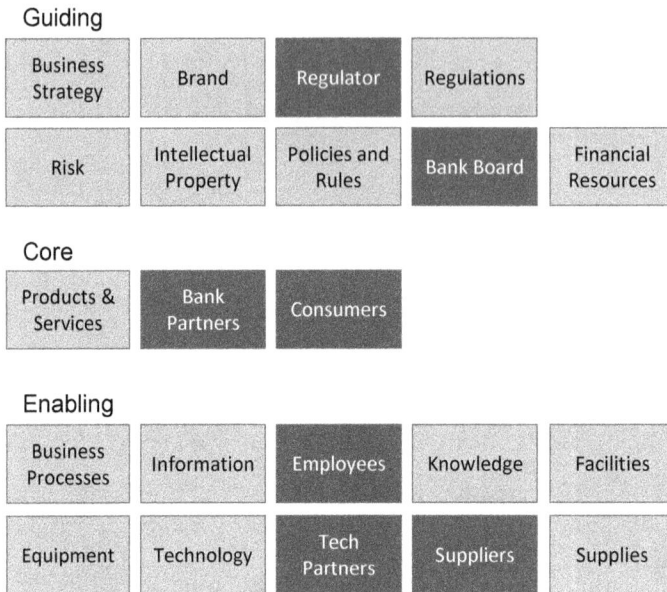

Figure 6-5. Scoped value chain concept model.

As we get into more detail, some concepts will appear on more than one page, but that is OK. It is normal to take a perspective and show the relevant concepts as a focused set. For example, we can show all concepts regarding human resources management. Obviously, the set will include concepts of Employee, Business Strategy, Policies and Rules, and go deeper with a set of concepts relevant to that function, such as role, compensation, location. Likewise, we could have chosen Products and Services as a focal point and examined its relevant concepts such as business case, price, and roadmap.

Another source of nouns can be found in the list of items exchanged with external ecosystem stakeholders from our earlier context diagram. Some of these will be key to the business's operations (the core), as shown in Figure 6-6. Please note that if we were interested in some aspect of the non-core parts of the business, such as IT, we would model that subset in our concept model.

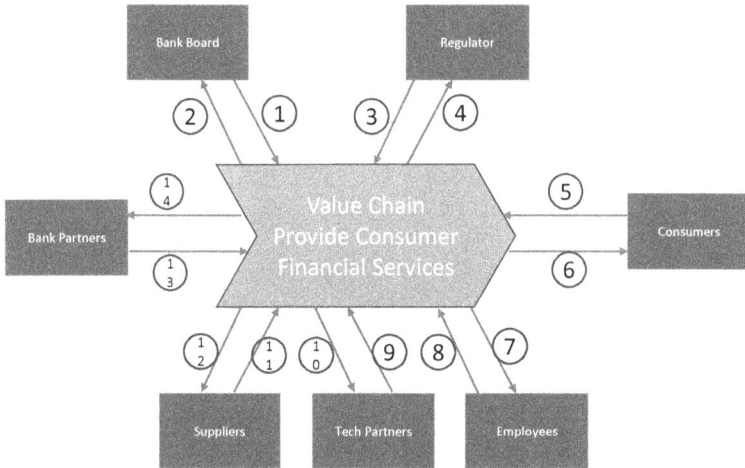

Stakeholder Value Item Exchanges

1. Capital, Targets, Board Decisions
2. Board Reports, Requests for Decisions
3. Regulatory Requirements, Certification Requests
4. Reports, Regulation Change Requests
5. Requests for Services, Fee Payments
6. Financial Services, Charges
7. Contracts, Requests for Supplies and Services
8. Contracts, Supplies, Services
9. Skills, Labor, Employment Commitment
10. Compensation, Employment Commitment
11. Community Concerns and Requests
12. Community Programs, Sponsorships

13. Service Agreements, Services for customers, Revenue share
14. Service Agreements, Customer lists

Figure 6-6. Context diagram as a source of concepts.

As mentioned, break the list of essential nouns into categories of core business and those that describe the guiding and enabling aspects. For this illustration, we will assume we are concerned mostly with business operations, so we will need more detail in this area. Some but not all of the concepts important at the operational aspects for the consumer bank example appear in Figure 6-7.

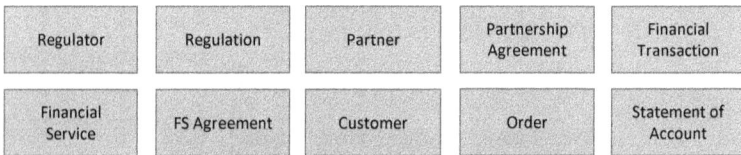

| Regulator | Regulation | Partner | Partnership Agreement | Financial Transaction |
| Financial Service | FS Agreement | Customer | Order | Statement of Account |

Figure 6-7. Concepts important to the operational aspects.

Once we discuss these, we may find even more relevant concepts to add. Now we have collected some dots describing what we need to know and manage, and we can start to connect the dots by defining the verbs that associate them.

Verb concepts

Verb phrases connect noun concepts to essentially create a sentence that is a statement of truth. The structure of such statements is 'Subject (noun)—verb—object (noun).' For example, '*a mortgage (noun subject) is secured against (verb) a fixed property (noun object).*' In SBVR, the set of these is called a 'Fact Model,' and it can appear graphically. A concept model includes both noun concepts and verb wordings that provide the foundational association between business terms without rule constraints.

Nouns and verbs

Although a fact model can (and should) serve as the basis for creating a data model or class diagram, its central business purpose at this point is to support business communications and help define relevant business information. Ignoring for now the non-core aspects, the graphical view of a portion of such a model appears in Figure 6-8.

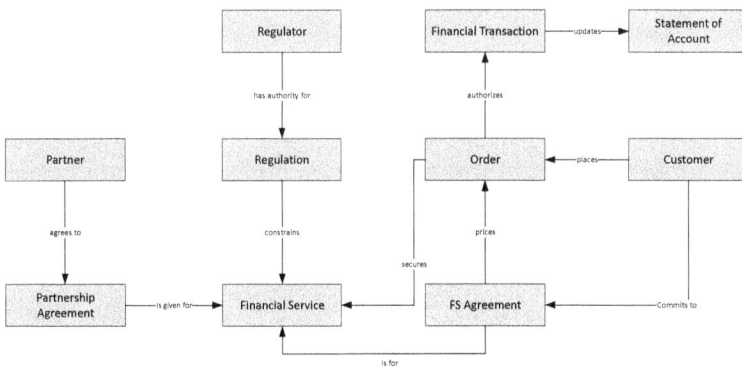

Figure 6-8. Sample Fact model.

The arrows are put in place to help read the diagram naturally. We read in the direction of the arrow (box name – arrow name from the base end – Box name). This does not imply sequencing or cardinality (see below). Many of the arrows could have been reversed, and the diagram read in the passive tense if it makes the reading and communication more straightforward. I prefer to have active tense directions if possible. Some people show wordings in both directions.

Such a model can easily be 'read' by business people for validation to be sure that we have captured the essence – the truth – of the business.

Definition of terms

As mentioned earlier, all terms in the concept model must be defined so they can stand alone and, as much as possible, not requiring a description that needs other terms. If possible, we recommend using commonly understood definitions, as defined by a commonly used dictionary, assuming the meanings are suitable for the business.

When terms are specific to an industry and have different meanings than the common vernacular, we use an industry dictionary or glossary reference. As a last resort, we would create definitions unique to your particular company or, regrettably, a specific group within it if we have to. At the time of writing, I am dealing with a company that uses the term 'supplier' except in one group that insists on naming these companies as 'vendor'. For others in the company that name means something different. Variations among company groups are where the arguments are the greatest.

An example of a well-formed noun definition is, "*A secured credit product is any loan that is backed by a borrower's asset.*" Note that, in the definition itself, there are other *underscored* terms that may also require definition. Do we know what a '*borrower's asset*' is or what qualifies to be one? Figure 6-9 illustrates several definitions for our concept model.

Notice that some of the terms defined here define other terms, as shown with underlines. If stored in a knowledge base of some sort, the embedded terms would be hypertext linked to their own definition. Of course, you cannot define the term with words that are essentially the same wording, such as, "*A partner is an entity with whom we partner.*"

The concept model, once done, is and should appear obvious and may bring forth the question, from some, as to why we bothered to take the time when we knew that already. As a foundation for so much else we have to fight for it to avoid complicated misunderstandings later. What

I have shown is the simplest form of a concept model. There can be more subtlety of course—there always is. A great read on developing concept models appears in Ronald Ross's book, *Business Knowledge Blueprints* mentioned earlier in this chapter.

- **Financial Institution**. An organization (public or private) that collects funds (from the public or other institutions) and invests them in financial assets.
- **Financial Services Agreement**. A contract to which we and our consumer agree to the set of financial services that we offer and the terms and conditions of each.
- **Financial Service**. The design of the policies, and legal standard business terms, that define what is sold to consumers and how services are delivered.
- **Generally Accepted Accounting Principles**. Generally accepted accounting principles (GAAP) refer to a common set of accounting principles, standards, and procedures issued by the Financial Accounting Standards Board (FASB). Public companies in the U.S. must follow GAAP when their accountants compile their financial statements.
- **Partner**. An organization that has or may sign a partnership agreement to deliver one or more financial services to our consumer.
- **Regulation**. A set of policies, rules and conditions that constrain the design of our financial services and govern how they are delivered.
- **Regulator**. An organization providing information regarding regulations against which we must comply and report.

Figure 6-9. Concept model definitions.

About the information model

Having a clear scope of concepts of interest and an understanding of the semantics of the business is extremely helpful in communication, analysis, and design and the avoidance of delays and corrections as design and change efforts proceed. The cost of not being on the same page with all models is a significant frustration that can lead to mistakes, design flaws with real cost, and time implications. There are several other models that benefit directly from the concept model. These are information, capability, business process, measurement, and business rules—all to be discussed in upcoming chapters.

Clearly, the business concepts will directly connect to information types. The concept model has the structure but is missing the cardinality (see below) needed for the full Information Model. It also is void of the attributes required to describe the specifics of the data details. The big buckets of information should use the names and scope of the concepts developed already, although they may be broken into sub types or have specializations (more particular usage). The hierarchy of definitions from concept to logic to physical data model, each with its own characteristics, must be traceable to the concept model.

Cardinality

The description of cardinality—sometimes called multiplicity—refers to the reality of the natural constraint of the connection between two concepts (aka entities at this level). The question is, "For each concept/entity, how many of the associated entities at the other end of the connecting line can exist?" In our example, "How many consumer banking customers requested a particular order?" The answer is clear that a particular order can only belong to one specific customer. However, if we look at it the other way around, it is similarly clear that a customer can place several orders and not just one. Therefore, in the model, we would have what we call a one-to-many relationship between these two concepts. There are several ways to graphically show the cardinality depending on the methodology or documentation standard you prefer. We often use the 'crow's foot' for the many end, and dash or double dash for the 'one' end.

In a different set of concepts such as Order and Financial Service, a particular Order can contain line item entries for more than one Financial Service, and a particular Financial Service is not constrained by only existing for a particular Order since many people can place their own Order for the same service. This is a one-to-many relationship both ways, which makes it a many-to-many relationship together. In some documentation approaches, especially when we consider the type of data storage mechanism needed, this may have to be resolved by another entity that sits between the two to clarify the connection. Perhaps we need another entity called 'Line Item' that connects to each of the others in a one-to-many fashion. If we are sure we will implement this information in a relational database, this may be helpful to know. Going to that level of abstraction finds us moving the conceptual view towards the logical level of Entity/Relationship modeling.

Figure 6-10 illustrates the addition of cardinality but without the line item entity that could have been added for relational data. Please note that we have added a couple of one-to-many relationships to be clearer in articulating the many-to-many relationships. Another aspect that may be considered at this point is 'Optionality,' meaning that we can articulate which of the relationships is mandatory—must exist—and which are not—that is may but does not have to. There is more to Cardinality and Optionality that is best served by other reading sources.[18] I will let the reader examine these on her own.

---

[18] For example, Data Modeling Made Simple, by Steve Hoberman, 2nd Edition, Technics Publications.

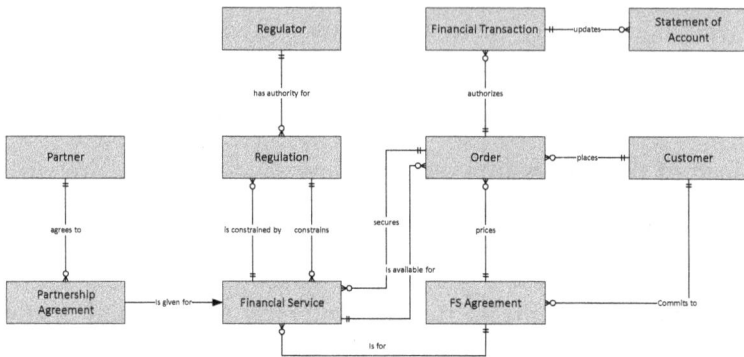

Figure 6-10. Concept model including cardinality.

Attributes

To establish the deepest level that we should go to and avoid getting into the detailed world of Logical Data Models, we can consider adding the main attributes to the entities we have established so far. Again, these may look somewhat different in the physical database design later for many practical reasons, but that is the realm of the database analyst and not our concern yet. Each attribute names a single piece of data that helps describe its entity. These descriptors can be a range of types, including text, numbers, codes, images, videos, and other unstructured data. Try to have attributes identified as belonging to only one entity if possible. This avoids update issues when multiple instances of information exist in several entities. In our example, some attributes for Financial Services Agreement may be:

- Agreement Number
- Agreement Name
- Agreement language
- Legal Jurisdiction
- Agreement Date
- Termination Date
- Standard Terms and Conditions

The attributes will have to be relevant but not exhaustively documented. If there is no need for them yet, you may leave them out for now.

Up next

Concept models are the backbone of the business architecture and are remarkably stable over time, helping the organization become more scalable and agile if defined once and shared. The understanding represented by the model pays off throughout any architecture effort or development project, whether Waterfall or Agile in nature. Therefore, I strongly recommend that one be developed and leveraged. You will not regret it. The following chapters will use the definitions and terms established here so you do not bog down in misunderstandings. The structured business knowledge gained through the concept model will hold together the architecture and be highly reusable. In the next chapters, I will discuss the process architecture and then the capability model, both of which strongly leverage the concept models developed here.

CHAPTER 7

Developing your Process Architecture

Previous chapters describing the Business Architecture Landscape, as shown in Figure 7-1, have dealt with the scoping of value chains and their connection to the ecosystem within which our architectures will fit. Notably, Stakeholder analysis was very useful in forming our strategic intent and definition of value.

This contextual knowledge becomes even more important now since we will tackle the connection of our business processes to our interactions with the outside world. This view ignores organization charts for now and focuses on the delivery of stakeholder value, keeping our end-to-end processes or value streams squarely aimed at doing the right things that support the mission of the value chain or enterprise.

I have also dealt with the importance of a common set of semantics and a shared business concept model leading to the information that the company must have and use. These semantics are essential to establish a relevant connected architecture since the rest of it uses the same terminology. The same wording is required to be sure that you have a relatable business process architecture.

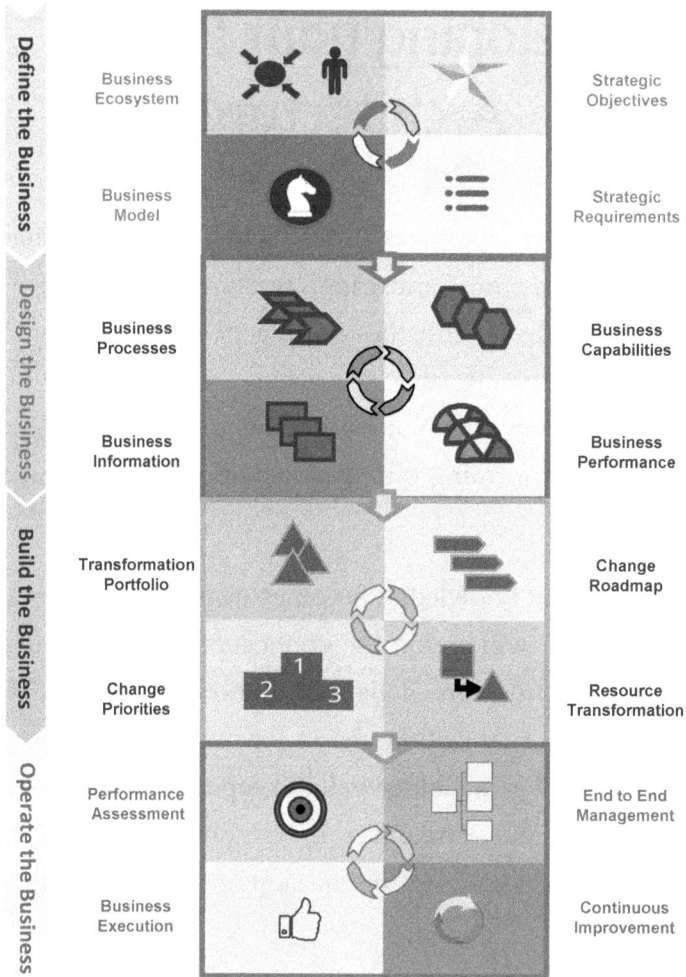

Figure 7-1. Comprehensive business architecture framework and foundational methodology.

I will continue to focus on realizing the external stakeholder perspective using our knowledge of the drivers, goals, and objectives of the North Star and especially the nature of the products, services, and information exchanged. These exchanges will give us the start and end of all comprehensive processes that create mutual value and launch value streams. We will remain independent of the organizational structure in doing this.

Business process explanation

The knowledge we should have now documented regarding stakeholders' expectations of value and experience, described in previous chapters, provides a context for our processes, which will directly connect to many of the other architectural domains.

Let's start by being clear about what we mean by the term 'Business Process.' A process perspective provides a critical foundation for effective business investment, operations, and change.

> *Simply put, business operations are the execution of instances of your core business processes.*

Your operational processes represent the work done by people or technology for a purpose. The process architecture organizes and describes the work required to deliver the business strategy. End-to-end processes models assure a business perspective in your business architecture. Once implemented, they deliver the day-to-day business results to outside stakeholders and provide the measurement structure needed to monitor and manage those results. To be relevant, organizations must start with a robust set of business processes that everyone understands. Then they can figure out what is needed to deliver operational business results successfully. The beginning of process relevance always focuses on running the business successfully.

A focus on processes comes from a deep-seated passion for making the business run better and not just building systems.

To be operationally successful, we must improve how processes execute every day to deliver value and achieve optimal outcomes. This is job one. It's what organizations are there to do. It's how they survive, thrive, and grow. This understanding must come before considering technologies or organization charts, no matter the latest technological or organizational fad. A business must start by striving to enhance the performance of business operations end-to-end for customers and other stakeholders. Doing the right work and making the right operational decisions is all about processes and business operations. It's how we get rewarded or punished in the marketplace.

Business processes are the pipelines that deliver operational results to stakeholders.

A solid process foundation is needed to connect the dots among strategic intent, business relationships, business capabilities, enabling technology, and human resources, to name a few. This end-to-end process structure is essential for achieving digitalization or customer centricity goals and ensuring that all business resources are shared and optimally aligned towards a common objective. To do this, organizations need to architect their intellectual and physical assets and shared capabilities using business processes as the glue tracing all connected work to enterprise intent and stakeholder outcomes.

A practical, shareable, and implementable business-process-driven change portfolio will ensure organizations choose the right transformation initiatives and optimize operational business outcomes.

Organizations can scope, analyze, and design new ways of working using process innovation and improvement practices and models. These will help organizations realize new business model intent and prescribe what's required technically, organizationally, and culturally to enable it.

Business Process Manifesto

The Business Process (BP) Manifesto[19] states that "an organization's business processes clearly describe the work performed by all resources involved in creating outcomes of value for customers and other stakeholders." In other words, a business process is not just a list of connected activities but a value-creating proposition for external service recipients. It emphasizes an end-to-end perspective, starting with those in our external world and working back to our internal operations. These manifesto principles emphasize this strategic point of view.

- A business process should create measurable value for customers and other stakeholders by delivering outcomes that satisfy their particular needs and expectations.

- A business process delivers outputs to and receives inputs from external customers and stakeholders as well as other business processes within the organization.

---

[19] http://www.bptrends.com/resources/bp-manifesto/.

- A business process should be guided, formally or informally, by the organization's business mission, vision, goals, and performance objectives.

The manifesto goes on to say that "a business process model represents the fundamental abstract structure and organization of a business process or set of business processes as described by their activities, their relationships to one another and to the environment in which they operate." This structural perspective emphasizes integrity, completeness, and decomposition of critical knowledge. Comprehensive process frameworks such as the Process Classification Framework® (PCF)[20] from APQC are built in this way. The manifesto also states:

- The complete set of business processes of an organization describes all the work undertaken by that organization.

- A business process model contains all the information required to describe the business process and its environment.

---

[20] https://www.apqc.org/pcf.

Relationship with business capabilities

Of all of the business architecture domains, there is most confusion and disagreement on the purpose or composition of processes and capabilities. It is intriguing to watch the unbridled emotion that sometimes surfaces between advocates in each camp, often arguing that we only need one or the other—not both. I strongly believe that these two areas are distinct and necessary to better understand the business. The prime misrepresentation by each camp is that the other camp's model is merely a subordination of its own. The contention is that by going deeper on one, you will find the other in the subordinated details.

I feel strongly that the two are domains of the first order, meaning that a business process is not a derivative of a capability at depth and a business capability is not merely an attribute of a process. Instead, they are different things, both fully decomposable and related through definable associations with one another. The BIZBOK now has recognized this fact and describes the two in the version released in April 2021.[21] This realization has surfaced based on the Business Architecture Guild's Business Architecture whitepaper release in late 2019, for which I

---

[21] https://www.businessarchitectureguild.org/page/publications.

admit to being one of the primary authors. Fortunately, the profession is adapting to a new way of seeing the association among the domains, and the battle seems to be settling down.

> *We execute, measure, manage, and improve processes. We build capabilities to serve that purpose.*

Another misunderstanding that was and still is somewhat present is that business capabilities describe the 'what' of the business and the Processes the 'how.' This is a twist on the idea that a process is a subcomponent of a capability — a harmful characterization I believe. All domains are 'whats', including processes, when it comes to business architecture. The capability 'payment processing' is what we have to be able to do regarding payments, not how. The process 'make payment' gives no hint as to how that is to be done, just that it has to be done in some way. There is no 'how' there.

So how do processes and capabilities relate? The diagram below (Figure 7-2) articulates an accepted view to serve both process and capability advocates at the Business Architecture Guild. It appears in the whitepaper[22] and also

---

[22] https://www.businessarchitectureguild.org/page/whitepapers.

in the current version of the Business Architecture Body of Knowledge.

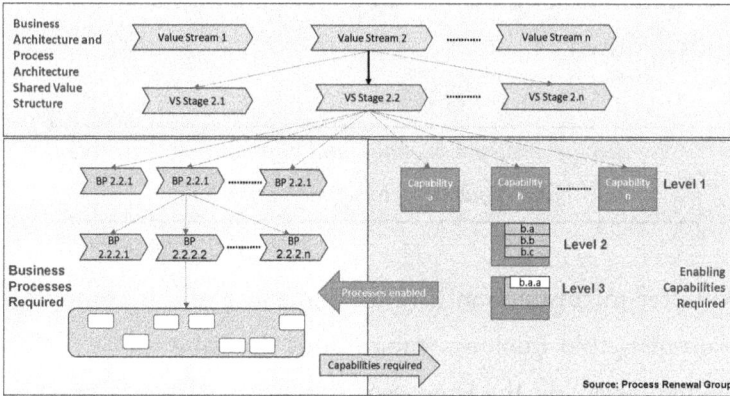

Figure 7-2. Process and capability.

The agreement is an important clarification of semantics. As I have noted in earlier chapters, semantics are important for understanding and consistency of communications, decisions, and actions. I will discuss the critical aspects of these meanings in more detail in an upcoming chapter dealing specifically with business capabilities. For now, the main message is that you must define processes and capabilities independently and connect them. One or the other separately will be insufficient. In Figure 7-2, we must understand what actions need to be taken to create stakeholders' value and understand the required capabilities to be able to do so. We have called these value streams that sit as components of a given value chain and, within each of them, values stream stages. Process professionals do not necessarily call these 'streams' or 'stages' but instead simply 'high-level processes' in a process architecture hierarchy.

The key is that both camps agree on the need to understand structured work that creates value. From that point, Capabilities can be derived and decomposed and also more detailed sub-levels of processes determined. The lower process levels will identify which set of capabilities, or sub-levels thereof, a process needs to execute effectively and also which processes a particular capability will serve. Each capability must consider all of the processes that will use that capability to know what that capability needs to achieve. This implies a many-to-many relationship between processes and capabilities.

We will discover that more than one process will execute each of several capabilities. For example, if I identify a credit check capability, I expect it to show up in multiple processes for which, risk assessment is required. But let's get back to the process architecture.

Key traits of a robust process architecture

To manage business processes as reusable assets, organizations need to establish a robust process architecture (enterprise or value chain process map) that leverages end-to-end thinking and stakeholder value delivery. A sound enterprise-level view of all processes at the higher levels (not workflow level yet) will exhibit some key traits.

Organizationally agnostic

Business processes typically do not correlate to an organization's formal reporting structure. Certainly, the work described by the processes in the architecture, at some level of detail, will be performed by people, equipment or technologies. However, end-to-end value creation is driven by our external party relationships, not our internal hierarchy, which may change much more often. A good test of the quality of an organization's process architecture is to ask if the process structure could survive a significant reorganization unscathed. If the answer is no, it is a poor process architecture and will have to be changed often when such changes occur. It will get out of date fast.

The business organizational structure can be changed but keep in mind that customers will judge your business by how well you meet their expectations of process delivery, nothing more or less.

Technologically agnostic

Technological services or implemented capabilities typically enable the processes of the organization. Given the availability of Enterprise Resource Planning (ERP) suites and other off-the-shelf software, it is especially tempting to follow the vendor's implicit design for the organization's processes. However, there is not always a one-to-one correlation between the two. Each process may have more than one enabling technology in use, and multiple processes typically employ a particular technology. The perspectives are different. Falling into the trap of following the technology in a one-to-one mapping effort to create the overall process map will not result in an end-to-end view of the organization's world that can deliver business outcomes to stakeholders. Unfortunately, this is a common trap that IT software developers often exhibit due to their laser focus on getting code to run first.

Value chains

Organizations can have multiple lines of business, products, services, markets, and geographies. Trying to mix and match all of these into one consolidated process architecture would be ideal. Still, it may be unwise due to the effort's disparate nature, sheer size, and complexity. Instead, it may be more feasible to build architectures around a single value chain at a time, each with its own unique value proposition. For example, retail banking is quite different from wealth management and what happens on the trading floor. To be sure you have well-formed value chains, check to see if the processes are truly different and serve different stakeholders, measures, and goals.

Consistent naming

True to the value creation proposition, processes should exhibit a high-quality and consistent active naming structure from top to bottom.

Organizations that have effectively named their processes typically use commonly understood language (i.e., no jargon), have ensured they are quantifiable and use an action-oriented verb-noun convention. Avoid nouns such as 'the order process.' Nouns are for data and things. Avoid gerunds or suffixed verbs such as 'marketing.' That's for departments. Avoid vague, lazy verbs such as 'manage technology.' Those are for functions or job descriptions. Instead, results or outcomes of value should be clearly visible in the name, such as 'settle claim' and not 'handle claim.' The closing event representing the targeted result of the process should be derived easily by inverting the name such as 'claim settled.' The process value goal or purpose should be apparent in the name. This naming convention is a passion for me and my colleague Alec Sharp, who also strongly emphasizes this requirement in his book, Workflow Modeling.[23]

Simple categorization based on process purpose

A process architecture oriented to an end-to-end view of the business is generally partitioned into three major categories, although there can be more: Core, Guiding, and Enabling Processes.

- **Core** processes deliver goods and services to the value chain or organization's customers, clients, or consumers. Core processes deal with what the organization does to action the customer relationship journey (from birth to death) and the product and service lifecycle (from concept through retirement). This is the actioning of the enterprise's Mission. It is what the organization gets paid to do. Therefore, everything else it does outside of the core must strive to optimize core processes and not be self-serving.

- **Guiding** processes set direction, plans, constraints, and establish control over all other processes. They

---

[23] Sharp, Alec (2009). Workflow Modeling: Tools for Process Improvement and Application Development. 2nd Ed. Artech House.

are not the heart of the business like the core but perhaps are the brains. Despite not being Core, they can be extremely important since a misdirection or inappropriate policy will ultimately show up in poor service to the customer and sub optimal business results.

- **Enabling** processes provide reusable and usually tangible resources that make it possible to do the work of all processes. Again, most organizations go into business to do the work of the Core, which cannot be effective without the right operational capability in place provided by the enabling processes. The enabling processes could be thought of as the arms and legs of the enterprise.

Many models or organizations use the terms "management processes for guiding" and "support processes for enabling." However, in my experience, these terms are not clear enough and are often confused with what managers or support departments do or are responsible for, not with the intention of the role they play as part of an end-to-end proposition.

Limited depth of structure

To remain architectural in perspective, the level of abstraction should remain high, and organizations should not delve too deeply into the details of the process activities yet. The distinguishing factor should be that the architecture describes 'what we do' and not variations in 'how we do it.' As such, architectures are conceptual in nature—a way of thinking and talking about our work. The process architecture should also be stable over time unless the business model itself is changed. For example, 'sell' does not say how the organization sells, but sales results can still be measured, and sales can be performed in many ways concurrently through varying channels and employing a variety of mechanisms. Once stabilized, the architecture does not have to change much, if at all.

While not a strict rule, starting with the value chain as level 0, approximately three and sometimes four subordinate levels of depth are usually sufficient in an architecture with perhaps ten or so processes per sub-level for each parent level process. The 'what' perspective stands the test of time. It also allows organizations to balance stabilization and standardization (process and performance) across the organization, including divisions and regions, and the customization necessary to accommodate the 'how we do things' among different groups where appropriate. Customization of 'how' things are done locally is often required due to regional and product differences and because of varying regulations, norms, systems, and cultures.

Measurable

As mentioned in the value chain section in an earlier chapter, a well-formed architecture-level process should be quantifiable. That's the first test and the first measurement indicator—determine how many instances of this process exist, appropriately factored, or filtered by different considerations of type, such as by location or product type.

If a good measure is impossible to find, then you may have a poor process structure on your hands. Perhaps it should be re-examined and re-scoped. At a minimum, architectural-level processes should always be measurable in terms of their effectiveness to service recipients and how well each one meets the expected value to be received in terms of needs met and experiences satisfied. A later chapter will deal with measurement in more depth.

Traceable

In terms of measurement, from the value chain down to lower levels of processes (more detailed), we should ensure that each process contributes to the value expectations of the recipients of the work performed. With a well-formed, end-to-end process architecture, this is easier than using a fractured functional or organizational view of the work, where we concentrate on or are constrained by internal handoffs.

Aligned

Like the goal of traceability through decomposition, each process in an end-to-end architecture must align with its interacting processes at the same level of composition. Outputs of upstream processes act as inputs, guides, or enablers to those downstream. There can be no disconnects or gaps among the processes in process architecture design. Processes that do not send to or receive anything from other processes are orphans and are not allowed into an aligned process architecture because they would not add to value stream outcomes. Typically, these are just not well designed processes, and the architecture would need revision to find the right fit for them. The flow of information may not be explicit in the process architecture, but it should be easily implied by looking at the process model from start to end.

Business process categories

Developing the top level of a process architecture often seems like a mysterious art. However, it does not have to be.

As described earlier in this chapter, if we start with the idea that we categorize three main groups of processes according to their usage or purpose, we will find core processes, guiding processes, and enabling processes.

There may be more segments of work processes within each of these groupings based on relative closeness to the core activities. Some industries lend themselves to extra distinction. Sometimes organizations break out additional categories to satisfy a need to make some processes more visible to the organization.

Figure 7-3 illustrates some further segmentation possibilities. The degree to which additional bands are chosen or added can be convenient to help the architecture resonate with readers since at this level, the diagram is helpful for communication and human adoption purposes.

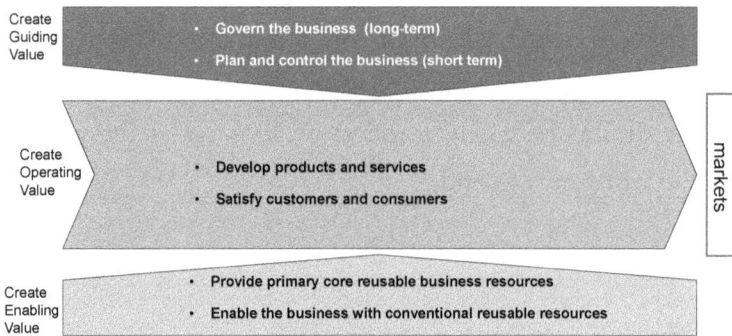

Create Guiding Value
- Govern the business (long-term)
- Plan and control the business (short term)

Create Operating Value
- Develop products and services
- Satisfy customers and consumers

markets

Create Enabling Value
- Provide primary core reusable business resources
- Enable the business with conventional reusable resources

Figure 7-3. Additional segmentation.

The core processes are typically focused on the customer and value delivery streams since that's what the organization gets paid to do. An airline would consider the processes associated with 'transport passengers to destination' as core, and I hope that includes 'with luggage.'

The core processes will also usually include everything the organization does to innovate and keep products and services in the market as long as they remain viable and remove them when they are no longer so.

Enabling processes include the essential support processes closely linked with the core as a separate band from generic enabling work. For example, 'maintain aircraft' would fall into the primary core business enabling processes associated with providing resources for 'transport passengers to destination.' We could call these 'core enabling' - and they would be different from the general enabling processes of 'provide staff' and 'build information systems,' which are very similar in all organizations regardless of industry. The farther away you get from the core, you can expect to see more cross-industry generic processes that you can find anywhere.

The guiding processes typically include the focused planning and control processes that managers employ to keep the core day-to-day processes working at their best. These can be shown graphically close to the core and separate from strategy and directional processes, which will have their own band—usually at the top. 'Develop flight schedules' is a good example of a 'core managing' process because 'transport passengers to destination' does not happen without it, and it happens and changes a lot. 'Set budgets' would be an example of long-term and more universal that is on a longer cycle and not intimately tied to the day-to-day flying of passengers on planes on routes.

Of course, there can be many variations on this model specific to a particular business. Still, this segmentation has served us well historically, and it gains executive buy-in without too much difficulty.

Exploiting the concept model

We can use the concept model to help figure out the top level of the process architecture within each category of Core, Guiding, and Enabling.

Every relationship proceeds through a life cycle of processes, moving external participants from unawareness and ultimately to relationship termination.

The lifecycle of the relationship with each appropriately segmented external stakeholder type naturally defines value streams and stages along the way—more on this later. Those relationship concepts appear in the concept model with a stakeholder name. All processes we conduct with customers, partners, owners, regulators, and the like are on the list of relationship type concepts presuming they are relevant for the business. In addition, if the other concepts to be handled, such as *'order,'* are already defined in the concept model, we can also define their lifecycle of activities and get all things that require action regarding an order into the process architecture map.

This means that a good cut at a process architecture can become determined, more or less, by the concept model structure and content. Even though we would not typically show the main concepts and processes on the same diagram, they appear here to illustrate the practice of deriving a skeleton based on business concepts. Figure 7-4 shows a process skeleton for the chosen value chain (Provide Consumer Banking Services)—there could be others for different value chains.

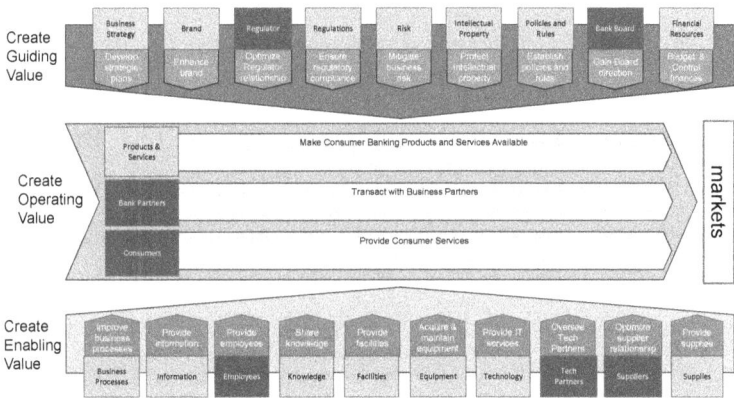

Figure 7-4. Process skeleton.

Terminology and professional history

The worlds of enterprise architecture and business process management have happily co-existed for decades. Still, when business architecture was on the ascendancy, the two communities exhibited disparate views on 'activity' as each expanded its point of view to include areas broader than what was traditional for each. As a result, some sparks flew over disagreement on what certain methodological terms meant.

Among others, the term 'value stream' became contentious. BPM people understood it to be essentially what Lean practitioners have used for decades to discover waste. This is different from what some newly minted business architecture groups have adopted. Business architecture for many bodies such as the Business Architecture Guild in its Body of Knowledge have not traditionally recognized a process architecture structure per se but prefer to list value streams instead. As noted earlier in this chapter, process practitioners would typically have classified these same things as high-level value-creating processes.

Value streams have stages (aka next level of detail of high-level processes) whereby some value item is produced to add up to or be required to contribute towards the realization of an end-to-end Value Proposition for a customer or other stakeholder. This is quite consistent with what a process architect would include at one of the upper levels of the process architecture and what he or she would call a high-level business process. As part of the conclusion of the earlier referenced Guild working group that I participated in, I feel comfortable treating the process architecture stack at the top as a value chain representing a line of business for a market that contains value streams that contain value stream stages. As noted, these are called levels of process architecture by process architects. These are the same things, and I will use the terms interchangeably.

At the highest level, we will use the term value chain when dealing with the core business and use the term shared service when it comes to the guiding and enabling blocks of work. Figure 7-5 will help to understand our naming and leveling for the various parties involved with process architectures.

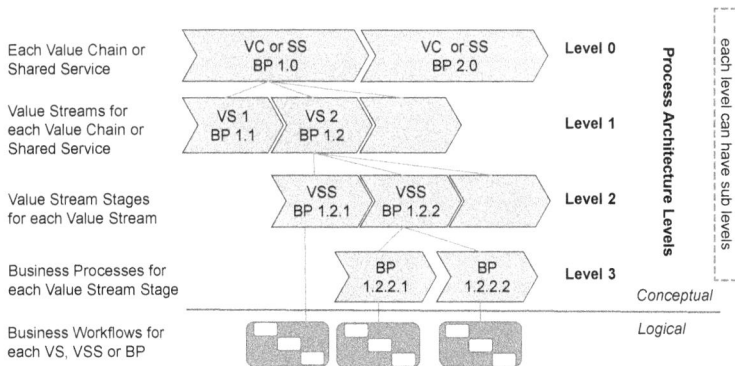

Figure 7-5. Important terms.

Cautions

A process architecture can take many forms and can be easy to do if you do not care about quality, usability, or reusability. Sadly, many that I have seen are not useful for actually operating or managing the business or realizing value. Most are too functional, meaning they often line up too conveniently with the organization structure or a set of professional competencies. Therefore, they are not versatile enough to withstand an organizational realignment or business model adaptation. That's what you get when you start by asking people in the organization, "What do you do?" instead of starting with the external stakeholders and asking, "What are the products, services, and experiences you need and want?"

Another potential pitfall is architectures created by blindly copying a pre-existing process reference framework. A Reference Framework is a templated list of actions that potentially prescribes a set of:

- High to mid-level Processes /Activities
- Business Concepts or Information Types,
- Business Capabilities
- Measurement Indicators

Frameworks can be extremely useful when used wisely. Many, however, do not deal with or describe end-to-end value creation well, although they will have a lot of the functional bits and pieces needed to go somewhere in the hierarchy. They have most parts but assembling them into a working value chain and value streams is often a problem. For example, I know that all the parts to build a car are in the car parts catalog by each one's function, but those parts are not organized by how you want the car to be built.

We build a useful process architecture from the point of view of the work to be performed to add value along a chain of activities all the way out to the external world. That means we should start from the outside and be agnostic to the organizational groups or the process parts catalog, at least for a while. We assemble these parts for a process purpose. Many frameworks are bundled functionally and void of a value creation lens. It is not unusual to see areas such as financial management shown as a process area even though many financial activities are embedded in many other end-to-end processes such as 'receive payment' in 'fulfill order' and 'make payment' in 'acquire goods and services.'

Nonetheless, a Framework can help to quickly define an initial rough cut at parts of a business architecture. A good use is to verify that an end-to-end Architecture developed using a value perspective is complete and that nothing has been missed. There are many such standard models specifically built for particular industries as well as those which are generic to most organizations. The American Productivity and Quality Center (apqc.org) and the Business Architecture Guild at businessarchitectureguild.org are excellent starting points. The frameworks will remind you to pick up the general process activities you may otherwise miss for the architecture model.

Working with the process skeleton

Figure 7-6 contains the overall skeleton with the selected Value Chain of Provide Consumer Banking Services shown at the core and shared services at the guiding and enabling levels. Now it is time to go deeper.

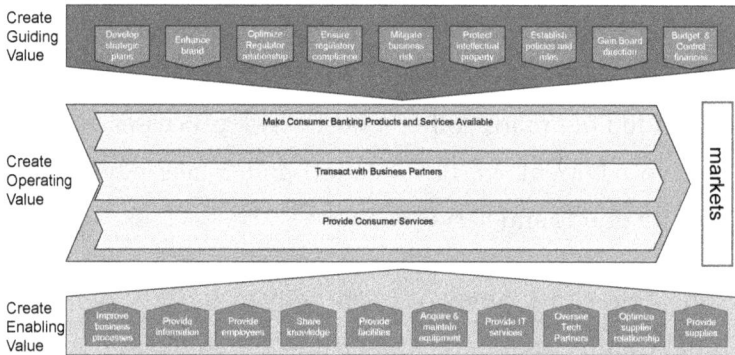

Figure 7-6. Value chains at the core.

Defining core processes

Let's briefly look at the development of the core processes for the illustrative example of a consumer bank with the core consumer services and guiding and enabling processes at level 0. Each level 0 process (value chain or shared service) comprises one or more level 1 value streams within the value chain and represents the value contribution to the end stakeholder goals of the value chain. Within each level 1 is a set of core processes.

Since the main focus of the core is the recipients of our goods and services, it is logical to look at what interactions we have with the customers over their whole journey experience with us.

The first step is to understand the lifetime customer journey (e.g., the life of the potential relationship if all goes well) and trace it from lack of customer unawareness of the organization or its value proposition to the end of the relationship. This will allow us to find the major transition points where value is attained (or at least attempted). Each transition point is where the state or status of the relationship changes, such as a lead becoming a signed customer that we can now transact with. We deal with them and they with us differently in the next state with a subsequent purpose and goal state in mind. We can define the process between states as work that we have to execute to achieve the next transition point. In this way, the closing state (and event timing) becomes the triggering state (and event timing) for the next process.

For customers, and indeed all external stakeholder relationships, there are three main stages that the relationship will go through. These are customer relationship establishment, customer business service operations, and customer relationship re-assessment. The customer relationship establishment typically happens once in the stakeholder journey to get things going, although it's suitability could be renewed or reconsidered from time to time. The customer business services operations processes typically occur on a regular iterative cycle, frequent or infrequent. The customer hopefully orders many times. For example, we may provide a service on a calendar basis once a month. The third phase – customer relationship re-assessment – occurs regularly, typically with scheduled periodic calendar reviews or actions due to a specific positive or negative trigger. This provides the opportunity to enhance the relationship or perhaps to terminate it. Of course, any particular customer will be in a state potentially different from the others at any point in time.

Once the main transition points (state - event) are defined, look for the activities needed to get to the next transition point for both the customer and the value chain. Figure 7-7 shows the bank customer (consumer). All relationships will follow a similar pattern, however.

Customer Process		Bank Business Process	Status
			Consumer Unaware
Establishment Stage	Recognize Company	Promote to Consumer Market	Customer Aware
	Request Information	Inform Consumer	Customer Informed
	Determine Interest	Qualify Consumer	Consumer Qualified
Operations Stage	Agree to Services	Gain Agreement to Consumer Services	Consumer Order Accepted
	Receive Consumer Services	Provide Consumer Services	Consumer Services Provided
	Request Account Closure	Close Consumer Accounts	Consumer Account(s) Closed
	Review Accounts	Report Accounts to Consumer	Consumer Account(s) Reported
	Review Transactions	Prevent Consumer Losses	Consumer Losses Prevented
	Settle Consumer Complaints and Claims	Settle Consumer Complaints and Claims	Consumer Complaints and Claims Settled
Re-assessment Stage	Evaluate Company Relationship	Evaluate Consumer Relationship	Consumer Relationship Evaluated
	Terminate Company Relationship	Terminate Consumer Relationship	Consumer Relationship Terminated

Figure 7-7. Illustration of a relationship lifecycle.

Since our business is all about our products and services, we must focus on gaining the best mix in the right market at the right time and for the right prices. This is a second perspective on the core—the product or service lifecycle (Figure 7-8), starting with the initial product or service (P or S) concept through to the end of the product or service life. Once again, we would identify all the transition points where the state or status of the product or service changes and then define the process that preceded the state change. Some of these will be pass-fail decision points.

Bank Business Process		State
Establishment Stage	Gather P or S Insights	P or S Insights Gathered
	Research P or S Ideas	P or S Ideas Researched
	Develop P or S Brand Promise	P or S Brand Promise Developed
	Identify P or S Need	Need for P or S Identified
	Approve P or S Proposal	P or S Proposal Approved
	Develop P or S Prototype	P or S Prototype Developed
	Develop P or S	P or S Developed
	Launch P or S	P or S Launched
Operations Stage	Promote P or S	P or S Promoted
	Establish P or S Consumer Agreements	P or S Consumer Agreements Established
	Forecast P or S Demand	P or S Demand Forecasted
	Plan P or S Supply Capability	P or S Supply Capability Planned
	Execute P or S Transactions	P or S Transactions Executed
Re-assessment Stage	Evaluate P or S	P or S Evaluated
	Enhance P or S	P or S Enhanced
	Decommission P or S	P or S Decommissioned

Figure 7-8. The product or service lifecycle.

Three main stages are in play, similar to the customer and other stakeholder journey relationships in the first example. These are product or service establishment, product or service operations, and product or service re-assessment.

Product or service establishment typically covers everything that happens to get a product or service into market, from conceiving a fragile idea, including many processes that each make a go/no go decision. Product or service operations deliver on a regular iterative product delivery/service cycle. Product or service re-assessment occurs based on a scheduled review or when specific triggers determine the opportunity to enhance the product or service or perhaps decommission it. Again, different products or services will be in different states at any point in time, but the pattern will be similar. Notice that relationship lifecycles also consider the stakeholder journey in the first column and how it maps to the organization's processes but the other concept lifecycles do not have the external journeys alongside. Also notice how the product cycle intersects with the customer journey at key points, such as Deliver Consumer Service.

Pulling it together at the core

Let's look at the journeys and lifecycles at the core. We can group some business processes into a higher level and find ourselves now with three levels of composition. Figure 7-9 shows how we might show the overall architecture for our consumer banking line of business with the core developed more deeply.

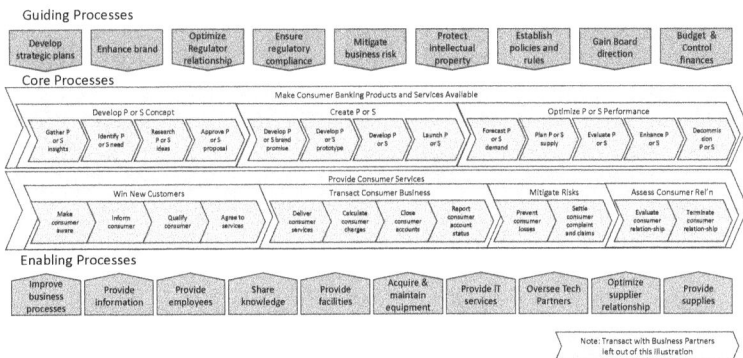

Figure 7-9. Overall architecture with core developed to lower levels.

Guiding processes

A Level 0 guiding process is a holding group for a specific internal shared service offering that should influence, constrain, or control many other processes. Each is required for each guiding or constraining stakeholder relationship, and each guiding concept that must be managed based on the concept model. Typically, this top-level contains level 1 processes/value streams for dealing with strategies, policies, budgets, regulations, and other governance issues and the entire journey for directional, governance, or compliance types of stakeholder relationships, such as owners or regulatory bodies.

Each has its own lifecycle with sub-levels (level 1, 2 on down) similar to the core customer journeys or lifecycles. The approach for relationship types of processes will be similar as shown earlier for the customer cycle, and the pattern will also show the three major stages. Non-relationship guiding concepts or items that we manage internally, such as strategies, budgets, or policies, all follow a lifecycle similar to stages seen in products and services. By identifying the guiding aspects of organizations, we can define the top level of the guiding architecture. Figure 7-10 shows the Level 0 shared service process 'Ensure Regulatory Compliance.' The other Guiding Level 0 processes will follow a similar pattern.

Ensure regulatory compliance	Bank Business Process	State
Establishment Stage	Identify Regulation	Regulation Identified
	Determine Regulation Strategy	Regulation Interpreted
	Interpret regulation	Regulation Strategy Determined
	Establish Regulation Implementation Plan	Regulation Implementation Plan Established
	Develop Policies for Regulation	Regulation Policies Developed
	Develop Processes to Ensure Compliance	Compliance Process Developed
	Implement Regulation	Regulation Implemented
	Monitor Regulatory Compliance	Regulatory Compliance Monitored
Operations Stage	Report to Regulator	Regulatory Reports Submitted
	Update Regulatory Changes	Regulatory Changes Updated
Re-assessment Stage	Deactivate Regulation	Regulation Deactivated

Figure 7-10. Level 1 processes for a guiding shared service.

Enabling processes

Level 0 enabling processes / shared services can be viewed as a holding grouping for everything in its sub-levels (1, 2, on down), which is the entire journey for reusable resource provisioning stakeholders, such as human resources (not the department), facility providers, or technology partner relationships. In addition, the internal provision and optimization of resources such as equipment and technology assets all follow a cycle similar to products and services with a clear life from beginning to end. Therefore, each level 0 enabling process will have clear stages—demarcation points in the journeys or lifecycles for their level 1 processes. By identifying the enabling aspects of organizations, we can define the highest level of the enabling architecture. Figure 7-11 shows the Level 0 shared service 'Provide Facilities.' The other Enabling Level 0 processes will follow a similar pattern.

Provide facilities	Bank Business Process	State
Establishment Stage	Determine Need for Facility	Facility Need Established
	Produce Business Case for Facility	Facility Business Case Approved
	Procure Facility Land	Facility Land Procured
	Design Facility	Facility Design Accepted
	Construct Facility	Facility Built
	Commission Facility	Facility Commissioned
Operations Stage	Operate Facility	Facility Being Used
	Maintain Facility	Facility Maintained
Re-assessment Stage	Evaluate Facility	Facility Suitability Evaluated
	Renovate Facility	Facility Renovated
	Repurpose Facility	Facility Available for New Use
	Decommission Facility	Facility Decommissioned
	Dispose Facility	Facility Disposed

Figure 7-11. Level 1 processes for an enabling shared service

Checking against reference models

Going back to frameworks or reference models mentioned earlier in this chapter, we can look deeper and find specific activities to incorporate into the architecture to expand the knowledge of industry-standard processes and sequences. These may modify the end-to-end process inventory at some level. Whereas the top levels of the frameworks will sometimes be organized differently from what is represented by the journey and lifecycle approach, the frameworks will become more and more useful, as each of the level 0, 1, and 2 processes are drilled more deeply into specific sub-process identification at levels 3 and 4. Figure

7-12 shows a hypothetical illustration of how looking at
the APQC list of processes allowed us to find additional
processes at a deeper level, some of which we can bring
into processes already in our architecture.

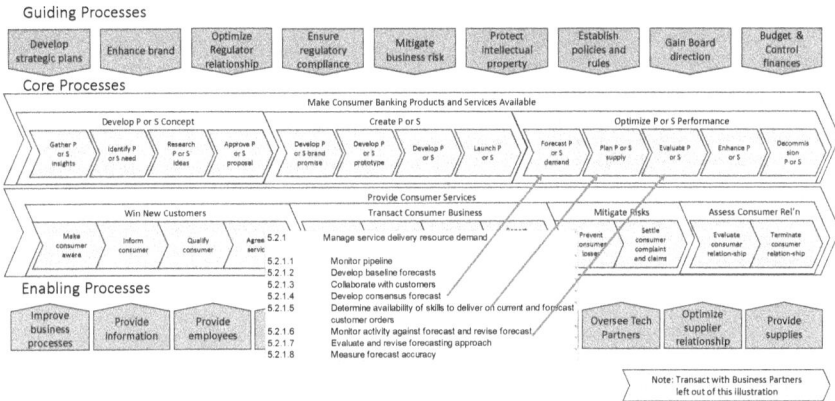

Figure 7-12. Adding in an APQC list of processes.

*The use of frameworks in guiding and enabling areas is
particularly helpful since these frameworks often have full
cycle views of organizational assets.*

Describing a process

Every process still needs a full description of its attributes.
Not all of the information will be available or known when
doing the early parts of architectural work. Still, at some
point-in-time, once it is better understood and some design
decisions have been made, the contents can be

documented. This information is an important complement to the graphic models and should be stored in an appropriate repository along with the pictures. An illustration for one of the processes in our banking model appears in Figure 7-13. The template is applicable for any level of process description.

Process Worksheet	
Organization: BPT Bank	**Value Chain:** Provide Consumer FS
L1 Process Name: Create P or S	**L2 Process Name:** Develop P or S

Process Steward: Manager Product and Service Development

Trigger Event: Prototype is ready for production development

Closing Event: New P or S is ready to be offered to consumers

Process Description: This process begins when the Create P or S Prototype process manager determines that the prototype is successful, and the p P or S group is asked to create the P or S version to be offered to the consumers. The Develop P or S group then works with others to create the software applications, marketing materials and training appropriate to enable rolling out the service to the branches, putting it on the bank website, etc. The process ends when marketing and sales take over responsibility for launching the new service.

Process Outcome: The new P or S, along with all supporting software, training materials and documentation is ready to turn over to marketing and sales.

KPIs: This process is measured by time to market from the moment the approval to create a new or changed product or service is received until the time it is ready to launch

Process Scope: Inputs from Stakeholders or Upstream Processes:
• Suggestions for changes/improvements to prototype
• Request to create a new service offering

Process Scope: Outputs to Stakeholders or Downstream Processes:
• New service offering
• New service offering documentation, training materials and supporting software

Process Scope: Guides from Other Processes:
• Budget limitations
• Corporate procedures for creating a new product or service

Process Scope: Enablers from Other Processes:
• Development staff
• Training staff
• New / updated software

Gain: What Strategic Outcomes Does this Process Support?
More products in market sooner

Pain: What Specific Performance Gaps does this Process have?
Lagging competitors in introducing new products

Figure 7-13. Documenting processes.

Up next

The business process knowledge gained and made available here should produce more than a nice picture, which it should do. It is the heart of the business, pumping blood through the organization's arteries and veins. The configuration is the structure of operational work and the basis for measurement and capability development. It tells you what is important to be good at, regardless of what your organization chart says. It is the basis of operational governance and change decisions. It is a view based on value creation and that's what we are striving to achieve. It lets us know the requirements for developing both unique and reusable capabilities. The performance management system will connect the strategy and process scorecard down to the detailed elements of everyone's work. These are the topics of the next chapters.

CHAPTER 8

Developing your Business Capability Map

I n the previous chapters of this book, I discussed some of the frameworks that professionals have been advocating, which are useful in developing our overall set of business architecture models, as shown in Figure 8-1. These have included the development of a concept model describing the things we need to know about and the process architecture describing what we have to do to satisfy external stakeholder value requirements. These models are essential for establishing a connected architecture that makes business sense and delivers stakeholder value.

This chapter will tackle a topic that has both intrigued me and frustrated me at times. There is a well-established enterprise architecture camp, often found within IT groups, and by nature, it needs to understand business requirements to conduct technology planning, prioritization, system design, and implementation. This need has led such solution-focused IT professionals to see 'capability' as their central concept of business architecture since it is their job to build IT capabilities to support the business.

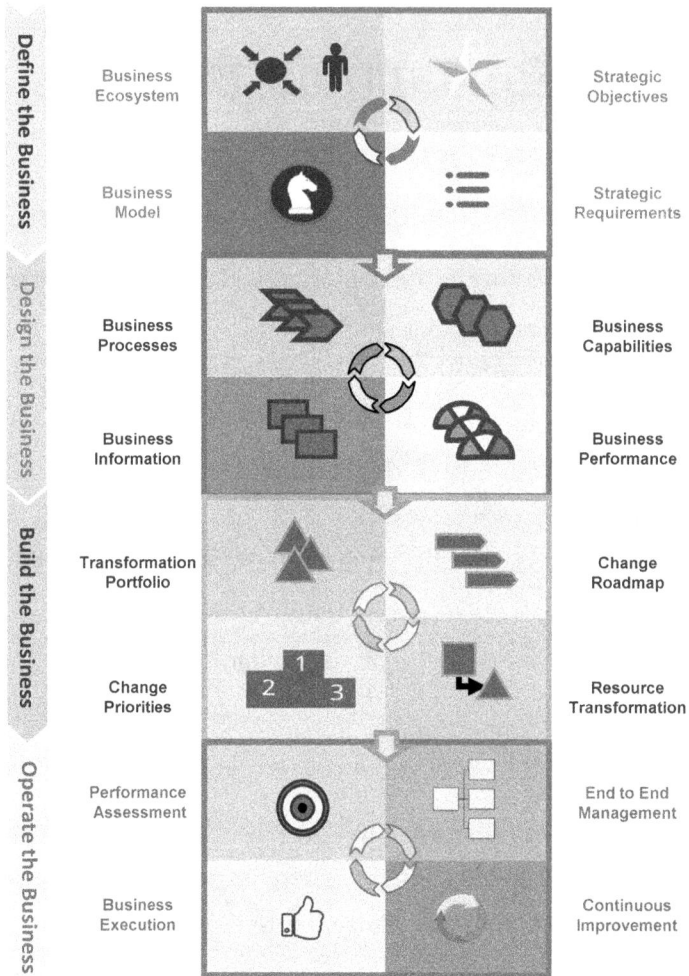

Figure 8-1. Comprehensive business architecture framework and foundational methodology.

This has been a great leap forward compared to the early days when they worried about technology specifications and solutions without surety of fit with business needs. However, other points of view, especially from process and business model advocates, see it a little differently. These groups aim to keep the approach business operations and work-oriented and not just about IT. Current examples of this phenomenon are the attempts to ensure that digitalization is about more than mobile phone apps and more about new ways of doing business enabled by digital opportunities. Many have used this opportunity to blow up existing business models.

The fit of capabilities in business architecture, shown in Figure 8-1, is still emerging and at this point, there are no indisputably accepted standards in place. However, several groups have strong opinions, and there is work happening on proposals for standardization. The Object Management Group's (OMG) effort to develop standards for a business architecture meta-model, which I have also participated in, is one notable undertaking. In addition, several large consulting and technology firms advocate their own views to maintain their differentiation in the marketplace.

The Open Group has postulated that capabilities are essential for both business architecture and IT solutions as a precursor or umbrella for all other aspects of IT architecture. In the TOGAF perspective, capability is a key area along with the value stream models. The TOGAF model is repeated in Figure 8-2.

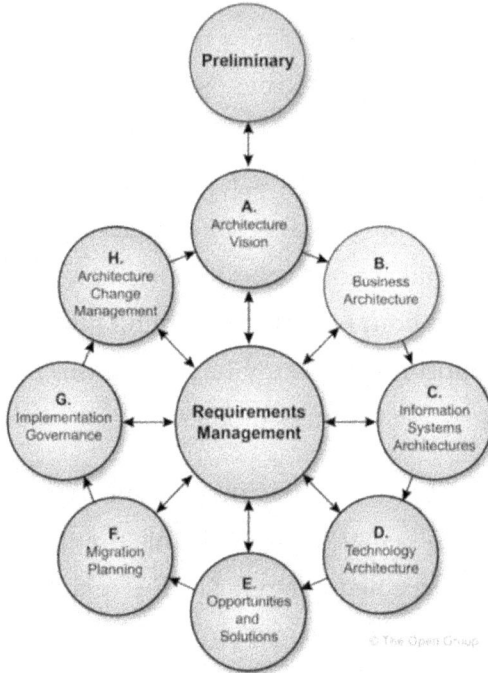

Figure 8-2. The Open Group's TOGAF positioning of business architecture.

The most comprehensive work available to define multiple business architecture views and a strong promoter of capabilities is The Business Architecture Guild in its Business Architecture Body of Knowledge (BIZBOK) as seen in Figure 8-3. Overall, I find it a very useful guide that is evolving and updated regularly as experience and new learnings are obtained. This is a good reference since it has a strong value delivery orientation, mostly consistent with our approach at Process Renewal Group. In addition, it includes a large section on capabilities and the value streams that need them to function well.

Figure 8-3. Business Architecture Guild's BIZBOK model.

What is a business capability?

In the common vernacular, 'capability' is typically associated with identifying how good something is to achieve some purpose. It is typically applied to some physical object such as a car or a toaster; some human resource such as the CEO or the call center agent; some piece of information technology such as a device or software app. The list goes on. It can also be associated with something more abstract such as a company or group like the ambulance service or a law enforcement agency.

The term in the English language is generally well understood when it is structured within a clear context giving it relevance. For example, are we talking about the capability of a person, organization, value chain, value stream, process, piece of software, facility, or piece of equipment? As defined by Merriam-Webster's dictionary, the term 'capable' means "having attributes (as in physical or mental power) required for performance or accomplishment."[24] Therefore, for layman usage, it is essential to know the purpose of an organization, business processes, or asset to assess if it provides suitable capability or is lacking relative to what's needed. For example, a hammer in the right hands is very capable of putting a nail into a piece of wood but not so capable of sawing that piece of wood in half if that's what's needed.

We need both a business context and a purpose to assess a capability.

Unfortunately, in my opinion, many business architects have applied a somewhat confusing, to many, definition whereby the degree of sufficiency towards an outcome is not what 'capability' necessarily means. The term has evolved to become an architectural domain in its own right

---

[24] https://www.merriam-webster.com/dictionary/capable.

with its own descriptors without regard to the actual level of its ability to perform relative to purpose. This is quite different than what many non-architects are used to and, therefore, the source of some dissonance, requiring a lot of explanation inside organizations. In architecture communities, the capability name is simply a tag for a placeholder of the capability concept without evaluating its needed or actual level of ability when formulated. For example, the capability name 'Credit worthiness assessment' does not alone indicate how good you are at assessing credit worthiness or how good you have to be at it to suit your plans, only that you need that capability in your business at some undefined level of ability to perform.

We execute, measure, manage, and improve processes. We build capabilities to serve that purpose.

The level of sufficiency will depend on your business need and your strategy. To some degree, process names are treated similarly in the process architecture. The process 'Resolve complaint' does not tell you how to do it, how well it works, or if it needs to be much better. It just says that conceptually there is a process that should be in the process architecture somewhere to determine if there is a performance gap and if we should close it.

Strategic capability versus business capability

Business capabilities should also not be confused as Strategic capabilities, or vice versa, as discussed in Chapter 5: Deriving your Strategy. The use in strategic situations typically is to establish what is required for you to put into place to realize an agreed strategic intent. This knowledge is mostly NOT drawn from a formal, comprehensive business capabilities model. Instead, these are strategic requirements that articulate the factors critical for the transformation success of the business to attain its vision and goals, as expressed by the North Star.

The inverse of strategic capability is strategic risk. For example, if the hypothetical banking entity illustrated in this book were to decide that part of its intent is to operate in other countries in the future, it would be critical that it establish a strategic capability to gain banking licenses in all the places it wished to go. These are the critical success factors that must be at the top of the mind of executives and appropriately resourced in the budget, perhaps as a strategic program. Business capabilities as we are about to discuss are more formally structured and can be mapped and decomposed.

Business context

Capability in a business architecture sense has come to mean what is required to build or improve to enable or contribute to the creation of value towards the intent of the organization or value chain stakeholders, especially those who receive our goods and services. As such, there is a closeness of 'capabilities' with value-creating 'business processes' or 'value streams' at higher levels. The capability map and the process architecture diagram can start to look alike when this occurs, especially at top levels of abstraction. Despite the closeness, it is important not to build these maps into one another. Figure 8-4 shows an archaic misconception often heard in out-of-touch architecture groups about how the two are interrelated.

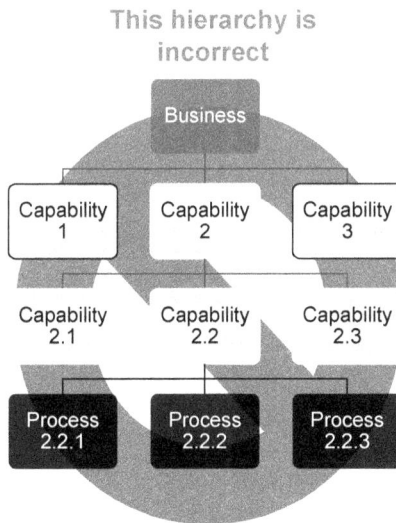

Figure 8-4. Capability – Process misconception.

The misplaced contention is that if one drills capabilities down, the processes will emerge at the detailed level of articulation. In my experience, this is simply not correct since good architectural principles, as re-iterated by John Zachman, simply state that you cannot decompose one type of knowledge (architectural domain, aka Zachman column) into a different one.

Maintain the integrity of the process and capability domains individually and associate them with one another through a meaningful set of connecting relationships. In architecture, we should be representing processes and capabilities in a connected many-to-many relationship. Both are needed.

In a recent personal experience of renewing a passport from another country, I experienced the needed connection between process and capability. After receipt of the application and submitting it electronically, the passport office processed the application, produced the document and handed it off to a courier to ship internationally back to me. A business architect I knew from the courier company had told me earlier that international shipping was one of their key capability differentiators. The passport office also swore they were quite capable to handle my rush application.

However, the passport somehow got lost after production,[25] and I had to go sort it out. It was clear that neither the passport office nor the courier viewed this as a single instance of a single value stream—the way I viewed it. Value was not created for me since they did not work together to support the entire passport renewal process as an end-to-end delivery — which would have assured my expectations would be met. When the envelope did not arrive as promised after several days, the architect in me concluded that there may have been individual capabilities in play, but they did not work for me, and it showed up as a failed instance of a process. I cannot tell whose capability or combination of them let me down. I just know it was a nightmare getting the outcome I needed. However, I was able to needle my friend in the courier company about his claim.

We need capabilities, but we also must get them orchestrated in the processes where they are needed and assure accountabilities for results to the customer. We will discuss more in an upcoming chapter that connects the dots.

---

[25] https://www.bptrends.com/real-world-business-processes-there-is-no-such-thing-as-a-bad-example-renewing-a-passport/.

Business capability traits

A sound enterprise-level view of all capabilities will exhibit some key traits listed in the Business Architecture Guild's BIZBOK.

Characteristics of capabilities:

- Provide a business-centric view of an organization
- Are defined in business terms
- Define what a business does
- Are stable
- Are defined once for an enterprise (or component thereof)
- Decompose into more capabilities
- There is one capability map for a business
- Map to other views of the business
- An automated capability is still a business capability, not an IT one
- If the mapping team cannot define a capability, it probably is not one

Business capability principles

As I outlined in an earlier chapter, all of the above principles are true for business processes for a value-creating process architecture. The main modeling difference at the highest levels of abstraction is that we express capabilities using modified nouns or gerunds and not verbs. Business processes (or value streams) are expressed in verb-noun constructs. Just like the process architecture, the capability map should:

- Be organizationally Agnostic
- Be technologically Agnostic
- Exhibit a consistent classification structure of Core, Guiding, and Enabling
- Initially be keep to a Limited Depth of Structure (typically 3 to 4 levels deep)
- Reflect 'What we do' and not so much the variations in 'how we do it'
- Be stable over time unless the business model itself is changed
- Be measurable when used
- Be traceable to higher-level capabilities and aligned with others at the same level

Starting from business concepts

The BIZBOK defines a capability as "a particular ability or capacity that a business may possess or exchange to achieve a specific purpose or outcome." A capability map should contain "a concise, non-redundant, complete, business-centric view of the business."[26]

We start identifying capabilities by taking a unique business concept orientation. Business concepts (aka business objects) provide a starting point for derivation. They are not capabilities themselves but allow us to ask what capabilities we need to make each concept effective. We discover these concepts by identifying specific types of relationships with external stakeholders and also others with particular objects of interest to the business (assets and other less tangible business concepts), as we did in Chapter 6 when dealing with concept models.

The key question to find relevant capabilities is, "What things do you have to know about that have to be managed by the business, and what do you have to be able to do with them?" To find a comprehensive list of possible relevant business concepts, we can identify all relationships and all 'things' to manage. In effect, we are striving to 'normalize' them down to their essence. That means having one place for everything and no redundancies. Just as we want unique concepts, we also want unique capabilities that may appear in more than one process / value stream. For our consumer bank example, we could find multiple types of relationships to manage.

---

[26] https://www.businessarchitectureguild.org/.

By agreeing on the relevant things to be managed, we ended up with the concept map of what we were interested in, as shown in Figure 8-5, originally shown in Chapter 6. Clearly, we would want to have a more extensive and complete map of all concepts to ensure that we could best organize the capability map, find more commonality, and assure no redundancies.

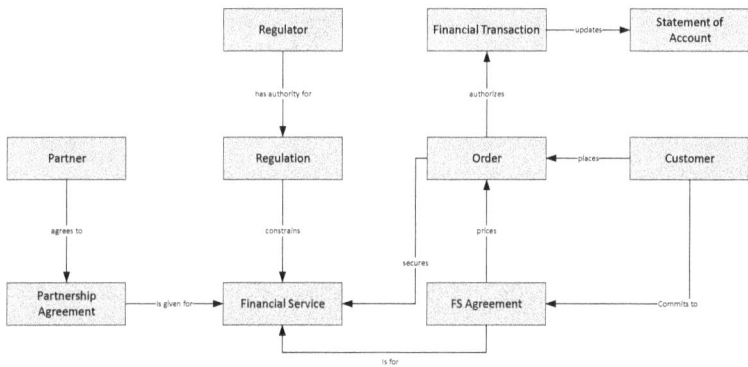

Figure 8-5. Concept model.

Each of these can have several sub-types, which appear as a decomposition of components. Figure 8-6 shows some derived capabilities inside the high level box and the boxes within each box, such as for potential Regulator Relationship Management and Regulation Deployment capabilities.

Please note that we use suffixed nouns or gerunds to name the capabilities. This grammatical structure makes a noun out of a verb action and appears as a noun in a sentence. You can expect to see suffixes such as …tion, …ing,…ent,

...al—all forms that are banned as process names since they are not active verbs. Another naming structure commonly seen is the tagging of the concept name with 'Management.' It's an easy and lazy way out that is often devoid of creativity or clarity of meaning. Try to be more precise if you can.

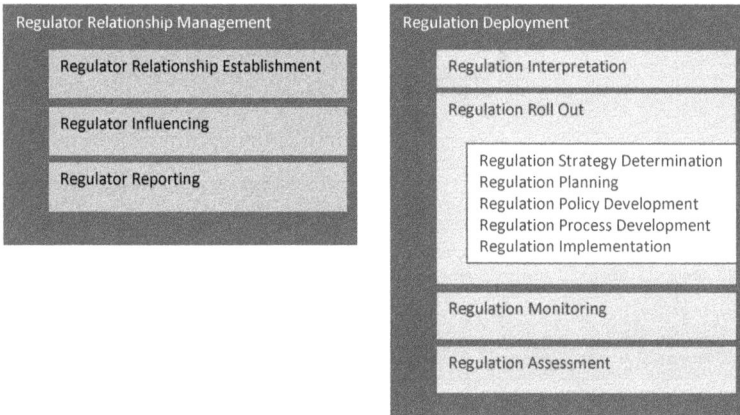

Figure 8-6. Derived capabilities.

In this example, Regulator Relationship Management appears as a unique Capability, which may be the case. Still, perhaps it is very similar to other relationships, and we may be able to share essentially the same capability along with them. Each may have some unique needs and value requirements, but many factors will be common. For example, are there attributes of a customer relationship similar to a partner, such as the basic identifying structure of companies and accounts? You will have to determine if these can be satisfied by a common set of capabilities or if each is truly unique. This type of tough question is typically hotly debated and is posed in Figure 8-7.

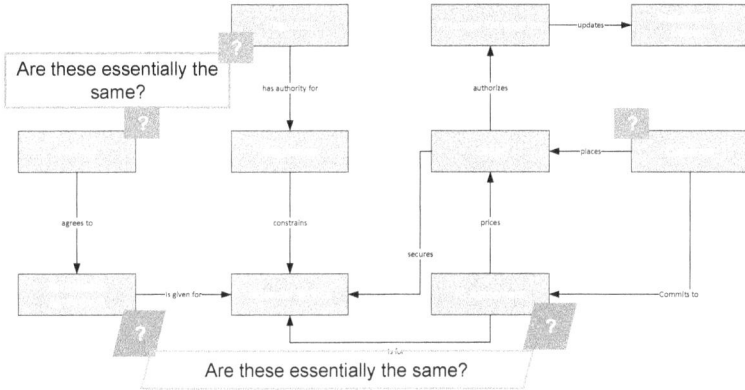

Figure 8-7. Tough questions.

How much of the customer cycle is similar to the partner one and what are the differences, if any? Figure 8-8 shows what this could look like if it were so. The variations to the side of the box are called capability instances in the BIZBOK.

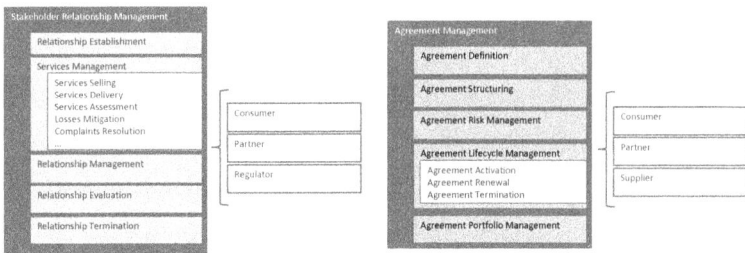

Figure 8-8. Capability consolidation and instances.

For the consumer bank, some other potential business concepts may be relevant. For illustration purposes, these appear in Figure 8-9. Again, some of these may have distinctions with sub types. You will have to determine how deep to go.

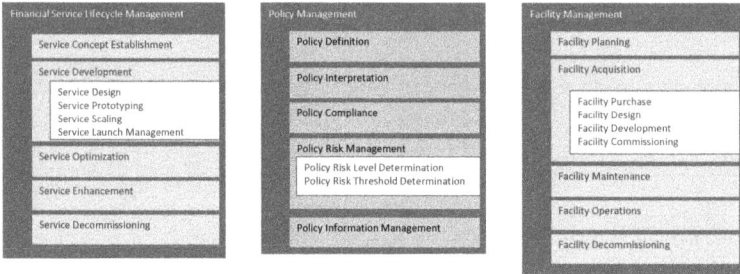

Figure 8-9. Other potential business concepts.

As an example of the importance of separating the relationships from the things the relationship is concerned with, we can return to Figure 8-6. Managing the regulator relationship requires a specific set of capabilities, but the internal management of a regulation cycle will require a different set. Therefore, it is important not to define these as one capability. Otherwise, we lose the goal of capability sharing and modularity, and change will be more complex if lumped together.

Burlton Capability Hexagon

There can easily be hundreds of level three and thousands of level four capabilities. Therefore, as we did with the process architecture, rather than going deeper on all aspects, it may be more appropriate to do a top-level skeleton (recall the concept map from Figure 8-5) covering all the macro objects, and only drill into the ones that we deem a priority. We will cover this prioritization of processes and capabilities in a later chapter.

In a business architecture, models are conceptual and are not physical implementations. This is important to understand since the architecture could be biased towards a given technology, organization structure, or any single factor. Pre-selected choices will certainly drive or constrain business behavior. Once the reality of having to bring a capability to life hits home, the conceptual capability does have to translate into real things through implementation and change programs which take time and cost to come true.

It is important to realize that a capability is a composite of several other domains once the decision is made to realize it. There is not a single type of resource that alone will deliver the needed level of performance. Therefore, it is not good enough to tell IT developers what is needed and no one else or let them make the call. To be truly capable of 'complaints resolution,' for example, many issues must be addressed, some of which will be more impactful than others depending on your current level of performance. The factors that will be on the table appear in Figure 8-10.

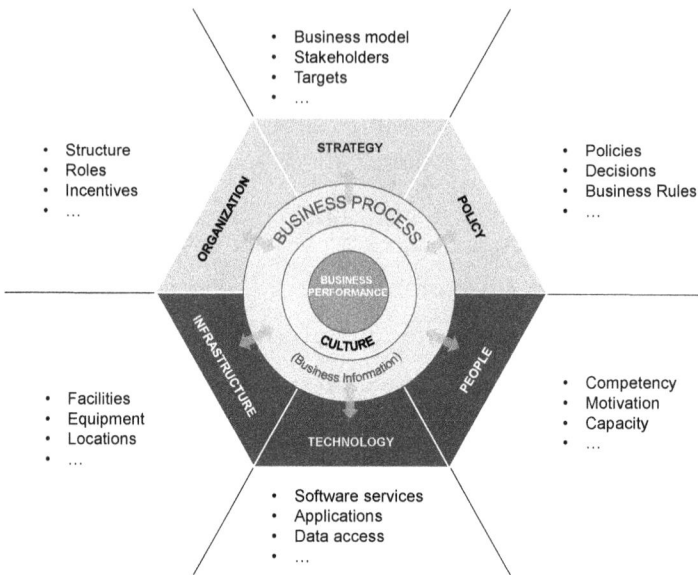

Figure 8-10. Burlton Capability Hexagon.

Performance bull's eye

The center of the hexagon is the definition of the measurable performance indicators and measurement data needed for the current assessment and establishment of the future target state. This provides the motivation for any ongoing development, execution, and improvement initiatives, and you have to be able to gather the data to assess it. It must drive everything.

Process ring

The hexagon assumes that we have a clear definition of the process boundaries and scope sourced from a well-formed process architecture that has followed the principles of the Business Process Manifesto and the architectural principles described in an earlier chapter. The process ring identifies the work actions and decisions from opening event to closing event, delivering value to the stakeholders served by the process or value stream, the items coming in and out of the process, and the dependencies among the component activities. This is the glue to which everything else will stick.

Business information ring

This ring identifies the input, output, and reference information to be transformed, used, or created by the business process and served up by the other aspects of the capability. It also includes the data gathered in the conduct of the processes to use for generating insights. The quality of this data will reflect the quality of the process. These are the artifacts of the business.

Strategy slice

This slice defines the strategic intent which will act as the alignment criteria by which the business capability is designed, measured, and assessed. It provides the basis for establishing traceability to strategy as well as connecting to the performance evaluation criteria. This direct strategic link is unique and assures the capability is linked to purpose.

Policies slice

This slice examines the constraints and the guiding impact from legislation, legal opinion, business policies, decision criteria, specifically articulated rules, governance requirements, compliance needs, and any other knowledge that guides or directs the work performed. Inappropriate policies and rules can cripple the effectiveness of the capability and the attainment of business goals and objectives.

Organization slice

This slice aligns the structural aspects of the organization in its reporting framework, governance, roles, jobs, and responsibilities. This also includes the formal alignment of roles and jobs to performance incentives and ideal outcomes and the ownership of results by organizational leaders.

People slice

This slice covers the enabling human ability to perform as needed in terms of competencies, skills, knowledge, education, and training needs. In addition, it defines capacities, experience levels, and any other human enabling requirements for the business.

Enabling technology slice

This slice defines how technologies of various types make the processes and, in turn, the enterprise, capable of realizing its strategic intent. It includes software applications, process automation engines, SOA microservices, APIs, databases, client devices, network infrastructure, and communications technologies. All of these can significantly impact the ability of the processes and enterprise to perform as needed.

Infrastructure slice

This slice deals with the needs to be supported by physically enabling resources such as work locations, physical plant, production and distribution facilities, and equipment and fleet required. The work environment, including working conditions and health and safety constraints, is also part of the set of facility requirements needed.

Culture ring

Culture is the set of behaviors exhibited by individuals in a group. This includes individual motivation alignment and the cultural aspects of human resource and group behavior. As such, all other factors could be constrained by the filtering effect of a toxic culture or made to shine by a culture of commitment.

Closing thoughts

I have a post-it note in my office that says, "Distrust anyone that claims that their one thing will solve everything." When it comes to 'capabilities' being the solution to all our architectural woes, I must heed that warning and not just go for the technology-solves-everything temptation. Also, when I see lists of vague, unaligned, and non-traceable capabilities that are uni-dimensional based on a single professional function and not sharable, I get concerned that, as professionals, we are being seduced into going for an easy way out.

The Burlton Hexagon, with its business process backbone connecting multiple dimensions of capability, is the most useful tool that I have found to sort out the capabilities and the right combination of resources needed for real business planning and implementation of change that will stick.

Up next

The business capability perspective discussed here is in its early days still, and there is still much controversy between business process, capability and IT camps. There are many ways to do business architecture, and you will have to make your choice of emphasis. Many organizations are still struggling to determine where to start and what to do. There is a lot of angst among business architects, enterprise architects, technology architects, business process professionals, and operational managers regarding what is needed and how to tackle the capability and process perspectives. We will shortly discuss how to deal with interactions among processes and capabilities, and the performance measurement aspects of a business architecture.

CHAPTER 9

Measuring Business Performance

Now it is time to deal with measuring what we have defined. How can we tell if our business model is effective? How do we know if our operating model choices were good ones? Are our resources being well used? Do we have the culture we strive for? How can we know what's working and what's not? What do we have to improve, what dots must we correct? Which of the landscape domains shown in Figure 9-1 are measurable? Which are worth measuring?

Defining a connected measurement framework makes sense now that we have things to measure and can connect them up in a traceable way. We now know the external opportunities and threats, the needs and expectations of the external business stakeholders, the ends and means of the strategy of the business value chains, and the aspirations we are striving for in the North Star target. We also know which business concepts to quantify, which value-creating business processes to monitor and manage, and which capabilities need to be in place to do so.

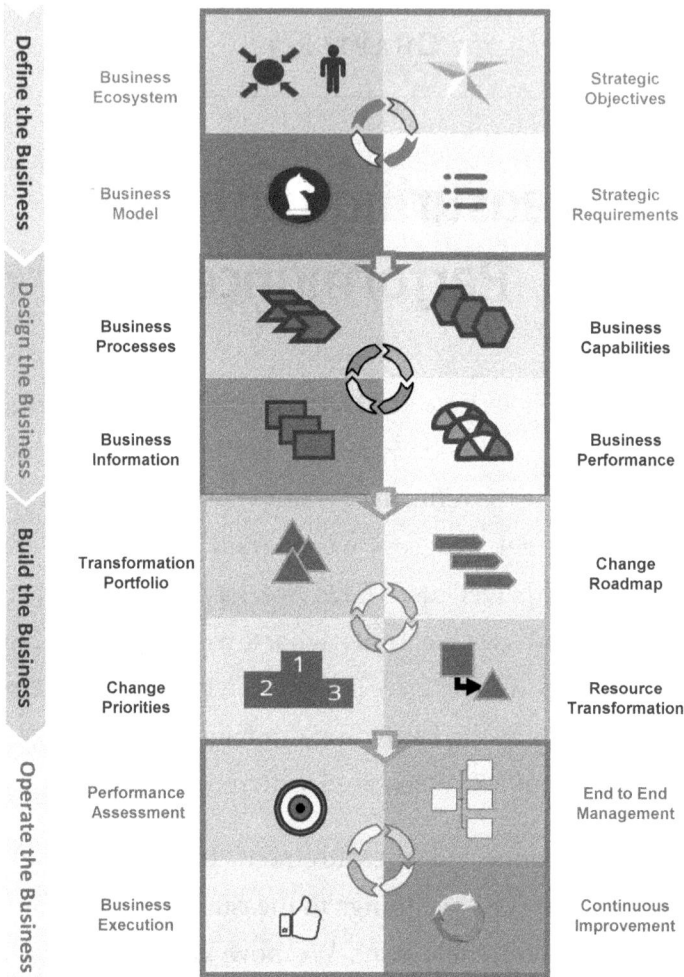

Figure 9-1. Comprehensive business architecture framework and foundational methodology.

Our strategy and business design work should have articulated what behaviors and cultural attributes we deem desirable or critical to attain our more challenging goals. So, what kind of measurement information do we need to decide on in the remaining work of architecture development, resource allocation for transformation, and day-to-day business operations? What do we need to know so we can manage?

Value of measurement

Anyone who has the experience of defining measures for us to live by will confirm that this is one of the hardest things to get right, although it seems deceptively straightforward at the outset. So, is it worth the aggravation? I say yes!

We can measure many things, but measurement should first and foremost help decision-making to act on both small corrections and more significant changes. Most organizations do not have a shortage of existing measures but often do not measure the right things. Despite having lots of KPIs, they usually have insufficient meaningful data to back up many of the decisions they need to make. One of the benefits of having the right performance indicators and trustworthy performance data is to be able to understand better what is happening in the business so we can do the following:

- Plan Business Strategies and Tactics
  - o Inform goal setting

- o Design transformation programs based on current data feedback
- o Make prioritization and resource investment decisions
- o Budget resources better

- Connect Operations to Strategy
  - o Develop traceability of scorecards from top idea to bottom details
  - o Develop leading and lagging indicators
  - o Assign responsibilities for performance to organizational units and process steward
  - o Monitor organizational alignment to value chain outcomes

- Evaluate strategy execution progress and adapt
  - o Control work and resources
  - o Learn what's working and what's not, and why
  - o Change tactics and strategy based on reality
  - o Monitor alignment of work assignments

- Assess the human aspects of work
  - o Align incentives of people with desired performance results
  - o Determine the behavioral fit and gaps of individuals and groups with the envisioned culture
  - o Motivate managers and staff

    o   Evaluate the human acceptance and readiness for change

- Make quick adjustments in operational execution
  - o   Monitor business operations and evaluate what's working and what's not
  - o   Reallocate resources operationally very quickly for control or improvement
  - o   Align individual performance incentives with formal organization targets
  - o   Change behavior and build culture

Quality of measurement

Measurement enables the business nervous system to function and keeps all work on track, so long as the measurement data is accurate, timely, trustworthy, and useful.

This requires us to have high-quality performance indicators. Similar to the concept of 'SMART' objectives, good measures have the following characteristics:

- **Relevant**. Supports the assessment of a vision or goal or something that one must know in order to track and make a management decision

- **Comparable**. Has a distinct Unit of Measure that can be compared over time periods, locations, or to other companies (benchmarking)

- **Time bound**. Is associated with a period of time or a point in time

- **Measurable**. Reliable data can be attained without bias or excessive time and cost

- **Reliable**. The more factual, the better, although external stakeholder perceptions may also serve as facts if collected in an unbiased way

- **Trustworthy**. People feel confident that the measurement data is accurate even if they may not like it

Often, we hear business managers and analysts talk in terms of some very vague or non-specific measures such as:

- We want to improve our reliability
- We aim to increase customer satisfaction
- We need to get better staff loyalty

None of these intentions has a performance indicator in it. These are goals to be attained but not measurable without some interpretation and specification. We need a unit of measure for which we can gather data.

- We want to improve our customer reliability *as measured by the percentage of orders that are perfect (the real KPI).* We define Perfect Order as an order delivered in full, with the right products delivered to the right place, at the agreed time, for the agreed price, paid on time.

- We aim to increase customer satisfaction *as measured by net promoter score.*

- We need to get better staff loyalty *as measured by percentage of annual turnover of employees.*

According to the Business Motivation Model from OMG, vague goals can become objectives by adding a target and a timeframe to the KPI for the goal.

An objective is a goal with a KPI and a target level by a defined time.

- We want to improve our reliability as measured by the percentage of perfect orders (delivered in full, right products delivered to the right place, at the agreed time, for the agreed price, paid on time) *to 95% within one year.*

- We aim to increase customer satisfaction as measured by increasing the net promoter score *by 10 points in eighteen months.*

- We need to get better staff loyalty as measured by decreasing the annual turnover percentage of employees *to 8% by the end of the calendar year*.

By structuring measures well, we now have a set of indicators to evaluate and report on periodically to monitor progress against our business and personal targets.

Top down or bottom up?

Please note that a Performance Indicator (PI) does not exist in its own right. It is always associated with something else and essentially becomes an attribute of or intimately associated with that object. So, the connective structure of the measurement system typically will follow some other structure within the business architecture that we may have already figured out.

Figure 9-2 shows some potential places to hang performance indicators depending on your needs. As you can see, there will be different performance indicators of interest to different parties. If you are driving towards strategic transformation, you will most likely start at the top level KPIs, work your way down the stack, and determine the contributing (lower level) more detailed PIs. This is aimed at the interests of the executive and board.

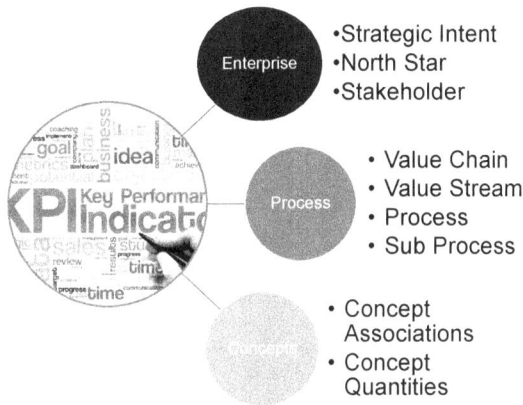

Figure 9-2. Potential places to hang performance indicators.

Suppose you are trying to get control over daily operations and are less concerned with strategic change. In that case, you may start with front line PI measures and selectively choose which subset could be the top level KPIs of the executive scorecard. This approach serves operations managers first. A third, and perhaps more realistic option, is to tackle some aspects of both approaches concurrently by conducting KPI determination for the very thin top level and then, for selected and focused priority areas, build bottom PIs and reconcile the fit building the total set over time.

There is no right or wrong approach, just the one that best deals with the prime issues that face the organization and concurrently supports your readiness and architecture maturity. This approach will greatly benefit both executives and operations managers in the area of focus.

Top-down view

Classical lagging measures have been used in businesses of various types for a long time. The problem was that they typically arrived after the fact and not much could be done about the numbers. In addition, these were mostly financial in their structure. In the early 1990s, Kaplan and Norton published several books and articles. The most notable is *The Balanced Scorecard – Measures that Drive Performance*, advocating a multi-variant approach to measuring business performance to get away from solely after-the-fact financial indicators. Their rationale was that it is typically too late to do anything about the financials once they were in. Instead, they advocated a number of indicator categories to be reported and evaluated periodically that were not pure lagging in nature.

They recommended indicators in different categories to get a better insight into what was happening in the in-flight business. Their view was to utilize a 'Balanced Scorecard' with four quadrants. The recommended categories appear in Figure 9-3. This structure is now considered to be a traditional balanced scorecard. This approach kept the financial view and added others.

The Customer view reflects what is important to the markets the enterprise is serving and shows how well it is doing in terms of well-established indicators such as market share and customer satisfaction. The Operations view—often called the internal process view—looks at internal efficiencies and quality, such as the average time spent by call center staff with a caller online. Finally, the Innovation and Learning perspective focuses on key indicators such as time-to-market and emphasizes learning and sharing knowledge.

Financial (generation and use of financial resources)	Customer (meeting the expectations of the customer)
Operations (Internal process excellence)	Innovation and Learning (New product success and human abilities)

Figure 9-3. Original balanced scorecard.

These additional types of measures have proven very useful for executives to track the company's overall progress. Along with Kaplan and Norton's companion innovation, the strategy map, organizations could develop plans that tackled multiple perspectives and strategize how to achieve the targets in each category going forward. One challenge with the traditional Balanced Scorecard became apparent when building a scorecard that would naturally cascade well down the organization chart. The four quadrants were pushed downwards to departments to find a traceable system of measurement top to bottom.

However, several of these quadrants were ill-suited to be segmented since the decomposition, except for the financial perspective, just broke up things that did not remain aligned when decomposed in organization chart terms. They ended up with suboptimal, self-serving incentives and unaligned motivation. The result of force-fitting lower-level work into the same set of Balanced Scorecard categories meant that intentions of end-to-end, cross-functional value creation were compromised by focusing on internal results and not on the ultimate outside stakeholders for whom value is to be created. End-to-end processes were broken into organizational unit sub-processes that were only a part of the whole. The drive to optimize work overall was lost, and sub-optimization ran rampant. In addition, Innovation and Learning issues became locally focused and not for collaborating with the whole business. Sharing of insights was hard to accomplish outside of a group.

For these structural reasons, among other challenges, the balanced scorecard has gradually fallen out of favor as a hierarchical management tool in the last few years as organizations become more concerned with end-to-end value creation. Seeing the value of multiple measurement perspectives, we at PRG felt that a value-oriented and cross-functional scorecard was in order. We felt that measures directly traceable to customer outcomes of value and other stakeholder needs and expectations were needed. Consequently, we looked at the prevalent value-oriented approaches that focused on results for the organization's external stakeholders and worked back from there. In the spirit of the balanced scorecard, the four main categories that we have found to be most useful appear in Figure 9-4. Realistically, depending on the industry, there may be a more focused attention on one category over the others.

Value-oriented balanced scorecard

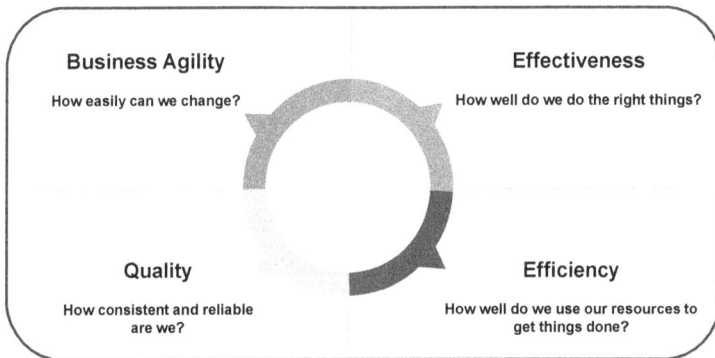

Business Agility
How easily can we change?

Effectiveness
How well do we do the right things?

Quality
How consistent and reliable
are we?

Efficiency
How well do we use our resources to
get things done?

Figure 9-4. Value-oriented balanced scorecard.

Effectiveness

Effectiveness questions how well we are doing the right things for external customers and consumers in the first place—how well we accomplish value creation as far as the recipients of our efforts are concerned. This category reflects the customer value creation point of view and the business' view of success with recipients. Although each industry and organization is different, typical indicators would be something like the following:

- Customer satisfaction rating
- Net Promoter Score
- Customer effort score
- Market share
- Wallet share
- Cost of non-compliance to customer expectations
- New business revenue
- Repeat business revenue
- Lifetime revenue value to us

Efficiency

Efficiency looks at how well your business utilizes its consumable and reusable resources to deliver its outputs. These measures are the classic production types that have been the subject of process improvement regimes such as Lean and Six Sigma over the years. They are not necessarily aligned with the question of, "Are we doing the right things?" and instead on, "Are we doing things we chose to do right?" Some indicators may be:

- Cost of service per transaction
- % of transactions that are straight through with no manual intervention
- Ratios of outputs to time and cost incurred
- Proportion of Waste (as defined by Lean)
- Average time to resolve a problem

Quality

Quality deals with how well we meet the expectation of the product or service recipient in terms of consistency and how well we meet standards and compliance requirements. It also covers the implications of a lack of quality. Some examples are:

- Defects/returns ratios to total counts
- Service Level Agreement % compliance
- Consistency of outputs as shown by ratio of variants to standard over locations and time
- Cost of non-compliance extra work to correct lack of quality or failed risk compliance (rework)
- Returns ratio (non-performing products)
- Complaints ratios to total orders
- Cost of lost future business due to poor quality
- Regulatory compliance costs (fines and restrictions)

Business agility

Business Agility covers the ability to change quickly and be effective when doing so. It includes operational agility, which tackles the ease of adjusting day-to-day based on fast-moving market conditions. It also covers reconfiguration agility that lets insights be turned into designs quickly and designs into products, services, and operations. Quick change includes all aspects of change, not just technology. Some illustrations are:

- Time to change a business rule while in operation

- Time to reallocate resources to an incident or crisis response
- Time to market for a product or service
- Number of insights generated annually and the conversion rate into executable offerings
- Proportion of customer special requests or variations turned down
- Cost of change for a product specification update
- Number of shared uses of a developed capability
- Lost time between human resource assignments (resources downtime on a change)
- Cost of staff retraining due to staff turnover

Scorecard structure

The structure of performance indicators should follow a value creation pattern, meaning value streams and business processes are quite often what we measure, or at least they are the place to hang measures in the reporting hierarchy. These measures will be strong contributors to the overall satisfaction of the stakeholders. As we dive deeper into the hierarchy, we will find the component processes (aka value stream stages) as the place to attach our KPIs. Some will deliver direct stakeholder value, but some will be indirect. For example, running a credit check before accepting a loan request is valuable to the business for risk purposes. It may be required due to regulation, even if the customer may not appreciate it. This hierarchy typically follows the process architecture structure, as shown in Figure 9-5.

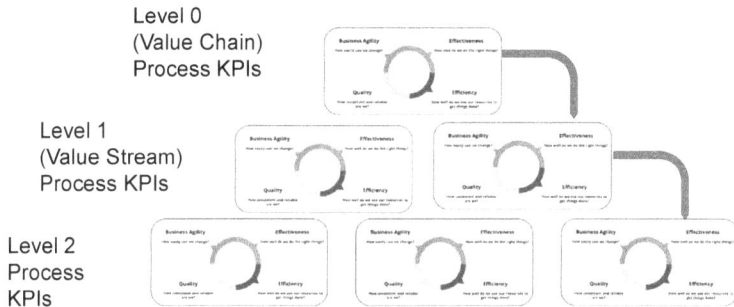

Figure 9-5. Process architecture measurement hierarchy.

As described in our process architecture hierarchy, we can measure many things. We need to have traceable indicators of:

- Strategic Objectives
- Stakeholders' relationships
- The North Star directional guidance
- The work we do (business processes/value streams)

We have to connect indicators into a cause/effect pattern. We can define our reporting dashboard requirements with the strategy structure connected to the process value structure. We also have to provide ranges of acceptable performance data levels that may signify danger, risk, concern, and safety, and immediate or longer term need to be tackled. These levels appear as red, yellow, and green lights on the management dashboard. With the KPI structure and the defined levels on limits of performance warnings, we should also drill down the stack to the underlying causes of concern regarding actual performance problems in the details.

Scorecard planning template

For the upper levels of the scorecard hierarchy, there are several attributes which we could describe. A template that works for each level of work hierarchy appears for one process in our hypothetical consumer bank in Figure 9-6 to illustrate the types of measures, the desired direction of the measurement data, the method of data collection, the current level, and desired level of performance of the indicator. Not all of this may be known when starting our architecture work, but we should strive to fill in the blanks over time.

Activity Level: Level 1: Value Stream	Activity: Win New Customers			
KPI	**How to get the KPI data**	**Current**	**Vector**	**Target**
Effectiveness # of New Customers annually	CRM and Internet banking System	21,650	Increase	30,000
Efficiency # of New Customers per FA	CRM	18	Increase	40
Quality Missing data on Signup - % of Customer Callbacks	CRM	28%	Decrease	3%
Agility Distribution of sales by FA channel	CRM and Internet banking System	87%	Decrease	69%

Figure 9-6. Scorecard planning template for a process.

Bottom-up view

Detailed measurement structure

One tool that can help us determine specific performance indicators is the concept model (Figure 9-7) that we previously used to determine information, capabilities, business rules, and processes.

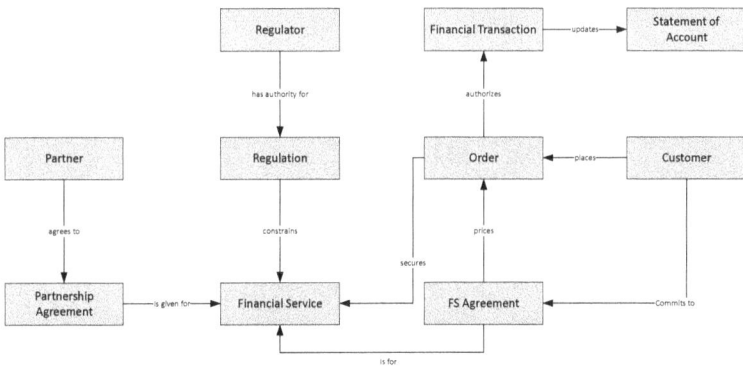

Figure 9-7. The concept model.

If we look at every box (noun is potentially a thing of measurement interest), we can quantify most of them with counts, amounts, or volumes. These will be useful if we feel it will be helpful to someone to make an operational or management decision about that concept. Please note that data captured is to support decisions required to operate or manage the business regardless of who makes them. Organizational structure is irrelevant to what you need to know.

Based on the concept model, a way to determine possible
PIs and KPIs appears in Figure 9-8. This matrix maps all of
the concepts of interest against the others. Note that the
same list appears in the matrix rows and columns.

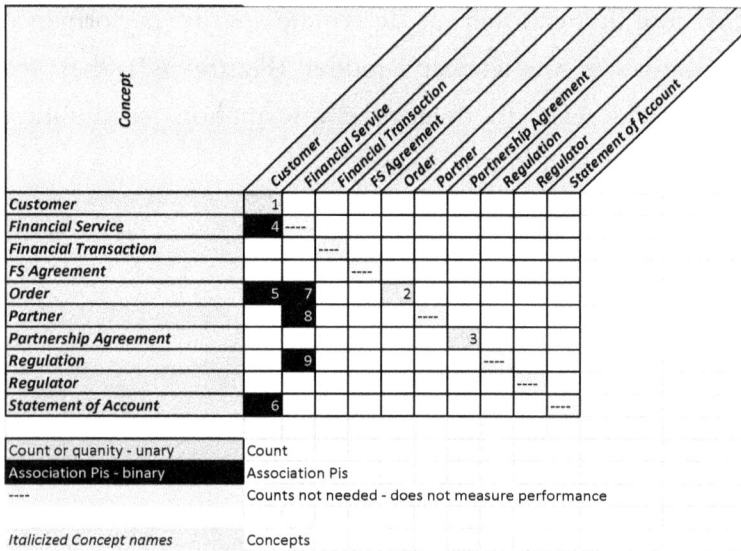

Concept	Customer	Financial Service	Financial Transaction	FS Agreement	Order	Partner	Partnership Agreement	Regulation	Regulator	Statement of Account
Customer	1									
Financial Service	4 ----									
Financial Transaction		----								
FS Agreement			----							
Order	5	7			2					
Partner		8				----				
Partnership Agreement							3			
Regulation		9					----			
Regulator								----		
Statement of Account	6									----

Count or quanity - unary	Count
Association Pis - binary	Association Pis
----	Counts not needed - does not measure performance

Italicized Concept names	Concepts

Figure 9-8. Translation of the concept model.

In this way, we can show the relevant concepts when
combined with other concepts. Not all combinations will
be meaningful, but some will be. We will identify those
combinations of interest by highlighting the relevant cells
connecting the row to the column. In figure 9-8, I have
illustrated some possible intersections (related concepts in
rows) relevant for Customer and Financial Service
concepts. We now have to figure out what the actual
indicator is for each intersection.

Quantifications (concept = thing)

The starting point for all measurements is to count or quantify things; an inventory if you like. Clearly, there are many things we could quantify, but typically we choose the ones of importance to us because of risk, strategy, or some form of operational motivation.

Numbers of orders (intersection number 2) are important, so we count them and quantify their financial amount. How many customers (intersection number 1) do we have? How many Partnership Agreements (intersection number 3) do we have and what is the projected revenue from them?

Physical items are the most obvious. How many branch offices are there? How many mobile phones are there? How many locations are there? Many non-physical items also need to be tracked, such as transactions. Do we know what the counts and amounts are? Can we determine other important attributes about each, such as the size of the branch office, the longevity of staff tenure, and the age of each of our mobile devices?

Each concept in this sample matrix appears in both the columns and the rows. So firstly, we look at the top left to bottom right diagonal of the same concept to itself and determine which concepts are worthy of being counted (relevance to managers) for tracking and decision-making purposes. In the illustration, we decided that only three of the ten shown are of interest for our decision-making. These are to be counted or quantified and reported. We generally refer to these types of concepts as unary since they involve only one concept at a time.

Segmentation (status and types of)

There is typically a breakdown for unary concept performance indicators into both statuses and types. In the performance data, you can expect these to be used as filters to segment or structure the reporting of information with relevance to the appropriate audience. Examples may be:

- How many customers of various types do we have? Types may include Strategic Customers, National Customers, Transactional Business Customers, and Consumers. Perhaps we wish to know the volume of sales by type. There could also be statuses of customers from leads, qualified, under contract, terminated, and renewed. Each of these will be of interest to those who conduct specific roles in the organization, such as sales promotion staff and customer loyalty and retention teams. The lists of types once again are called filters. These filters are usually of great interest to data analytics staff, so we have to gather data about them for research to gain insights.

- How many employees of various classifications do we have? Types – another filter – include unionized worker, management exempt, contract, and executive. Statuses include applied, under consideration, offered, hired, onboarded, promoted, terminated, and retired. Different programs and processes will be in play for each type. If the value of an indicator is out of a defined limited range, it may lead the organization to respond with specific plans and actions. Performance data will also have type and status filters that can expose the important subsets to various parties.

Associations (things per thing)

When a concept is relevant in combination with other ones, we refer to these as binary. Intersections of a concept with a different concept appear below the diagonal line in Figure 9-8. Not every combination is of importance, however. For example, item 7 in the sheet shows that we have chosen to know about Financial Services as related to Orders. We can view these from both ends of the relationship. We may wish to know:

- How many, or what percentage of orders include each type of Financial Service?
- How many Financial Services, on average, are there per order?

Another combination of relevance appears in item 5:

- How many orders are there for each Customer?

- What is the value of all orders from particular customer segments?

We can now derive the places where PI or KPI data must be captured in the process execution and define the IT requirement for data capture. As with unary concepts, many measures will be broken down further by status and type:

- Number of orders received, and the total dollar amount filtered by region (USA, Canada, Europe, Asia Pacific) and payment type (cash, credit, invoice, …)
- Number and size distribution of financial service transactions filtered by channel of customer interaction type (web, customer center, mobile in person, kiosk, branch…)

Possible measurement associations can often be seen directly from the concept model by looking for the direct linkage of concepts (nouns) by the wordings between them (verbs). Some examples would be:

- Number of orders received by and the total dollar amount for each consumer category (link from the consumer to order)
- Number and size distribution of financial service transactions for each financial service type (link from the financial transaction to financial service)

Looking at every direct link in the concept model between concept pairs will allow us to question whether or not there is some associative measure of importance to decision-making or execution of the business. Be careful, though, since not all are useful.

Timing of things

I often see organizations initially defining measures in non-comparable ways over time. When nailing down useful KPIs, the timing factor has to come into play to see trend lines and conduct comparisons. The examples above are still not yet fully formed since we have not defined the period we will compare and contrast them. Are we counting and reporting daily or annually? The numbers will be hugely different in scale, and the reporting period and systems requirements for gathering and consolidating quite different also. By adding the time factor, we can now compare apples to apples meaningfully in all places and periods where we grow and sell apples. Reframing the previous examples would give us useful measurement data to work with:

- Number of orders received by consumer category and the total dollar amount for the category *per month*
- Number and size distribution of financial service transactions for each financial service type *per quarter*

Ratios

Most of the binary associative performance indicators are based on counts or amounts of one concept factored by the counts or amounts of other associated things. For example, 'number of orders per customer category per month.' It is typical to see many of these performance indicators as a ratio. Many meaningful indicators are best expressed as a comparison of one count by volume of another, such as:

- The percentage of all financial transactions delivered by partners per month
- The ratio of returned orders over total orders by sales channel per month

Again, the usefulness of the performance indicator is gauged by how well it informs those who need to know to decide, act, and change something about how to perform work.

Performance indicator template

There is a lot to consider, document, and keep track of when it comes to KPIs. The following (Figure 9-9) is a template that I have found useful to keep me focused. It is to be read top to bottom in each column – not horizontally. You may have to adapt it to suit your specific purposes.

Focus Area	Customer Related KPIs		Order Related KPIs		Financial Service Related KPIs	
Primary Concept	Customer	Customer	Order	Order	Financial Service	Financial Service
Secondary Concept			Customer	Financial Service		Order
PI / KPI	# of customers	Customer gross sales volume	# of orders per customer	# of orders for Financial Service	Profitability of financial service	# of Financial Services per Order
Filter 1 By Timing or Status	by Customer status	by Customer status	N/A		by Time in market	N/A
Filter 2 By Type of Breakdown	by Customer type by Region	by Customer type by Region	by Customer type by Region	by Financial Service Type by Region	by Financial Service Type by Region	by Region
Organization Level Interested	All	All	Regional Managers	Product Owners	Executive Product Owners	Branch Manager
Frequency of Reporting	Quarterly, Yearly	Monthly	Monthly	Quarterly, Yearly	Quarterly, Yearly	Yearly
Comment	Description of value/usage of the KPI for decisioning					

Figure 9-9. Performance indicator template.

To keep the sheet flexible, the attributes for Filter 1 and 2 should be defined separately from the table, as illustrated in Figure 9-10. These are the breakdown for sections of the reporting data.

Customer Status	Customer Type	Region	FS Owner
lead	Strategic Customers	Canada	Ourselves
qualified	National Customers	US	Other Partners
under contract	Transactional Business	Europe	
terminated	Consumers	Asia Pacific	
renewed			

Figure 9-10. Define filter attributes separately.

Going beyond the data (who cares?)

So far, I have delved into counting and comparing the things and associations that are discrete and for which data is more readily accessible as a byproduct of doing the work. Now comes an even harder part—the soft part. With the unrelenting push toward customer focus comes the question, "How do we know how they feel about us?" Customer journey mapping, customer satisfaction surveys, and the drive to improve customer experience are all attempting to reflect this phenomenon.

In an earlier chapter, I discussed the issue of stakeholder expectations of value and the fact that great experience in how things were done was not so useful if the main value delivered through the product or service was not up to par. For example, "The staff were nice and fast but gave us the wrong advice," is not good for future prospective business. So, we have to evaluate both effectiveness and experience factors in light of the customer expectation.

Gaining useful data

Examples of useless KPI data are everywhere today. I refer to this as measurement theatre. An example, In my opinion, is hotel ratings listed online by various travel sites. The super high-end hotels often do not get the best ratings because the expectation of visitors to the hotel was perfection due to the high price they paid. In the same survey ranking list, you will often see much lower-priced hotels with great ratings because no one expected some of the features and services of a five-star property in a two-star hotel that was one-quarter of the price. Comparables here are much harder to rationalize due to factoring in people's expectations. Perception-based measurement feedback can be biased or influenced for the better or worse.

So, we should evaluate the satisfaction level and the experience perception of the external stakeholder but with caution. If we can capture data through counts, amounts, and associations, that may be the best that we can do. Sometimes proxy measures are an easier way to judge satisfaction. For example, easily measurable indicators of timing and frequency of repeat business may be a more reliable and useful indicator of satisfaction.

Reconciling the measurement indicators with your current measurement scorecard

We all know that a clean sheet is unrealistic when defining measurements. Invariably, there are many measurements being reported today but are they currently useful? A good idea is to reconcile the old with the new by comparing each to your process architecture to see if all your current measures have a home and see if any can be retired for better options based on the balanced point of view.

By cross-correlating the list of KPIs to the process hierarchy, we can answer several questions:

- Are there too many KPIs for this bucket of work?
- Are there too few KPIs for it?
- Are existing KPIs sufficient or do we need some new ones as well?
- Can we drop any current ones in favor of some new ones?
- Do we have KPIs which have no process associated?
- Does a KPI cover too many processes, or should each have more specific indicators?

This is a good sanity check you can do with the management team to gain commitment on a better way of measuring and managing data.

Measurement opportunities, challenges, and biases

Gathering the data: How much is enough?

Measurement can be overwhelming if taken too far. Our challenge is to capture just as much as we need to make good operational and management decisions. It is easy to get caught up in trying to get absolute precision in all your measurement data. If you are fortunate to have measurement data capture built into all your IT systems, or were smart enough to have designed them to capture everything already, then congratulations, you are on your way.

The challenge is that for all the things you want to know that are not systematizable, you will have to design data capture into your processes, build the capture mechanisms and go out and capture that information. At worst, you will have to sample the population of transactions. The question becomes one of the need for statistical significance of the measures. You will have to decide what a sound sample looks like according to the rules of sampling theory to remain unbiased and assured. You also have to decide what degree of precision you need, since if you are not careful, you will expend more energy gathering the data than the effort required to do the work itself. There is a fine line between not enough and not worth it. Furthermore, some data may be wonderful to have, but the methods to get it may be convoluted and the results easily biased and unreliable. Perhaps some simple proxy may be better and still give sufficient insight into what's going on.

Attention to how you acquire the data is an important consideration.

Alignment with personal motivation

There will always be arguments over what data to collect since managers know that someone (herself?) will become accountable for it if we capture it. Performance indicator data and the associated targets tie to an organization's formal or informal incentives for its people.

So long as the individual's indicators align with everyone else's indicators and are traceable to overall strategic objectives, personal incentive will push behavior and decision-making in the intended direction. Sadly, this traceability and alignment are lacking much of the time, and indicators are not well connected. If done poorly, laser focus on the official personal and organizational objectives can lead to significant gaming for personal reasons as well as result in sub-optimization, lack of traceability to end-to-end results for the stakeholders, and misalignment with strategic intent. Of course, everyone drives toward targets, but often these are the wrong targets since they are biased towards divisional motivations and personal preferences.

When deriving the hierarchy of measures to be sought, it is imperative that it not be done based on the organization chart but instead on the process architecture structure and the results of value streams, agnostic to the formal organogram.

With the right set of performance indicators aligned to value delivery, rather than an arbitrary formal hierarchy that fractures value propositions, we can ask who can take accountability for monitoring and advocacy for whatever needs to be done to attain intended end to end results. Then and only then can we see how the organization structure maps to the performance hierarchy.

A challenge with perception-based measures is that it has become easier than ever to ask the customer their opinion than ever before. So, what is a good measurement strategy? With so much online booking of services and digital delivery, it is simple for the service provider to generate surveys for perception-based feedback and scoring automatically every time. Since I travel a lot, I expect survey requests flying at me for everything I experienced, and, for me, it is simply annoying.

On my last pre-pandemic trip, I had survey e-mails from airlines for each of four flights, from the hotel I stayed at for the few nights I was away, and from my restaurant booking site for three restaurants I visited. I responded to exactly none of them. Asking too much can become intrusive. My concern is that we have probably reached the stage of survey overload (at least for me) that reminds me of the customer comment card in hotel rooms in the past. The only time I filled them out was when I was over the moon with the great service I got because someone went out of their way to satisfy a key requirement of mine that I just had to congratulate them, or if something happened that was so poorly dealt with that I had to vent. Anything in between got no action from me. I have reached the same point with online surveys now. I typically just delete the request, and I think I am not alone. I have to wonder how representative the samples are of reality. I call this measurement fatigue. Are too many surveys of customer experience detracting from their actual experience?

Furthermore, we have lost the ability, in my opinion, to truly score the results. Differences between individual vendors and service providers seem to all start at 4 stars and go to 5. What happened to the territory from 1 to 4? If you note that your Uber driver only has a 4.8, you are conditioned to ask yourself what's wrong with the person since it was not a perfect 5. Differences are so minute and offer minimal valuable distinguishing feedback that I cannot trust what I see as a consumer. This is made worse when the supplying organization games the numbers by telling the customer what the score should be when they will be surveyed or has interveners who jack up or down the ratings in ethically questionable ways.

Observer effect

In science, the term 'observer effect' means that the act of observing will influence the phenomenon being observed. In business, it means that the act of measuring itself will bias the measurement data. For example, we know from high school physics days that the insertion of a thermometer into a substance will not accurately capture the temperature of the material because it will change it. Physics geeks are quick to talk about the Heisenberg Uncertainty Principle that postulates that you cannot determine both the speed and location of an atomic particle at any point in time since if you get one, the other is not knowable.

The classic business example goes back to the observations noted by Henry A. Landsberger in 1958 after evaluating a series of studies conducted some decades earlier at a Western Electric's Hawthorne Works near Chicago.[27] The Hawthorne Effect characteristics showed that when people are watched, they change their behavior. At the Hawthorne Works in the 1920's researchers adjusted working conditions in multiple ways to observe worker productivity. No matter what they did, such as

---

[27] Hawthorne revisited: management and the worker: its critics, and developments in human relations in industry, Henry A Landsberger.

brightening the workplace and then later dimming it, the performance improved but only for short periods. Landsberger concluded that the main factor was that workers were getting attention from experimenters and so modified their behavior. It was not the innovations per se. As an Industrial Engineer, formerly forced to do time studies in full view of the work subjects, I can assure you that the workers did not work the same way when I was not there watching. We all played games with one another because we all knew that the other party knew what we were trying to do. So, the act of measuring will bias the data unless you are very careful in your data gathering methods.

Visibility of measurement data alone can be a blessing if done appropriately. For example, on a recent process improvement exercise, we noticed significant disagreement regarding the straight through processes (STP) rate for loan applications at a large bank (% of applications without manual intervention). We got estimates from 40% to 70% from different groups, including executives. Once we sampled 100% of the universe of transactions from the preceding year, we found it was about 55%. We added the measurement indicator to the scorecard for all loan origination locations and for all staff to see. The results jumped to closer to 70% within two months with zero process or technology changes. Being aware of the data can be a powerful virtuous motivator affecting behavior in its own right when aligned.

Discovering bias-free ways of getting the data and aligning with motivation is as important as the data being sought.

Measurement and behavior

One of the benefits of measurement is aligning process work to results assigned to people, analyzing those results, and discovering causes of poor process and individual performance. This allows us to help people do better. However, a problem comes when the organization wants a culture different from today, and the hard measures are not sufficient to capture the behaviors of the individuals that collectively reflect that culture.

The jury is still out on appropriate measures to indicate behavioral consistency with what's needed. There is no simple scorecard to show this. We still believe that defining the behaviors desired under a set of circumstances is a key part of defining solution requirements. Designing the observation and coaching roles required (Figure 9-11) as part of process design and development is a critical aspect we often miss. It is an essential complement to measurement.

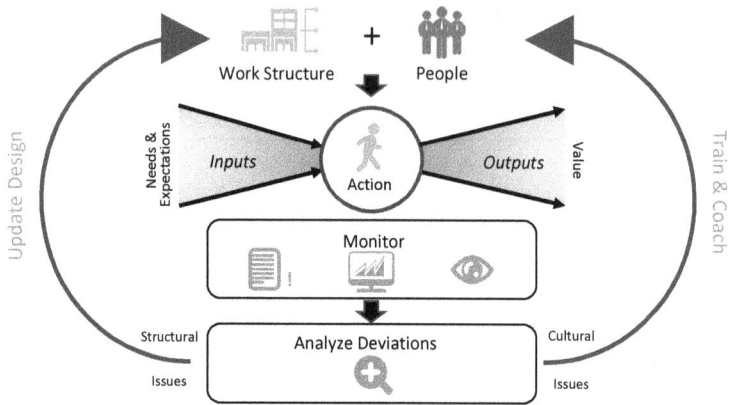

Figure 9-11. Observation and coaching roles required.

Measurement and organizational maturity

Making a serious commitment to aligned and traceable measurement is a big ask and may be the hardest thing to get right. You all probably have lots of measures already but need a real commitment to baseline measurement as a more formal and never-ending discipline. Based on the business architecture and the organization's operating model, we can imply the perpetual roles and responsibilities for measurement outcomes to be established and honored.

Typically, that requires certain aspects of the architecture to be in place. It is hard to assure traceability if no clear strategic framework exists and no concept model and business process architecture are available. If they are not in play, do your best to get some measurement thinking and some common-sense indicators in place while you build out the operating model. If you have these models, then determine your performance structure, indicators, and targets, and strive to make measurement a key part of working and managing. Everything will reconfigure itself to be focused because there will be a 'why' to aim for.

Up next

Measurement ability builds on the business model and the operating model. Gaining alignment and assuring a traceable measurement dashboard and data capture mechanism will be frustrating but worth it. Aligned measurement will help us better focus on customers and end-to-end management. With clear strategic requirements framed earlier in our journey and good architectural models for concepts, processes, capabilities, and measurable performance, we will be able to connect the dots and prioritize the changes of greatest strategic importance. That will be the topic of the next chapters.

CHAPTER 10

Aligning Architectural Domains

As the chapters have progressed, we have discussed many ideas, models, and methods, as seen in Figure 10-1. The framework recognizes the iterative and interactive nature of the major phases of developing a business architecture. The approach is certainly agile if we want it to be. The discovery and population of the knowledge gained for each domain of interest can only really be well understood incrementally in the context of the others.

Despite the need to keep each domain independent in specification, in real use they are interdependent. Over time, with this set of business knowledge domains evolving and becoming more robust, we will be able to use knowledge of the domain components and their interdependencies in a value chain to enable rapid anticipation of the impacts of change and the response to it. We must understand how specific instances within a domain potentially interacts with others.

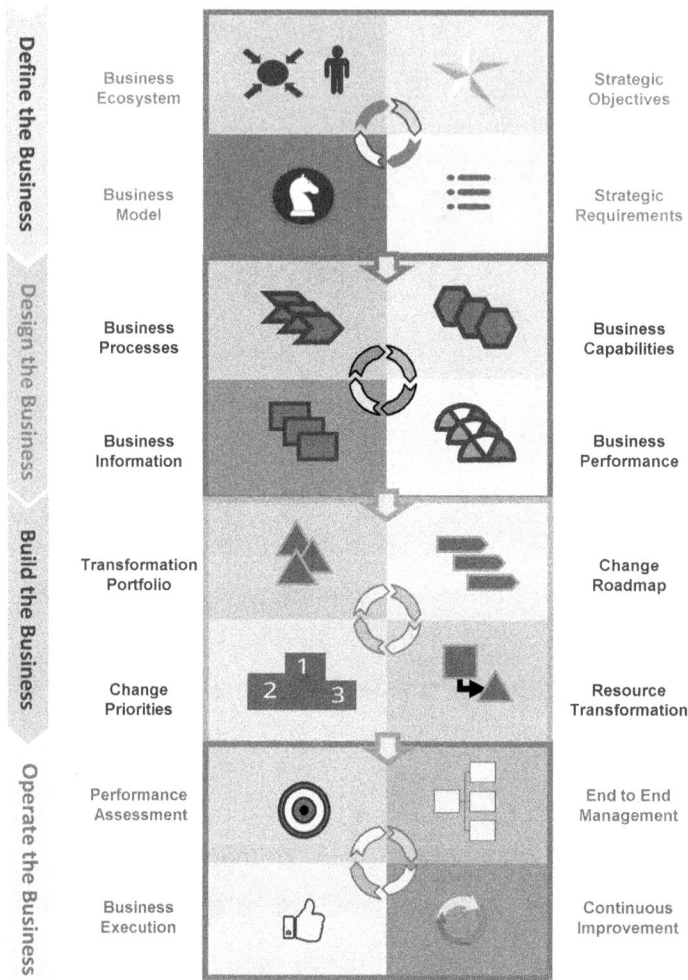

Figure 10-1. Comprehensive business architecture framework and
    foundational methodology.

Our approach tacitly presumes that we have or can gain
the business knowledge that describes the business
architecture's various aspects. Implicit in this is the base
assumption that we are not developing independent

architecture components simply to conduct a single domain project or solve a single problem.

> *The integrated architectures create holistic solutions that provide longevity, sustainable business advantage, and ease of change.*

Single domain understanding will be helpful for a single-purpose change, but I contend that architecture should be about more than a simple transformation. For example, suppose we only focus on introducing a new product, service, or even a new business model without thinking longer-term. In that case, as soon as we finish a particular transformation effort, we will immediately begin re-architecting all over again for the next transformation fire drill. Not keeping models and knowledge up to date means starting over each time.

Clearly, our organizations are leaving the so-called industrial age where we used to have a long time in the market. Now we are well into the knowledge age where constant turmoil and short product and service time-in-market will be the norm. Drivers such as digitalization, agile, fickle consumers, new technologies, radically different and cross-entity partnership business models, social media culture, and real-time expectations are driving old ways of working to the scrap heap. No evidence suggests this trend will stop or slow down any time soon.

It is clear that if 'we do not know what we know' regarding how all the pieces connect, then continuous change will be risky with large impacts and dramatic unintended consequences. The expression 'the main cause of problems is solutions' will surely be a continuing reality. Some approaches, such as Agile software development, are helpful but will not be sufficient in and of themselves to solve a multidisciplinary problem. A bigger boat is required. One that will let us be continuously relevant and be capable of perpetual business agility.

We have to know how the architectural components connect and use one another to create value.

Scope of alignment

We can attempt to cross-reference the business knowledge domains to one another in one of two ways. The difference is in the scope of what we choose to take on. We could be and should be wherever possible, connecting the various models as we go. This involves linking knowledge gained in the Define the Business Phase with the Design the Business phase artifacts. However, getting all models developed to depth and assuring all aspects are connected may prove an enormous, impractical, and unappreciated effort.

There are so many information concepts, processes, and capabilities, among other domains, that the effort easily becomes an exercise in modeling for modeling's sake and certainly may be perceived as such. As a result, we can easily lose focus on business value creation. This approach is usually a recipe for losing your business support since managers will not see any tangible results soon enough despite the invested effort. An alternative approach would be developing skinny higher-level models and, getting through a strategic prioritization exercise (see Chapter 11 for how to do this) to identify a few key processes and connect only those other domain components needed to move forward in a focused but cross-connected manner.

The full architecture and its connections can evolve as you deliver valuable change. Whichever scope you decide is best for you, the rest of this chapter will establish what connections are most useful and how to build the implementation plan.

Main connections

As we have covered in earlier chapters, many interconnections could be made across component business architecture models. Some of the main pairings appear in Figure 10-2.

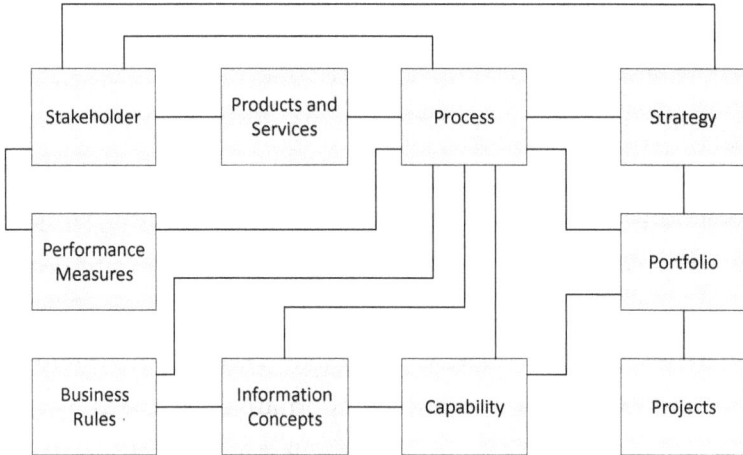

Figure 10-2. Architectural Interconnections.

Business architecture wiring

Let's look at some of the key knowledge areas we need to know about and how they connect. Practically speaking, no single domain model is sufficient to tell us the impact of change. The purpose of the architecture is to establish a set of base constructs that will remain relatively stable over time and tell us what will happen about how each impacts other items of interest if we change it. That means that the interconnections become as important as the components being connected. Nothing stands alone.

What is the business strategy and how does it connect?

Earlier chapters have outlined the starting point of the strategic intent and strategy of the business as the raison détre of business architecture. Especially important is the connection of strategy to external stakeholders and their expectations of value that they have of our products and services delivered by the business processes that deliver that value.

What are business concepts and how do they connect?

For me, the business concept model is the foundation for business processes needed to act on those concepts. They form the structure of business capabilities which must realize the needed ability to make the business work, the key performance indicators to assess the state of business performance, and the information to keep the organization alive. In addition, the model of the operational business concepts provides a rigorous foundation for structuring business rules to be used in making business decisions within some of the processes. Knowing the essential elements of the concept model is the start of understanding change since we can ask, "If I change this concept because of a business model change, what else will be impacted?"

What are the business processes and how do they connect?

Business processes connect to many of the other domains.

A business process defines our work to contribute to delivery of value externally to stakeholders. The processes are measurable vehicles to translate the strategic intent into operational action and deliver products and services better to stakeholders.

We can build the business change portfolio around processes. This is critical to know about the traceability of investments in change back to strategy.

A business process creates, updates, deletes, or refers to information concepts defined in the concept model so that interconnection is critical.

Many business processes make business decisions such as approve/deny. There is the need to know which processes use invoke which business rules to do this well. These business rules, in turn, are built around the concept model's structure (lines between concepts) as a set of constraints. Therefore, we also need the information defined by the information concepts as input to the decision-making.

However, the most prevalent process connection of interest to business architects and process practitioners seems to be with the business capabilities.

What are the business capabilities and how do they connect?

A business capability map is a business domain in its own right. If it's on the map, you'll need that capability in your business at some level of performance appropriate for your business. This may be low to high.

Capability in a business architecture sense has come to mean what is required to enable or contribute to the creation of value, directly or indirectly, to meet the intent of the organization or value chain stakeholders who receive our goods and services.

The capabilities are used in value streams/business processes implemented through human, technological, and other types of resources to conduct the work to be done. Therefore, the Portfolio of Changes will have to include various capability development projects; the most expensive and often the most time-consuming parts of the portfolio.

Business Process-Capability connection

My work with the Business Architecture Guild's BPM working group articulates how this important interconnection can be structured. As noted earlier, some business architects use the name value stream rather than business process. This is simply a semantic issue, and there is no difference in content or intention if well designed. However, we must be careful not to confuse the term 'value stream' as used by different communities such as Lean Six Sigma (LSS) practitioners.

Wikipedia states that, "value stream mapping is a lean-management method for analyzing the current state and designing a future state for the series of events that take a product or service from its beginning through to the customer."[28] It is used as the basis for eliminating non-value-added work (waste) to benefit the customer and the business.

Our usage of the term is a high-level end-to-end business process delivering value to stakeholders that is triggered by some business event.

If your process architecture is value-centric, you need available capabilities to bring value streams to life and

---

[28] https://en.wikipedia.org/wiki/Value-stream_mapping.

deliver results. Once again, Figure 10-3 shows the connection. The business process needs appropriate capabilities made possible with the application of technological and human resources suitable to get things done. Poor capabilities will, by definition, lead to poorly performing processes and poor performance measurement results. Any individual process will typically require multiple capabilities. Also, a capability ideally, if well-scoped and structured, may be used by more than one process or value stream. Please note that this is implied but not reflected in Figure10-3 explicitly. The connection is many-to-many.

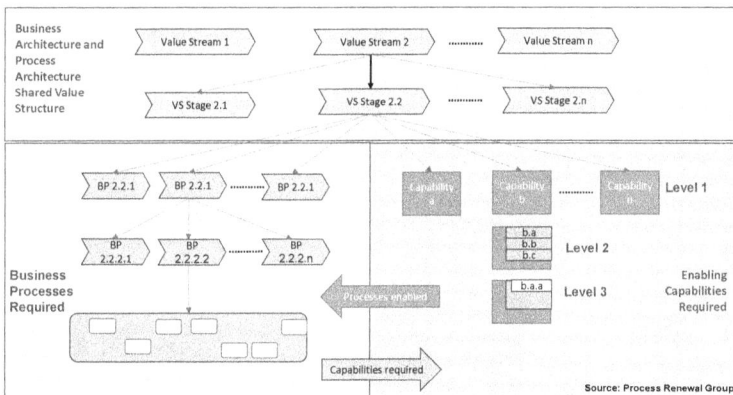

Figure 10-3. Process-Capability Interconnections.

There are logical value creation points within the stream that a process practitioner may call a sub-process or an activity, but some business architects may call a value stream stage. As we advocate and described in an earlier chapter, a value-oriented conceptual process architecture would look very similar to a set of value streams at higher levels of abstraction, so it is easy to understand the potential confusion in naming. From now on, we can use the value-oriented process architecture to hold and structure the value streams and stages. You are free to use the term that best resonates within your organization.

An extrapolation of Figure 10-3 appears in Figure 10-4. It is important not to build these domains into one another or ignore one or the other since both are required to operate and design a business. In architecture, we should be representing information, processes, and capabilities in many-to-many relationships. For example, Process 1.1.1.3 needs capabilities a.a.a and a.a.b to do the job, but capability a.a.b is also needed by Process 1.1.1.2, so we better be careful to accommodate the needs of each in capability design.

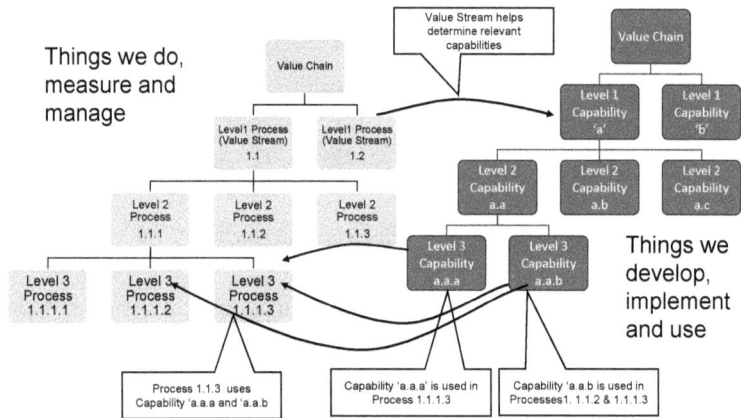

Figure 10-4. Illustration of Process – Capability Interaction.

A subset of our illustrative process architecture appears in Figure 10-5. In it, we can see that these processes require several business capabilities to function. Also, notice that multiple processes use many capabilities, so when we design each capability, we have to keep in mind the needs of all the relevant processes that may action it.

Once we have a value-oriented process architecture and a comprehensive capability map, we can connect the dots so that once any of these are found to be lacking or a new strategy for it becomes apparent, we are in a position to determine all of the impacts of the changes and get them into the roadmap of change. This includes impacts on the process operationally due to capability adjustments and also capability changes required to build due to process improvement or innovations.

Extending this picture to fully formed capability and process diagrams will obviously not be simple to read graphically. I have only shown this snippet to help the reader understand the idea. Matrix views may be a better way to show the connections captured. Using repository tools based on an appropriate meta-model is essential once you build these architectures to ensure integrity and keep your sanity. Native Visio and the like cannot handle this integrity requirement after the initial versions are crafted due to the difficulty of tracking changes and keeping up to date.

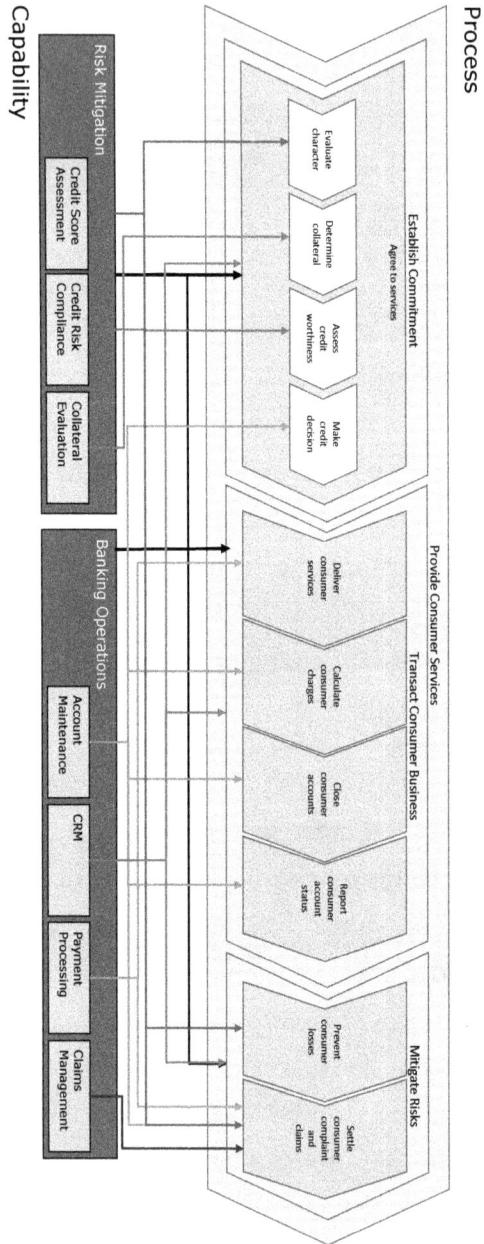

Figure 10-5. Subset of our process architecture.

Value-oriented business processes are about defining actions to create ultimate value for one or more of their recipients. However, just using these models alone may not sufficiently pinpoint the gaps, needed improvements, or investment required in holistic change. This can lead to redundant resources being developed to do work because of multiple requests from different organizational units or process owners for similar solutions that a common capability would tackle.

Looking from a capability map perspective alone does not provide a context for the importance or effectiveness of a given capability, especially in how it and other capabilities, in concert, can impact and propel stakeholder value delivery through the processes within which they are applied. Both views are required to work together to make the right changes happen. If there is both a good capability architecture and process architecture in place, mapping one to the other will be straightforward.

Burlton Hexagon

We have discussed capabilities, processes, and information as defined domains. As we all gain more and more experience with them, our professional body of knowledge reference will become richer. However, realizing a new capability or a changed process in terms of making a difference in the value creation of the business may require many other architectural components and resources to be changed. The Burlton Hexagon in Figure 10-6, discussed in detail in Chapter 8, shows the relationships among several of these that are critical in solution implementation to bringing the complex capability components to reality and improving the processes that execute them. Several of these aspects will undoubtedly show up in the Transformation Roadmap.

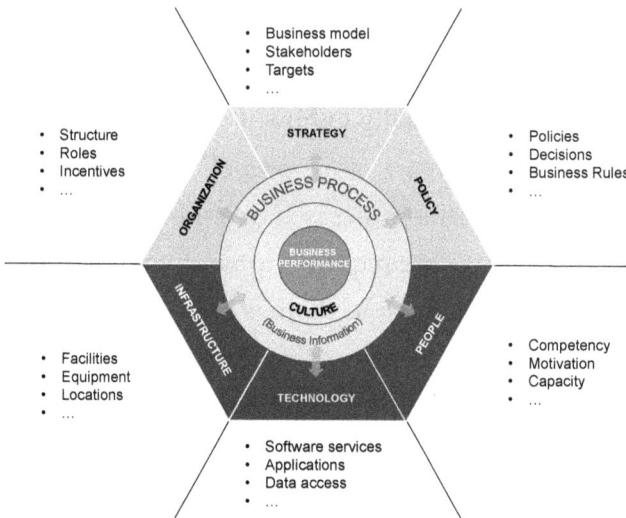

Figure 10-6. The Burlton Hexagon.

Tooling needed

Knowledge retention and the ability to trace and connect the various domains are critical requirements for business agility. Despite all the prognostications that Agile software development methods may not need this degree of knowledge rigor; nothing could be further from the truth if you want to be truly agile as a business and not just fast with software releases. In reality, if this knowledge of interdependent parts within various domains were available, I am convinced that Agile software teams would use it and do better and create more aligned work.

The problem is that there is often little commitment to sustain the knowledge after a project or epic, so it often remains unavailable later, rendering it useless as things continue to change. It takes commitment and is hard work. This will always be the case so long as we are project-based and not sustainable knowledge-oriented, thinking only short term. A large part of the challenge is that we often do not have the software knowledge base and tools to track what we've got. Diagrams that are solely pictures will not suffice. Intelligent tools are essential. Full function toolkits with strong impact analysis and what-if functionalities are essential.

With so many input sources in so many knowledge domains, it is ludicrous to expect anyone or any group to keep everything in their heads or even in static documents. Sophisticated tools such as QualiWare, BiZZdesign, Capsifi, IRIS, Mega, Trisotech, Orbus, and at the next level of decomposition if you are process-centric, Signavio and Bizagi, to name just a few, are needed. With all due respect to Microsoft desktop tools such as Visio, PowerPoint, Excel, Teams, SharePoint, and the like, they are not choices that can collect the dots, much less connect them and sustain all the interconnections without monumental effort. You will not be able to make queries to find change impacts, and the models will quickly be full of hard to notice inconsistencies and redundancies, soon becoming outdated and unused.

Business knowledge and maturity

The current reality is that most organizations are business knowledge-poor regarding business architecture artifacts and understanding the impacts of change. What we do have is frequently not current, and the parts are disconnected. It is foolish to think we can solve this challenge overnight, even with tooling.

A journey is needed to make us more able to manage architectures. This journey's key progressive steps cannot be skipped.

I have seen many organizations try to go from low architecture ability and maturity to become world-class overnight. It does not work, and the effort can meet with significant cultural and political resistance, not to mention that it takes time to gather and structure what they need to know and develop the culture of using the knowledge to full effect. Achieving useful business architecture capability is a matter of knowledge, maturity, and readiness.

Figure 10-7 is inspired by Watts Humphrey's Capability Maturity Model. With it, you can ask yourself where you may be today and how far you want to go. It may not be necessary, practical, or possible to strive for level 5 where the air is truly rarified for good reasons. If I aim to put a working roving vehicle on Mars and have it function for a decade, level 5 may be critical. If I am selling vegetables at a farmers' market, perhaps not.

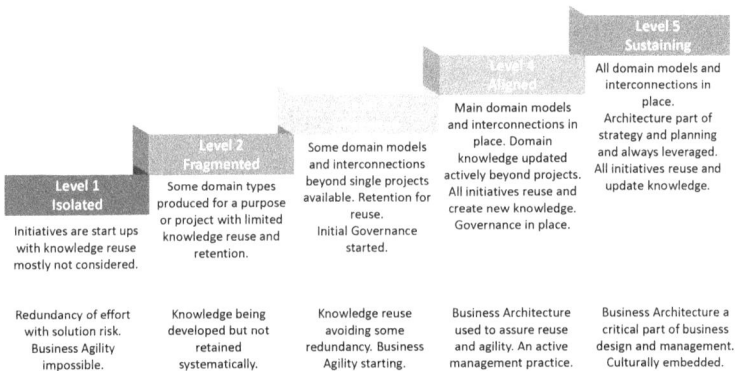

Level 1 Isolated	Level 2 Fragmented	Level 3	Level 4 Aligned	Level 5 Sustaining
Initiatives are start ups with knowledge reuse mostly not considered.	Some domain types produced for a purpose or project with limited knowledge reuse and retention.	Some domain models and interconnections beyond single projects available. Retention for reuse. Initial Governance started.	Main domain models and interconnections in place. Domain knowledge updated actively beyond projects. All initiatives reuse and create new knowledge. Governance in place.	All domain models and interconnections in place. Architecture part of strategy and planning and always leveraged. All initiatives reuse and update knowledge.
Redundancy of effort with solution risk. Business Agility impossible.	Knowledge being developed but not retained systematically.	Knowledge reuse avoiding some redundancy. Business Agility starting.	Business Architecture used to assure reuse and agility. An active management practice.	Business Architecture a critical part of business design and management. Culturally embedded.

Figure 10-7. Business Architecture Maturity: How far do you want to go?

If we truly know where we are and what we have, we can chart a path to our goal of leveraging accessible business knowledge. On the other hand, if we think we know enough about what's going on or feel that we do not need to know what we have and the ramifications of change, we are surely risking our future—one that will continue to surprise us. Can we survive long enough to find out?

Up next

The business information, business capability, business process perspectives, and the other domains described here are still in their early days of maturity in most organizations. Many are still struggling to determine what to do first. There is a lot of angst among business architects, enterprise architects, technology architects, business process professionals, and operational managers regarding what is needed. The ability to drive measurable operational process work and develop the optimum set of capabilities requires a practical framework where the pieces fit shown.

Next, we will prioritize selecting processes, capabilities, and information to gain the biggest advantage in allocating our scarce human and financial capital for change. But, of course, we cannot do it all at once, so let's choose according to our strategic drivers and performance gaps.

CHAPTER 11

Prioritizing Change

So far, we have tackled the efforts to Define the Business and Design the Business. Now we are entering into how we can Build the Business, as shown in Figure 11-1. In the overall scheme, we have collected, connected, and will now begin to correct.

Without the structured models as a baseline and strategic intentions and measurement of performance in place, it is impossible to develop a portfolio of change other than one based on personal opinions, bottom up lobbying, and internal politics. This chapter is intended to leverage all of the architectural knowledge we have gained by applying the methods of the previous chapters so we can establish a set of high-level change priorities that will deliver the best transformative initiatives—ones that allocate our scarce financial and human resources towards the best return. We will base it on a repeatable strategic and architectural method. This chapter will take on alternative approaches to prioritization. , It will establish change priorities based on strategic business importance and process performance gaps. One version will be fast. Another will be more comprehensive. This chapter will also examine where to start—with information, processes, or capabilities. From there, we will sort out the dependencies on one another to get a comprehensive view of changes. The results will allow us to do confident project scoping and define the requirements for changes.

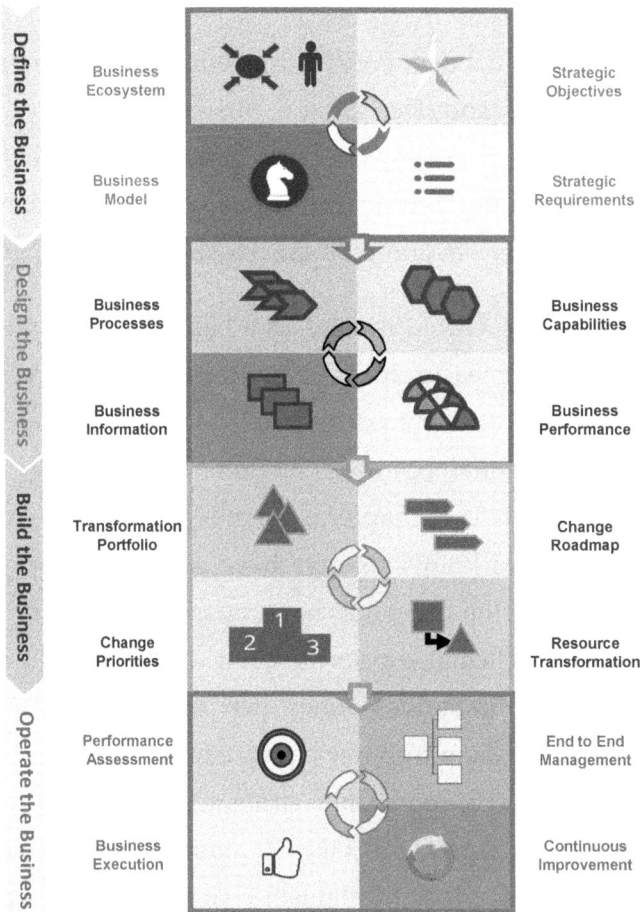

Figure 11-1. Comprehensive business architecture framework and foundational methodology.

In prior chapters, we focused on two main types of business knowledge. The first is to understand the business drivers in the business ecosystem, business intent, and strategy as crystallized by our North Star. This is all about intention. It does not describe how we design a structured response. It does, however, provide us with a set of consistent criteria that we can and should use to choose among the many investment alternatives.

The second knowledge set at the heart of the business architecture covers the various aspects of how well we are currently able to perform so we can deal with the intentions and future operations of the business day to day. It deals with the resources and assets we will need to move to the intended higher state. It will intelligently match the structural process, capability and information components against the intentions and business strategy. The payoff will provide a great start to a sound investment strategy that maximizes the business return of our spend and most expeditiously gets us closer to our goal state.

Because market conditions change constantly and required change resources are not sitting around waiting to be assigned, this assessment is critical to conduct periodically in a small, repeating cycle. At a minimum, it should be done slightly before or iteratively with, the annual prioritization, portfolio management, and budget timings. Ideally, it will be done more often than that, perhaps quarterly, as the real-world races by and perpetual ecosystem changes and the reality of the status of changes underway become apparent to us.

Structure of change prioritization

There are some choices regarding the primary organization or structuring mechanism of planning for change. The three most common from the Design the Business Phase of the landscape are business information, business capabilities, and business processes as the hub of choice, starting point, and organizing mechanism. We can make strong arguments for each, and at the end of the day, we will have to have plans to change each and determine which ones will require structured efforts, programs, and projects, to renew them. So, ultimately, it's not one or the other but all.

Information first

The scenario calling for an information-centric approach is when the need for absolute data integrity drives the organization, and everything else should serve the primary data mission. If the organization is built on reporting information and data compliance, you may choose to start there. Examples are organizations or value chains that value:

- Compliance and regulatory reporting of critical data about a stakeholder such as customer and employee privacy. Customer privacy includes General Data Protection Regulation (GDPR), Know Your Customer (KYC), and Anti-Money Laundering (AML). Employee privacy includes employment information and tax compliance.

- Master data management integrity, such as reference data with a single point of the truth.

- Data lineage, showing traceability of actions on data for audit and risk management, governance purposes, and compliance such as Basel 3-4 for capital, liquidity, and credit risk, Markets in Financial Instruments Directive (MiFID) for protection in investment services, International Financial Reporting Standard (IFRS) for insurance contract liabilities, etc.

Once we prioritize the information areas, we must find the processes and capabilities that act on the critical information as reference data.

Capability first

The argument for a capability led approach, typically made by enterprise architects and some business architects with a IT mindset, is that ultimately we have to plan for and make expensive changes in enabling capabilities (typically technologies). Therefore, we must get right at it and define and correct any weaknesses directly without dealing with business operations per se. This argument has appeal when:

- Many capabilities are used in a lot of processes requiring a high degree of reuse and common practice

- A piece of comprehensive software is currently ineffective and some of its embedded capabilities are used in many processes and will have to be replaced

- IT is the predominant means for operating the business with a high dependence on ERP, MRP, and CRM or other types of technical services

- You have to transition away from a software application perspective to a microservices one

Process first

The argument for the business processes first approach is that the design of the operational work that we execute every day has to be sorted out first to define and connect sub-processes to enhance ways of working and business performance. End to end connectivity of work is essential since processes get measured in business terms, and we want to improve business performance for our customers and other stakeholders. We have to determine and enhance how our processes interact with stakeholders in the outside world as the prime concern.

This is most likely when:

- Traceable strategy realization is essential

- Value for stakeholders is the driver

- Measurable performance enhancement must be managed

- KPI and measurement centric

- The time is right, and the organization is mature enough for cross-functional management and governance

- The organization is not at the lowest level of process maturity—higher than level 1.

All factors are co-dependent, and processes create and consume information and require capabilities to be applied to deliver better business performance and relationship outcomes. However, customers only realize our capabilities (good or bad) when executing process work. Therefore, the ultimate goal of our architecture efforts must be to end up with more effective and efficient business operations that are inherently adaptable. This is the view of business operational managers who are accountable for measurable results.

For the reasons above, I will illustrate a process first approach that will focus on operational business performance to determine which capabilities deserve priority enhancement and investment compared to possible alternatives. Not all organizations will start here. We will cover examples of different starting points in Chapter 13.

My personal preference is to start with processes for many of the following reasons.

- Capabilities do not solely act directly to deliver the performance of operations—only when processes employ them to do work.

- End-to-end processes are tied to performance measurement and capabilities provide the ability for them to perform. Large process performance gaps imply large capability gaps.

- Realization of Strategic Intent is measurable when delivered through processes in action, not organization charts. Therefore, processes become a logical place to look at first to ensure traceability to overall stakeholder and business objectives.

However, capabilities allow processes to perform. We have seen that a typical process requires several capabilities to be available. Still, each of the capabilities that it is dependent on may also support multiple other processes, so looking at both is essential to avoid unintended consequences.

We will start with processes and connect to capabilities in a symbiotic way.

Fixing weak capabilities without knowing which processes employ them does not guarantee better net business performance or attainment of strategic intent. Non-strategic capability weaknesses may be quite acceptable and not be a problem. Strategic considerations of inherent value contribution must be examined to avoid investing in the unimportant. Suppose we use the example of a 100% online bank, and we assessed its Facility Management capability. See Figure 11-2. In that case, we might find that several sub-capabilities are weak. However, just going after them without the performance context does not help since, in this scenario, bricks and mortar banking branches are largely irrelevant to our mission and our vision of universal access and digitalization. It is not enough to look solely at capabilities. Capabilities in the context of processes and performance priorities will serve us better.

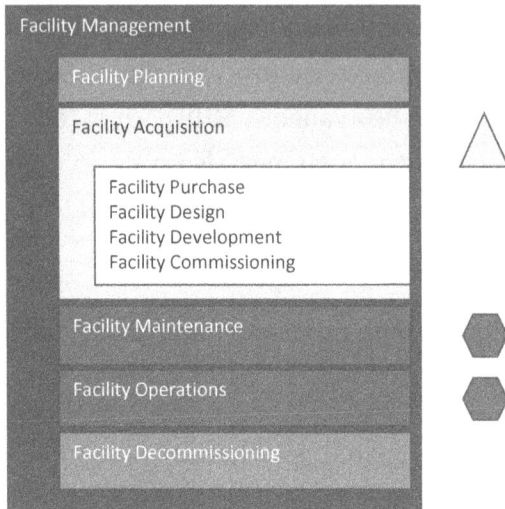

Figure 11-2. Strong and Weak Capabilities.

Reviewing strategy and the North Star

We discussed the requirements for stakeholder relationship optimization and striving towards the organization's strategic intent as the purpose of all architecture work. We will map the intended state against the gap to the current state to make choices and actively use the knowledge we have gained.

External stakeholder analysis

Our enterprise is so strongly connected in our business ecosystem that focusing on the customer journey and experience is essential. Digital strategies, for example, are pointless without connecting the digital customer interactions with our behind the scene processes. Customers are among the wide set of external parties our enterprise must interact with to thrive. Critical stakeholder knowledge includes the following characteristics:

- A recognition of the required nature of customer relationship that should pervade all thinking and planning, including the Value Proposition with its classic choices of Operational Excellence, Customer Intimacy, and Innovation that will help us choose among investment choices and design needs.

- Understanding who the stakeholders are is essential—who cares about us and who do we care about?

- What's happening at the interface points? What tangible or virtual product, service, and information exchanges do we have with outsiders?

- What expectations of value we have of others, and them of us?

- What measurement indicators and performance data is needed to evaluate the stakeholder relationship performance, including what are the gaps between the current state and future objectives?

- What aspects of the relationship are healthy and unhealthy?

- What are the required capabilities for relationship success?

We must do it at this point if we have not done the investigatory work earlier, as advocated in prior chapters. Remember our rule that criteria must always come before decisions and design.

Consolidating strategic intent and stakeholder analysis

There is a myriad of opinions on what to prioritize. Unfortunately, we often base these on individuals', groups', or executives' functional roles and personal performance motivations. Going with an opinion-based approach can be a minefield. It rarely results in what's best for operational business results. That's why we tackled the thorny issue of gaining acceptance to the strategic and stakeholder criteria for end-to-end outcomes as a basis for choosing among alternatives earlier in the architecture before we started to prioritize investments. This allows architects, planners, and business leaders to derive an outcome-based program of change and not a divisional or functional one.

If you recall, the North Star is a packaging of stakeholder analysis and strategy discussions that provides from four to seven weighted statements (aka goals) with vectors of increase, decrease, or sustain to indicate the needed movement. It also has weighting factors to show the relative importance of each criterion. Figure 11-3 shows the example of our consumer bank's North Star that we developed earlier.

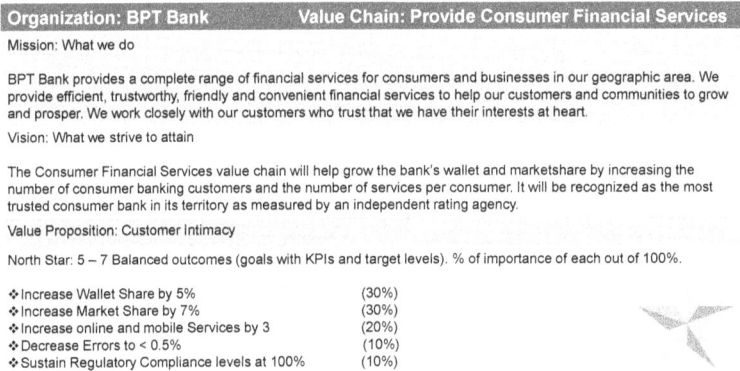

Organization: BPT Bank	Value Chain: Provide Consumer Financial Services

Mission: What we do

BPT Bank provides a complete range of financial services for consumers and businesses in our geographic area. We provide efficient, trustworthy, friendly and convenient financial services to help our customers and communities to grow and prosper. We work closely with our customers who trust that we have their interests at heart.

Vision: What we strive to attain

The Consumer Financial Services value chain will help grow the bank's wallet and marketshare by increasing the number of consumer banking customers and the number of services per consumer. It will be recognized as the most trusted consumer bank in its territory as measured by an independent rating agency.

Value Proposition: Customer Intimacy

North Star: 5 – 7 Balanced outcomes (goals with KPIs and target levels). % of importance of each out of 100%.

❖ Increase Wallet Share by 5% (30%)
❖ Increase Market Share by 7% (30%)
❖ Increase online and mobile Services by 3 (20%)
❖ Decrease Errors to < 0.5% (10%)
❖ Sustain Regulatory Compliance levels at 100% (10%)

Figure 11-3. North Star illustration.

Reviewing performance gaps

Performance gaps indicate how far away we are from measured results targeted for the end of the planning horizon of the strategy work. This is a key point since the gap is not from where you are to where you should have been today, but to where you choose to aim for by some defined planning horizon. So, there may not be a current gap today but a big one compared to the future aspirations.

If we had been diligent enough in the past, we would have had all the performance data we needed, relevant for each of the processes that we have architected. Perhaps at the end of our architecture journey, if there ever is one, we would have all of the measured performance statistics we need, but that is a dream in almost every enterprise.

Realistically, we will have some relevant data, and we should use what we can. We can also run data analytics to get whatever else we can derive or infer to help take away personal biases regarding performance. However, we will still need to rely on market feedback from the stakeholders themselves and not allow internally biased players to solely hazard an opinion. Look at customer service calls, social media observation, and feedback from those on the front lines. These anecdotal sources of success or dissatisfaction will still be important to inform the assessment.

Fast track pain and gain

As indicated earlier, your best investment bets are with those processes that potentially can deliver the highest stakeholder results and strategic value (Highest Gain) and simultaneously are the worst performers today relative to what's needed going forward (Highest Pain). The combination of High Pain and High Gain deserves our attention and is the best bet for overall business performance improvement. A comprehensive assessment of all of the possible factors inputting to defining the need for change is often not saleable in the early days of business architecture efforts, especially the first time through. In these cases, we recommend a fast-tracked approach to prioritization based on a triage tactic whereby we assess everything in the process architecture down to level 2 processes, but usually not deeper, for all core processes and to level 1 for most guiding and enabling processes. This is a rough guideline. You may choose your scope differently.

Process gain

Using the North Star as a general reference point, we would select the processes (as represented by their numbers in the chevron in Figure11-4) that potentially contribute the most versus the least and those in-between. This is a triage since we try to ensure equal processes in each zone to avoid everything being lumped as most important to our intentions. We do this while deliberately ignoring the performance gap of each process for now. We will get to that next. A poorly performing process is not necessarily important in and of itself just because it is not working as well as we would like. Raw strategic contribution is what we are looking for here.

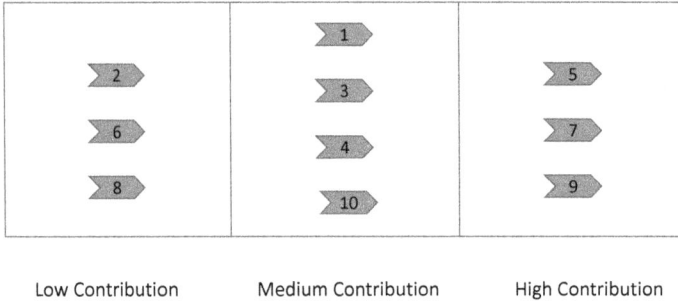

| Low Contribution | Medium Contribution | High Contribution |

Figure 11-4. Process gain.

High contribution items will contribute most to the North Star and the customer value proposition. These are the ones that will differentiate us in the marketplace and make us distinctive compared to our competition. We require world-class capability and performance for these.

Medium contribution processes are those whereby we have to be at par with others in our industry or market space. Being worse will be noticed and hurt us with our customers who expect a reasonable base level of performance. On the other hand, being better may not help much and just cost us for not much leverage. Customers may not even notice superior performance here or care. They will not value these any more if we were world-class with them. It's not that important to them, but they will notice if we are worse than expected

Low contribution processes, relatively speaking, are not valued as much by customers, nor do they contribute much to marketplace success. They may not even be apparent to recipients. If we are just adequate, that's not an issue. Internally, no one likes to hear that their work area is not as important as some other things happening in the organization. All areas are important, but excellence in some is more valuable than others to realize our strategy. Note that this is a relative triage into more or less equal thirds, and we force-fit these to be able to focus on attaining strategic intent and achieving what matters most.

Likewise, we will take the same processes (as shown by the numbers in the chevron in Figure 11-5) and map them to the degree of performance gap they exhibit today compared to what we would want them to be in the future. As mentioned, we can achieve this by comparing feedback from performance tracking or analytics, or it can be anecdotal, whatever you can get your hands on.

When considering Pain, we apply some established criteria to help formalize what otherwise could easily become a politicized exercise.

Process pain

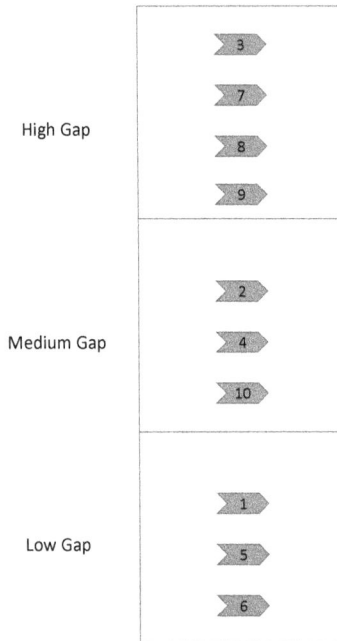

Figure 11-5. Process pain.

Some senior staff want to gain resources for investment into an area they care about, so they claim it is very badly broken to raise the priority. Others, for personal reasons, do not want others to see their area as poorly performing, so defend their turf and push away changes. We ask:

How well could the process achieve the defined Process Ideal Outcome(s)?

- Are the desired results of the process achieved now?
- Will it be able to meet future needs?

Is the process executed consistently by all performers in the business?

- Is the process repeatable across the Enterprise or done differently by different groups and locations?
- Is the process formalized, that is, structured and defined in a shareable way?
- Do people involved understand their roles and responsibilities?
- Is there a clear direction and set of reference materials on what to do?

Are the resources efficiently utilized?

Note that resources are not just human. We must consider — technical, financial, and other aspects.
- Are resources over or under-utilized?
- Are resources efficiently utilized during normal and exceptional circumstances?
- Is the process efficient, or is there wasted activity?

Mapping of pain and gain

Combining these two perspectives will give us a process prioritization grid, which may look like Figure 11-6. This combines the two triage exercises into an actionable heat map that focuses on the processes in the top right corner that are the best fit if we can gain the resources needed to rebuild them, renew all capabilities, and tackle the information changes. High Gain and High Pain is where the action should be. Once some other feasibility issues are considered such as technical feasibility, operational feasibility, dependencies, financial feasibility, cultural feasibility, and even political feasibility, we can focus on the technical, human, and physical resources requiring investment and the right change program so we can develop our roadmap.

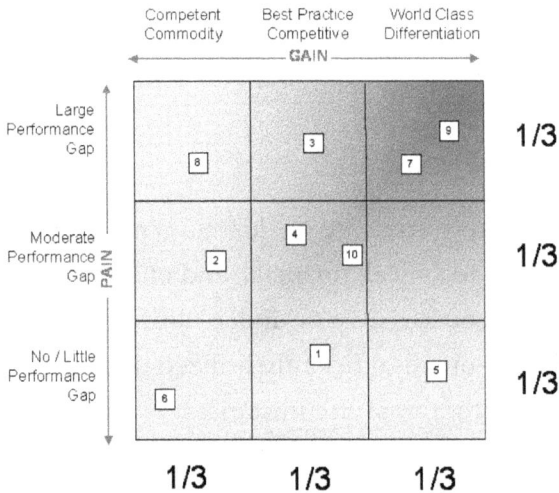

Figure 11-6. Process Pain – Gain prioritization grid.

We may also use this fast-tracked positioning to act as a macro filter to get a short list for a more comprehensive assessment of priorities, leaving out low gain and low pain. We will conduct a more comprehensive analysis of the top right four blocks of the nine-block, which appears in Figure 11-7.

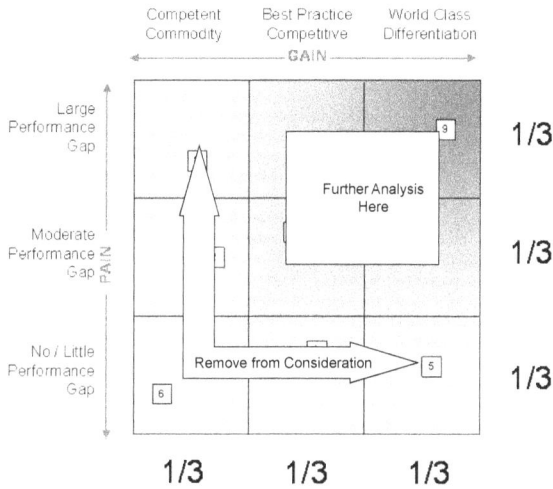

Figure 11-7. Macro filter for prioritization.

Comprehensive pain and gain

Comprehensive gain

The fast-tracked approach shown in the previous section of this chapter developed a rough cut at the prioritization. This may serve you well if you are not highly mature in business architecture or it's your first time on the journey. It can also filter the set of processes to be further assessed so it acts as a first step. A more comprehensive approach can compare the processes one by one against the criteria point by point of the North Star and performance gap factors.

In this approach, Gain calculations are made process by process against each separate point on the North Star and factored by their pre-agreed weighting contribution. The In our example, Gain calculations are assessed according to a scale from 1 to 5 with each number having the following increasing contribution for each process:

1 = No contribution

2 = A Little

3 = A moderate amount

4 = A large amount

5 = A significant amount

Of course, you will have to define what these values mean and work through a few examples together before applying them to the full set of processes that you are tackling. We must all be on the same assessment page and consistent about what 'moderate' really means relative to 'a little.' After applying the gain criteria, we factor each process by the weighted contribution for all North Star points' total set of contributions. This appears in Figure 11-8 for a particular process, 'Create Product or Service.' In this case, it is agreed that the chosen process contributes 'A Moderate Amount' to the North Star aim of 'Increase Online and Mobile Services,' with a score of 3. When multiplying the 3 by the weighting factor of 20%, its value is .6. Doing the same for each North Star statement, we will end up with a net score of 4.1 out of a possible maximum of 5. When we compare this to the other processes evaluated, we discover that this process ranks first in Gain contribution. Therefore, we would map it to the far right on the Pain/Gain Grid horizontal axis relative to all the others ignoring the vertical dimension of Pain yet to come.

PROCESS GAIN WORKSHEET		Scoring for all criteria: 1=None, 2=A Little, 3=A Moderate Amount, 4=A Large Amount, 5=A Significant Amount														Page 1	
Organization: BPT Bank																	
Value Chain: Provide Consumer Financial Services		Strategic Outcome Statements and Weighting															
		Increase Online and Mobile Services		Sustain Regulatory Compliance		Increase Wallet Share		Increase Market Share		Decrease Errors							
		20%		10%		30%		30%		10%						Adj. Score Total	Rank
Process Name	Process #	Score	Adj. Score	Score	Adj. Score	Score	Adj. Score	Score	Adj. Score	Score	Adj. Score	Score	Adj. Score	Score	Adj. Score		
Develop Strategic Plans	1	2	.4	2	.2	4	1.2	4	1.2	2	.2					3.2	6
Mitigate Regulatory Risk	2	1	.2	5	.5	2	.6	2	.6	4	.4					2.3	10
Create P or S	3	3	.6	2	.2	5	1.5	5	1.5	3	.3				4.1	4.1	1
Identify P or S Need	4	4	.8	1	.1	5	1.5	4	1.2	2	.2					3.8	4
Enhance P or S	5	3	.6	2	.2	4	1.2	4	1.2	4	.4					3.6	5
Provide IT Services	6	4	.8	2	.2	3	.9	3	.9	4	.4					3.2	6
Deliver Consumer Services	7	4	.8	4	.4	4	1.2	4	1.2	3	.3					3.9	2
Settle Consumer Complaints and Claims	8	1	.2	3	.3	4	1.2	3	.9	2	.2					2.8	8
Promote P or S Brand	9	3	.6	2	.2	5	1.5	5	1.5	1	.1					3.9	2
Provide Employees	10	2	.4	2	.2	4	1.2	2	.6	3	.3					2.7	9

Figure 11-8. Weighted gain contribution.

Comprehensive pain

As with the Gain formalization, we calculate the Pain using the factors indicated for lack of performance shown earlier in this chapter. Once more, we will have to define what the scoring amounts really mean, gaining a common understanding of the difference between 'Sometimes' and 'Rarely.' For example:

1 = Always

2 = Mostly

3 = Sometimes

4 = Rarely

5 = Never

This appears in Figure 11-9 for 'Create Product or Service.' In this case, it is agreed that the chosen process 'Never' achieves its ideal direct outcome, which is a score of 5. Doing the same for each Pain criterion, we will end up with a net score of 13. If we wanted to normalize the scoring, we would divide each by 3 so that the Pain and Gain both were taken out of a max of 5 and the size of the axes is the same resulting in a square grid for ease of readability. When we compare this to the other processes evaluated, we discover that this process ranks first in Pain, and we would map it towards the top of the Pain/Gain Grid vertical axis relative to all the others.

PROCESS PAIN WORKSHEET		Scoring for all criteria: 1=Always, 2=Mostly, 3=Sometimes, 4=Rarely, 5=Never				
Organization: BPT Bank						Page 1
Value Chain: Provide Consumer Financial Services		Process Performance Pain Criteria (1 – 5) Relative to the ideal state of the process				
Process Name	Process #	The process achieves its ideal direct outcome Score	The process can be executed consistently Score	All resources are efficiently utilized in the execution of the process Score	Pain Summary	Pain Ranking
Develop Strategic Plans	1	3	2	2	7	10
Mitigate Regulatory Risk	2	4	3	2	9	8
Create P or S	3	+ 5	+ 4	+ 4 ⟶	13	1
Identify P or S Need	4	2	4	4	10	6
Enhance P or S	5	3	5	3	11	2
Provide IT Services	6	5	3	3	11	2
Deliver Consumer Services	7	3	3	5	11	2
Settle Consumer Complaints and Claims	8	3	5	3	11	2
Promote P or S Brand	9	3	2	5	10	6
Provide Employees	10	3	2	4	9	8

Figure 11-9. Weighted pain contribution.

As in the fast-track version, these will be mapped on the grid to visualize the top right corner prioritization, as shown in Figure 11-10.

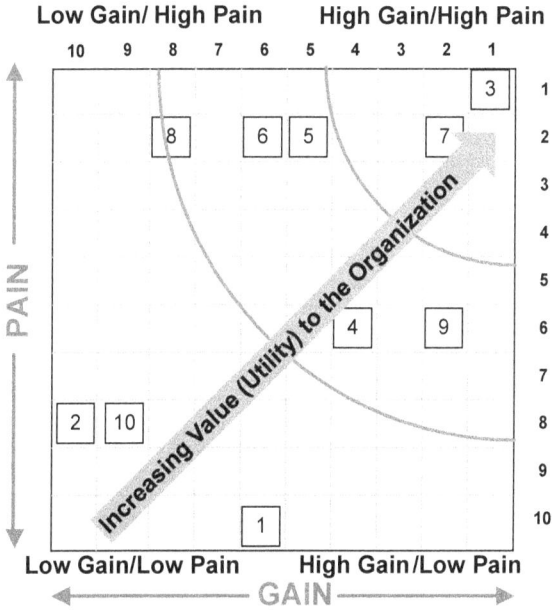

Figure 11-10. Comprehensive Pain - GAIN version.

We can show this by placing raw scores from the calculations for each axis of Pain and Gain. Alternatively, we can show relative ordinal ranking based on the scores. This latter approach makes it more obvious to see the differences, so it is my preference. Based on this model, we can draw utility arcs to show the initial thoughts on the grouping of the change program and possibly the budgeting buckets with a relatively higher percentage of investment resources going to those closer to the top right.

Up next

The coming chapters will examine and develop the priorities developed in this chapter into a detailed plan for capability development and implementation for resource allocation and a roadmap for transformation.

CHAPTER 12

Building the Change Portfolio

So far, we have tackled the efforts to Define the Business and Design the Business and now have entered the Build the Business quadrant by prioritizing Process, Capability, or Information led high pain and high gain processes, information types, or capabilities. Again, the quadrants appear in Figure 12-1. In the overall scheme, we have collected, connected, and now we will continue to correct the dots.

Without the structured models as a baseline and defined strategic intentions and performance measurement in place, we could not have established our priorities in a structured manner. But these priorities are not quite yet the portfolio of actual changes to be made in the sections. This chapter helps articulate what is needed to plan and schedule a set of specific changes that will require people, money, and time to get the job done. As a result, we will allocate our scarce financial and human resources to deliver the best return on that investment.

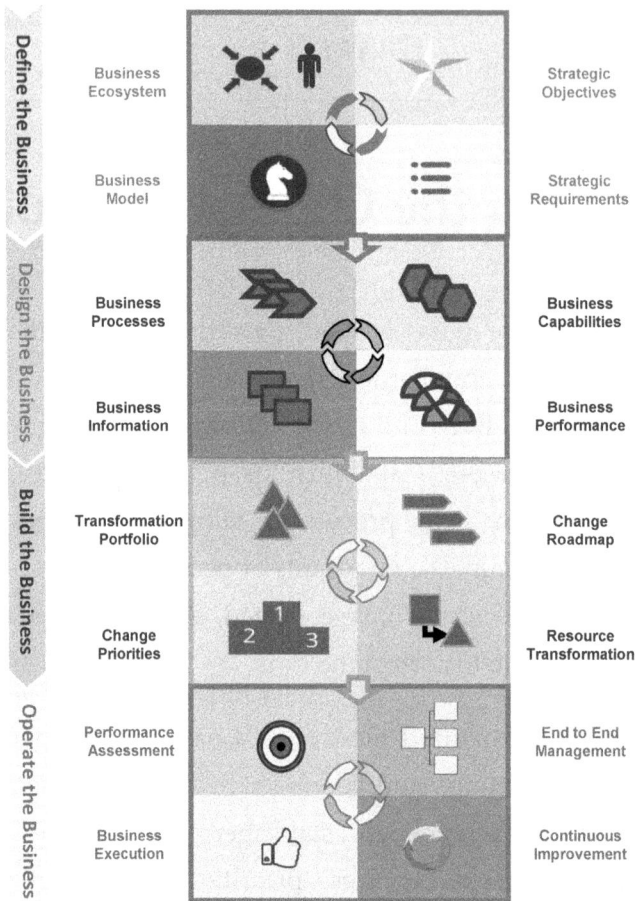

Figure 12-1. Comprehensive business architecture framework and foundational methodology.

Interconnections

When making strategic prioritization choices, we can prioritize according to information types, capabilities, or processes as our starting category, recognizing that we would still have to align the others regardless of which one went first. We chose processes as our major organizer for illustration purposes. For now, I will stay with that to show the interconnections and need for a complete set of items to deal with. If you start with something else, you can follow the same logic. Examples of different starting points appear in the next chapter. Figure 12-2 shows that these three primary domains are the first order.

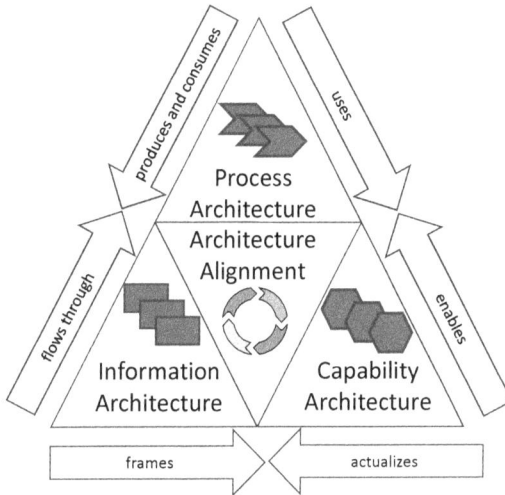

Figure 12-2. Three primary domains.

We must address all three domains regardless of our starting point. Our processes create or use information. They also employ the capabilities developed to get work done in the way it is envisioned. Capabilities define the resources needed to enable the processes to work with the appropriate rules and tools. They also transform the information via the tools enacted. The information flows through the processes to be available when needed, and it defines the nature and requirements of the capabilities to manage such information.

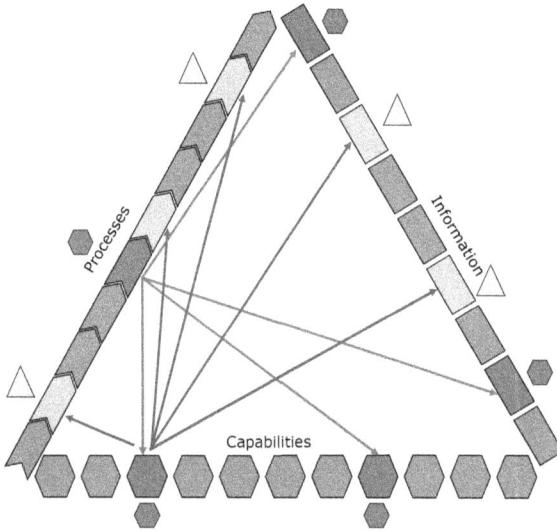

Figure 12-3. Three primary domains.

Looking at a conceptualized situation in Figure 12-3 whereby a particular process had been identified as a top priority to address, we can see that we must consider the other domains to lay out the whole portfolio and subsequently the roadmap. In this case, the one process chosen needs to have four sufficient capabilities available to perform to the needs of that process's customers. It also uses or produces information in two information concept areas. In the illustration two information types and two capabilities are connected and need adjustment and sufficient investment to make the process work properly.

However, there is a typical problem shown in this example. Three other processes also use one of the weak capabilities that needs to be renewed. We must be sure that in changing that capability based on the needs of the first process, we do not damage it as far as the other three are concerned. Likewise, that capability may deal with multiple data sets used by other capabilities and processes. This is where you will wish you knew how all the parts impact one another—how they are connected— before starting to make changes and unwittingly introducing unintended consequences that will have to be fixed or undone later. These unknown complexities may lead to delays in implementation or capability and process failure.

Looking again at a subset of our hypothetical process architecture and capability map from Figure 12-4, we see that 'Settle Consumer Complaints and Claims' is a very poor process. It needs several capabilities, as shown in the line below the processes in the diagram. Some of these are working well enough for the process, but the 'Credit Score Assessment' capability is causing many heartaches. If we fixed this process solely for 'Settle Consumer Complaints and Claims,' we could easily provide an updated capability that no longer works well for the other processes such as 'Evaluate Character' and 'Prevent Consumer Losses' because we did not consider those needs.

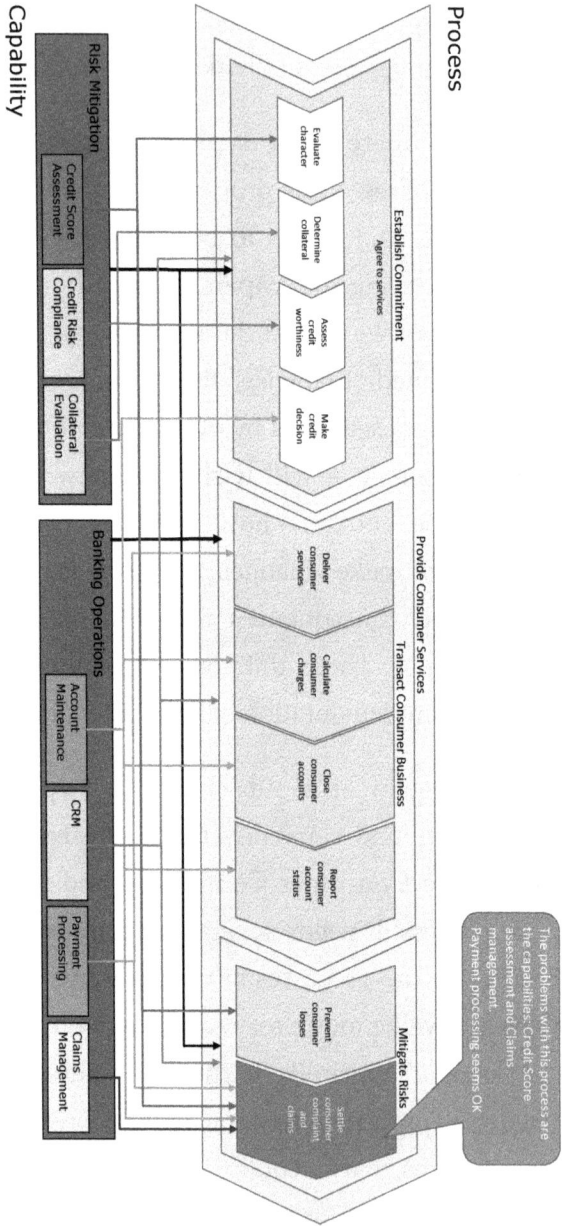

Figure 12-4. Process architecture and capability map interactions.

Defining capability items for change

The message is that we have to assess the potential impacts and interactions among several items to enact the right change. The Burlton Hexagon can play a critical role in sorting out the changes to be implemented that may end up in the change portfolio and roadmap. Figure 12-5 contains a heat-mapped version of the change areas that are needed most versus less so and not at all. Also shown is a sample articulation of what specifically those changes may be.

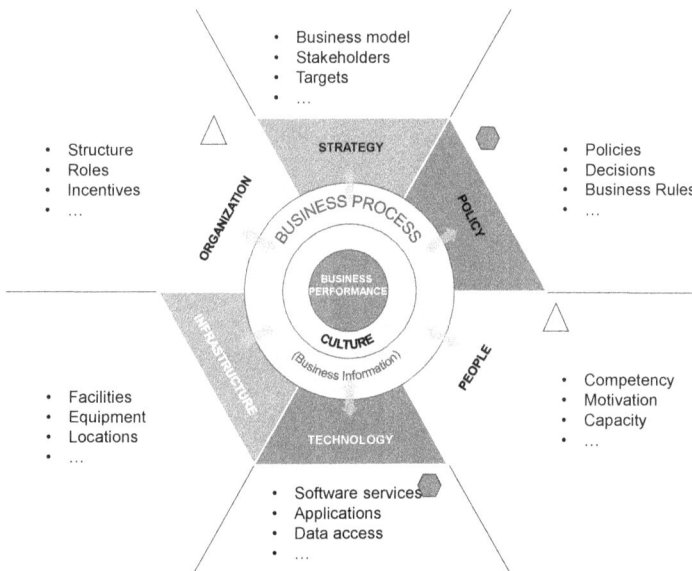

Figure 12-5. Heat-mapped version of Burlton Hexagon.

We can define specific changes in terms of developing solutions relevant to the categories of the hexagon—the work packages. There may be more than one aspect of change for any hexagon category, as shown in Figure 12-6. At the same time, we may not have to tackle something in every category if it's not needed. Building the solution may involve combining aspects of the same category or group several under one team, if that makes sense.

Category	Insights
Business Performance	Measure the amount of customer claims we have to pay out due to mistakes in banking operations
Business Process	Document the process and make it consistent
Business Information	Share the transactional data daily with the group that does the claims work. Provide access to what really happened.
Culture	Get the teams to share in the motivation of eliminating errors and delays and reconciling issues sooner. Have them meet weekly.
Strategy	No issues.
Policy	Update our customer service policy to be more trusting of the customer.
Organization	Seat the claims people close to the customer care group and have them report to the same manager.
People	Train our claims staff on how to deal with difficult customers.
Technology	Replace the transactional systems and claims system to one that has the holistic view of customer history.
Infrastructure	Not an issue.

Figure 12-6. Categories of the hexagon needed for change.

For example, an organizational restructure, a change to managers' performance plans, and an update of the business governance scheme—all part of the Organization sector—should be done by the same team as one project rather than three separate plans. So, we will group them in the roadmap. Likewise, we may find that certain work packages from different categories may have a natural affinity and should be combined. Perhaps some technology changes are better combined with some process redesign if, for instance, a technology largely automates and dictates how that process will work. We could easily combine a human competency upgrade with business rules and a culture change program and have it tackled as one. See Figure 12-7.

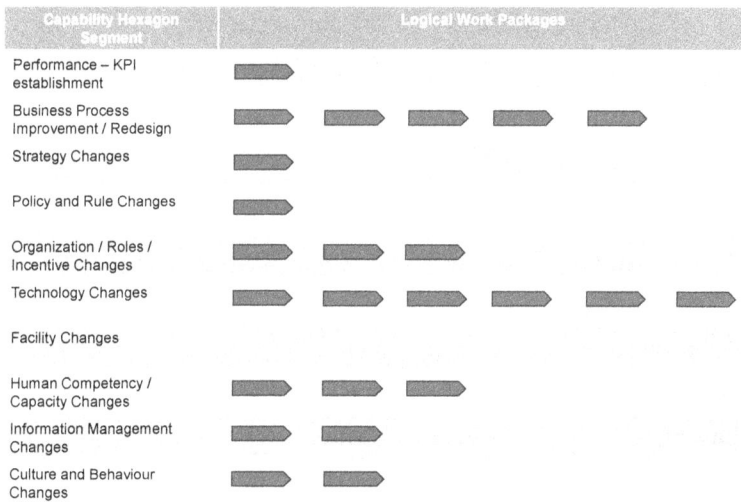

Capability Hexagon Segment	Logical Work Packages				
Performance – KPI establishment	▶				
Business Process Improvement / Redesign	▶	▶	▶	▶	▶
Strategy Changes	▶				
Policy and Rule Changes	▶				
Organization / Roles / Incentive Changes	▶	▶	▶		
Technology Changes	▶	▶	▶	▶	▶	▶
Facility Changes					
Human Competency / Capacity Changes	▶	▶	▶		
Information Management Changes	▶	▶			
Culture and Behaviour Changes	▶	▶			

Figure 12-7. Multiple aspects of a change program

Logical dependencies

Once we have the right projects, the next consideration will be the logical dependencies. It would be unusual for larger transformations to be able to start all aspects of change concurrently. We would normally expect to do some before the others and see them spread over a timeframe. Once we know the totality of change projects, we can turn our attention to the nature of the dependencies among them. Anyone that has done any project activity planning in a project management tool will understand the classic dependencies among one another:

- Does one project have to complete before starting another (a finish to start connection)?
- Does one activity not have to wait to start but cannot finish if the other has not (a finish-to-finish relationship)?
- Can one start after another has started but only after a certain amount of time has gone by (a start to start with a lag)?
- Can they start together (start to start)?

Laying this out on a logical sequencing diagram will move us to the next question. See Figure 12-8.

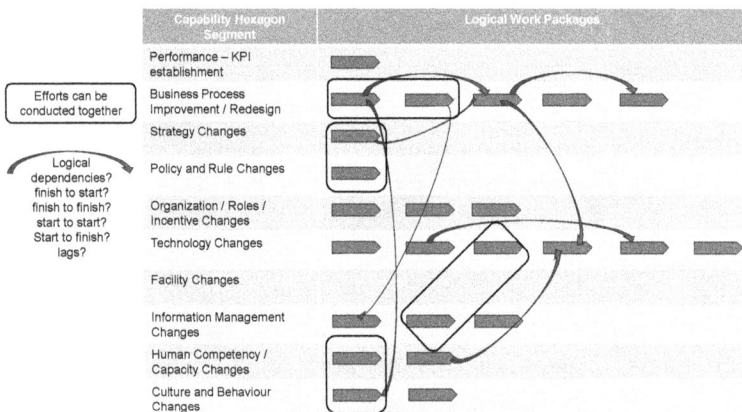

Figure 12-8. Logical dependencies among components.

Estimates, resources, and calendar constraints

The next step in determining the timed program of change is to determine the human and financial estimates required to get the work done. Each work package will need to determine what project roles are needed and what type and level of each professional worker is needed to fill that role.

In addition, you will need to estimate what amount of that resource will be needed for each part of the effort. Do not forget at this point, to consider the resource availability that will be needed from business stakeholders and operational managers to participate in the effort while they continue to execute their day-to-day business. There are always these types of constraints that will affect the timing of initiatives.

There will also be a critical consideration of the reality of the calendar. There are times when people are just not available due to statutory holidays such as Thanksgiving in the US and other seasonal, cultural, or religious events elsewhere. From a different perspective, there may be unmovable deadlines including the requirement to comply with regulatory requirements, such as tax or reporting mandates by a particular date, or facing the inevitability of severe penalties if compliance dates are not met.

Lastly, you have to consider what other programs are happening and what other commitments are being sought from those needed to do the work or get involved in the initiatives. If you only have one database administrator and that individual is committed to existing efforts, you will have to get creative, find new resources, or accept the timing impacts on your program. Likewise, if the business must make available the experts who know the business best but they are tied up with operational activities or by their involvement in other change efforts, you had better call upon your masterful negotiation skills to get it agreed all around. It is wise to allow for a contingency factor to keep the program on course as unexpected events crop up.

These have to be sorted out through understanding all needs and constraints, negotiation, and balancing to find a Roadmap that works. This will not be easy, and please do not commit to something that you are not confident can be pulled off. If you doubt it now, you will have no contingency during the effort when a surprise comes along—and it will. Governing the oversight of the program roadmap is not going to be a one-time event so re-examine the plan regularly during execution and always strive to be realistic and ever-current. Remember that 'hope is not a plan,' so start with what you trust and believe and nothing less. Figure 12-9 should reflect all we have done prior to this point.

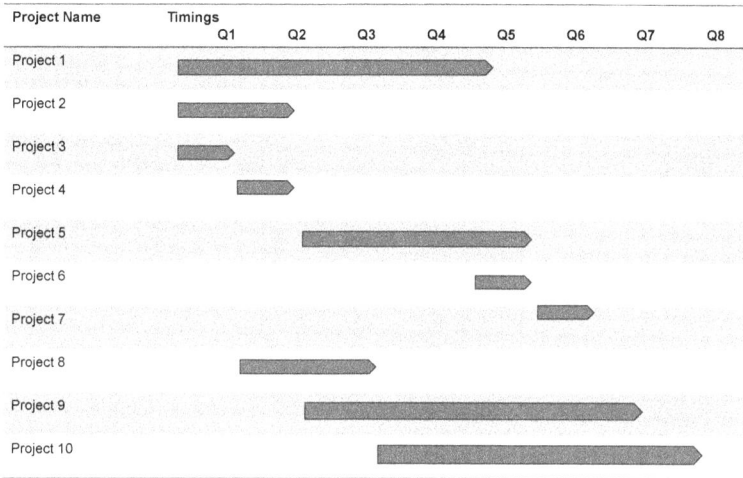

Figure 12-9. Program plan.

Up next

The next chapter will look at organizations that have taken different implementation approaches. Each faced unique challenges and addressed their efforts differently, but all took a holistic point of view, showing that there are alternate ways to take on the challenge.

CHAPTER 13

Freedom within a Framework

In the prior chapters, I have outlined the attributes required for each perspective or domain of business architecture that will assure high professional quality and integrity. In Chapter 2, I referred to the insight of George Box's words, "All models are wrong, but some are useful." Our aim as architects is to be useful, knowing we will not get it perfect and that a long and winding journey is ahead of us. The profession of business architecture is fraught with dogmatic views on how to do things, driven by academics and professionals who seem more concerned with theory than pragmatism.

In reality, I have never faced the same business scenario or drivers more than once, and the path has never been the same. Business architecture is not an end in its own right, but a means to a number of possible ends, each unique to an enterprise at a point in time.

We must solve particular problems or meet acknowledged needs and figure out the appropriate journey, albeit using many reusable techniques sitting in a sufficiently adaptable framework to tackle almost any specific challenge. This should enable us to use appropriate stable approaches and vary when necessary.

Erich Fromm (1900–1980) was a German-born American psychoanalyst and social philosopher who had said in the 1940's:

> *True freedom is not the absence of structure — letting the employees go off and do whatever they want — but rather a clear structure that enables people to work within established boundaries in an autonomous and creative way.*

This is a good mantra for practitioners who must prove business architecture value within their companies. It is the message that I will support in this chapter.

PRG Business Architecture Framework

The Process Renewal Group's Business Architecture framework appears in Figure 13-1. The diagram shows its main logic.

Each of the four main phases shows a circle of learning in the middle that iteratively builds the knowledge over time, but there is no one preset starting point, sequence, and pre-defined depth to pursue. There is logic, but the situation at hand will dictate how to go about it.

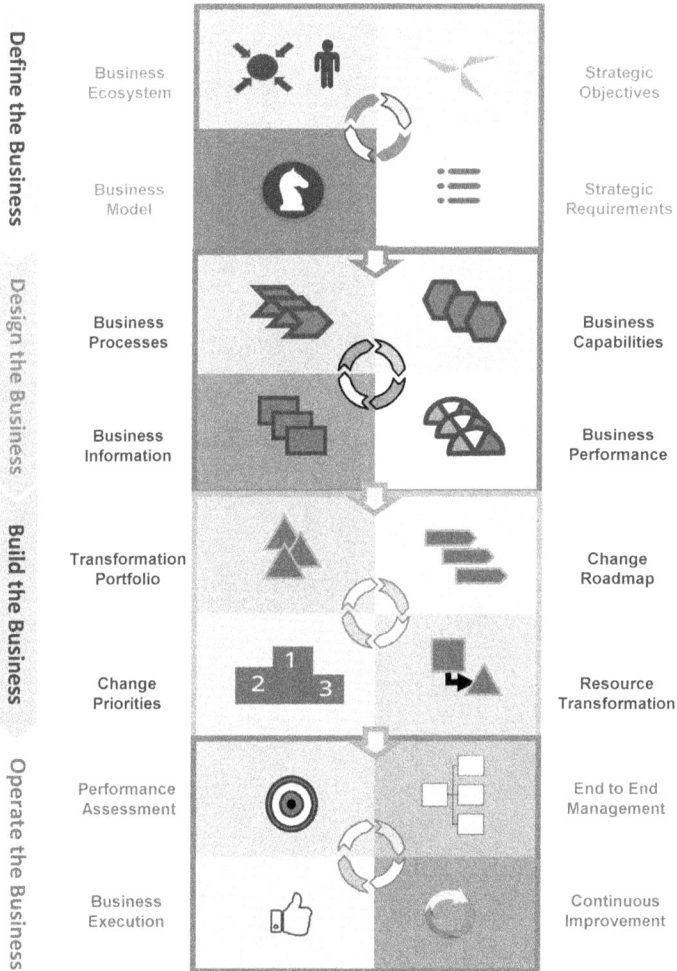

Figure 13-1. Comprehensive business architecture framework and foundational methodology.

Working with the end in mind at the end of the framework, the overall approach simply implies that you cannot optimally *'Operate the Business'* day-to-day if you have not carefully and effectively built the processes, capabilities, systems, and human competencies to do so. It is unusual that we are driven by the goal of architecture perfection for its own purpose. Instead, conducting Business Architecture is lumpy, not smooth, and evolves over time.

There is always the need to quickly and effectively continue to improve the mechanisms utilized to conduct daily work and to question the value of what we currently do. Therefore, all phases, as indicated by the center circular arrows in each phase, should continually help move the organization forward in an appropriately adaptable way.

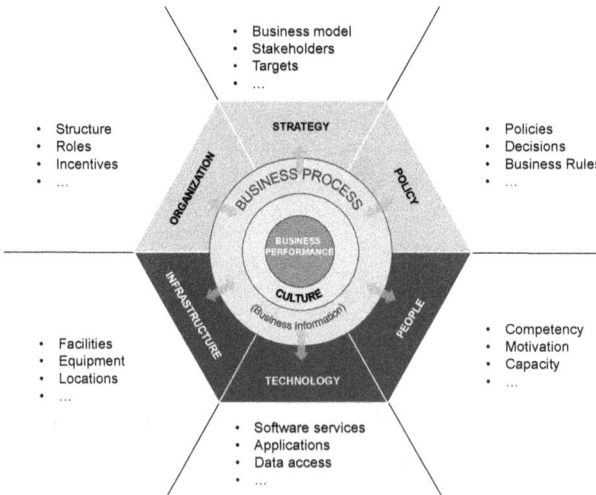

Figure 13-2. The Burlton Hexagon.

Moving from bottom to top in the framework, we need to be sure that we build the right things when we 'Build the Business.' That means we must have ways of identifying the reasons that those things may need to change to populate the transformation portfolio with the right projects to tackle the right changes in the required aspects of the Burlton Hexagon. Then, these must be agreed upon, estimated, and subsequently resourced to schedule a roadmap.

All resources must be committed and available when required to launch the changes as defined by project plans. Then, project teams of various hexagon components in play can conduct and control projects, such as process articulation, technology development, and training production. We can also implement changes to allow operations using new capabilities to start up and keep going. In reality, there are many ways to go about drilling into the various aspects of the framework based on the issue or opportunity that has justified the architecture development with the emphasis needed.

We can view the PRG Framework as a model of key conceptual domains representing the knowledge areas critical to defining the business solution. In Figure 12-3, this diagram represents the types of knowledge we need to capture. The image is not a methodology to be read from any particular starting point but to be understood from one concept box to another by reading the box name and then the connecting box one at a time following the arrow. This shows the fundamental nature of understanding the knowledge needed and the logical connections among the pieces. So, regardless of method, the information in boxes is needed at the end of the day and the relevant connections are made between each shown pair. Again, on tackling the architecture, there will be an emphasis on different aspects based on the mandate given to the architecture team. We show the rectangular shapes in the 'Define the Business' phase, the rounded corner rectangles in the 'Design the Business' phase, and the parallelograms in the 'Build the Business' phase. However, information about any concept can be picked up and enhanced at any point.

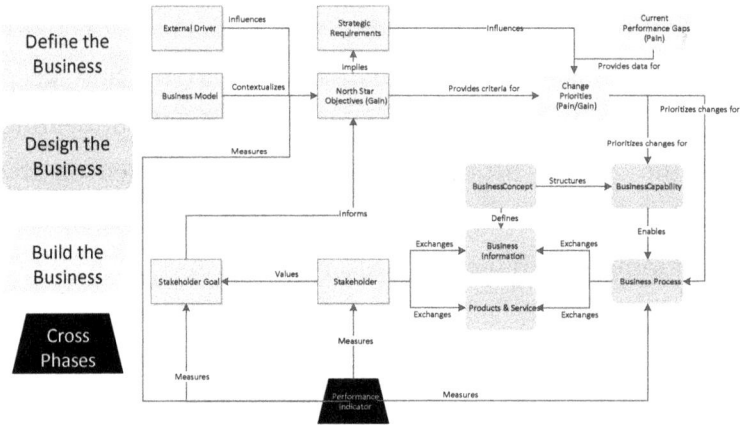

Figure 13-3. The PRG Framework.

Arguments from incumbent professionals

From the dawn of professional management, vociferous arguments have waged over the best methods to conduct enterprise-level analysis and design. A few examples are top-down versus bottom-up, strategy driven versus lean operations, and MBO's versus team empowerment. In the business architecture community, there have been angry debates about process-led (usually from the industrial engineering and business operations crowds), capability-led (usually from the IT enterprise architects), and data as prime (usually from the data quality and master data management folks). So, who is right? Well, the true management consultants would utter their time-tested response of, "it depends." In reality, these all play off of one another, as proposed in Chapter 12 and shown once more in Figure 13-4.

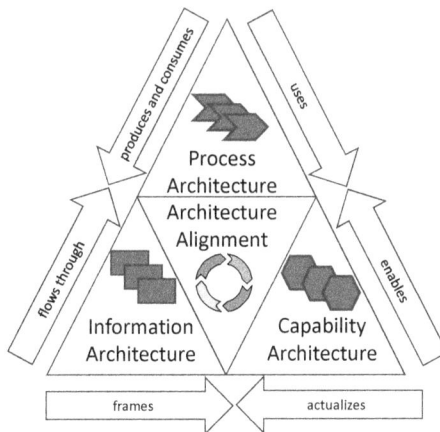

Figure 13-4. Three primary domains.

Understanding the 'it depends' is critical because no one gets to do business architecture without some benefit expected as a return from its investment. That expectation of benefit will drive the style and approach to its realization. As discussed in earlier chapters, there will be differing degrees of emphasis on process, capability, information, or in some balance in the middling zone. Iteration will occur as each domain informs and validates the other iteratively (agile thinking). So, what are the factors that may get us to get going in a defined initial direction?

Drivers for business architecture adoption

The approach to take requires examining external and internal drivers first introduced in Chapter 4 as STEEPL.

External point of view: Pressures

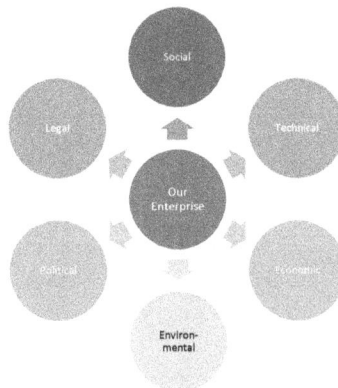

Figure 13-5. External pressures.

Understanding the ecosystem of your enterprise is required to know what is needed in the content and depth of your business architecture. It is also a major factor in deciding how to develop it.

Let's look at each factor and see some sample natural architectural responses for certain pressures.

Social

The predominance of a fast-moving younger market for our products may lead to a response that emphasizes the need for continuing data analytics and ready access to timely and accurate information. This will lead to a data-first approach requiring trust that there is a reliable source of the truth. If your interest is in influencing that market, you will have to know a lot about those in it and reach them easily with the right offerings based on market insights gained from working with rich data sets about them and the market they are in. The implication is to get your data management sorted early since it will be your core asset.

Technological

If your market is financial services, you have to accelerate your move to running with digital solutions and end-to-end digitalized self-services ASAP. This driver argues for the reuse of planned capabilities to shrink the time to market rapidly as well as processes that connect all the dots end-to-end. The technology can then be configured to achieve seamless value delivery and ease of reconfiguration without long delays in development and implementation.

Economic

If you are an airline in today's world, you cannot survive with cost structures completely out of synch with customer revenue volumes. Survival is a major concern, and costs must be taken out to avoid bankruptcy or bailouts. Sound processes will lead the charge because the execution of work is where money is spent. We have to become more efficient while possibly making some other tough capacity reductions.

Environmental

During the pandemic, training companies and educational institutions had to change their delivery methods rapidly and move to virtual delivery for student learning and competency validation. This means they had to establish many new education and administrative processes for everyone, including students, enabled by existing or newly acquired technology. Here processes and capabilities are the key starting point.

Political

With persistent political turmoil and an uncertain future everywhere, government and semi-government agencies must be very flexible, meaning they must build their capabilities for both business and technical ease of re-configuration and their processes built for agility. Assuming this reality is recognized, capabilities and processes are initially both on the table together.

Legal

The flood of regulations and new and updated standards such as Basel in banking, IFRS17 in insurance, and GDPR in any industry require significant changes. They impact data capture and reporting for compliance purposes and avoid punishing penalties for misreporting. To handle it, we have to build new data cohorts and combinations for reporting on data with integrity. Therefore, information management is the key first position.

External point of view: Tendencies

Your industry and marketplace's nature may also bring some inherent architectural style.

Some styles lend themselves naturally to certain industries. Although there are exceptions to the pattern, you can expect business architects in similar businesses to intuitively bend towards similar industry models, reflecting their predominant way of thinking about value creation.

Architecture method and style

I will borrow a phrase from Bruce Silver, a noted thought leader in the process and decision management world. Bruce observes that a variety of approaches to professional practices can be applied utilizing the same modeling notations and tools. Bruce refers to these as 'Method and Style,' and some styles work better than others in different circumstances. By extension, there are ways to produce high-quality model deliverables and ways to miss the mark. Some industries are better served by certain architectural methods and styles than others. Again, "It depends." I am convinced that data-centric, process-centric, or capability-centric are all possible initial choices for certain industries.

Data-centric

Data-centric is a good style for organizations with information capture and distribution at the heart of what they do. You could say that data is their core product or is extremely critical and closely tied to it. Good examples are social media companies, entertainment distributors, and news and knowledge access entities. In addition, some organizations rely almost completely on information to make decisions or manage risk without frequent interactions with external parties. These would include insurance and re-insurance companies that rely on reliable data and algorithms to make investment risk or loss mitigation choices. Others may include social survey and polling firms and rating agencies where data is the basis for selling their services. Recipients of their offerings would be knowledge-oriented decision-makers, often with a financial concern.

Process-centric

Process-centric organizations are many. Service-oriented organizations depend on highly interactive processes to maintain a continuing dialog and tackle various cases and situations as they evolve. The effective adjustment of the flow path while in flight with outside parties and bringing new information to it requires agile processes. Examples are medical organizations such as hospitals and clinics where the patient journey is managed flexibly to reach the immediate patient action.

Government agencies providing citizen services are similar, despite the reality that some are not good at what they are supposed to do. Professional service firms also must execute services in an adaptable manner since the need varies from time to time. Their methods are embedded in or called upon from their processes. Those who process customer information transactions like banks will also have a high degree of process orientation.

Another type of organization that tends towards a process orientation is manufacturing and distribution, which features challenging supply chain costs and risks. Many of these organizations are actually a network of players that have to be working in unison to ultimately deliver physical items to a customer. This is also true of an information supply chain. This type of organization needs smooth, lean operations and seamless service without delays, errors, and rework. Food manufacturers and their grocery clients selling to consumers both need great processes to work in a just-in-time manner. Time is of their essence. Delivery companies need a process perspective to deliver as promised. However, the item may have traveled through more than one country and seen many business partners, distribution centers, and transportation hubs.

Capability-centric

Fast change industries need to have a grip on their processes and have quality data. Still, their driving foundation is typically the capabilities that have to be well-defined and built quickly and, most importantly, change easily. Great capabilities can typically be composed into a configuration that can be disassembled and reused in other configurations. Modern research and development (product-oriented) organizations will strive to design component parts that can be assembled into various products. Think of IKEA and LEGO products as an analogy but apply the same thinking to enabling the business itself. These organizations are driven by speed and ease of change and avoiding re-invention of enabling resources each time a change is required. Typically, this challenge is common in technology companies with significant reuse of system functionality or microservices configurable to a client problem.

Financial service companies are similar, especially when they have many lines of business and markets. For example, there is no point in having a payment capability that is uniquely defined for each of the consumer bank, business bank, and wealth services—a payment is a payment for all. In general, organizations with multiple business lines may wish to define common ways of conducting much of the similar work using the same capabilities but allowing for necessary variations. In addition to needing great customer services, telecommunications companies are typical of industries that have to change often. They would benefit from finding stable capabilities and isolating the variable aspects to avoid changing everything each time something small has to adapt. Business Agility is the driver within these industries.

Internal point of view

In addition to the natural tendencies of particular industries and types of external pressures to prioritize business architectural domains, there are internal reasons why a particular approach may lead. Your fundamental value proposition within a market, your embarkation to a different business strategy, and your strengths and weaknesses will also play a role. In each industry, there is room to differentiate. Not everyone will strive to be the closest to their customers. Some may choose to be more cost-effective and unobtrusive. Instead of focusing on service, they may focus on price. There is room for all propositions in any industry. Usually, though, each organization will have a style close to an industry norm.

Value proposition

Your main value proposition articulates which orientation your organization is primarily striving to attain in its marketplace. Operational excellence, customer intimacy, and innovation are three classic ones. Each one provides an implied method and style.

Operational excellence

Operationally excellence-oriented organizations have an unrelenting cost concern. They want no wasted effort or time delays in the workflows while assuring that the quality of their products and services are uncompromised. They are passionate about everything being right and that all work is done in the right way while optimizing resources. Their focus is on having no gaps in the workflow and effective handoffs where required. Connecting the Business Process dots is their main concern. Data quality is usually the next concern, especially if poor data results in extra work, time, and process cost.

Customer intimacy

Consumer intimacy strives to get and keep customers for the long run. The lifetime value of the relationship with them is the major concern with every customer. The relationship feels personal. In this sense, the products and services may vary over time, and any specific product may become secondary to the retention of the relationship. It is more about the strong trust developed between players. Quality of service is paramount. The experience is important—even critical. All employees must exhibit behaviors that show that they have the customer's best interests at heart. To make this proposition work, we must have significant knowledge about the partners in the relationship, appreciate the relevant wants and needs of the customer, and deal with them positively and proactively. Deep knowledge based on the customer's place in life and relevant preferences is essential. Data orientation is a normal first concern when you know a lot about those you are serving. Great processes to keep interactions smooth may also be important.

Innovation

Organizations facing time-in-market and time-to-market pressures must become very good and fast at changing what and how things get done. Those who continuously bring innovative products and services to market as a strategy, such as mobile devices, to catch up to or get ahead of their competitors and continually adapt must establish the necessary building blocks. Establishing a set of configurable capabilities (reusable parts of the business), will be the challenge and priority.

Change in strategy

	Helpful	Harmful
Internal	Strengths	Weaknesses
External	Opportunities	Threats

Figure 13-6. Change in strategy.

Organizations these days find themselves rapidly moving into and out of positions of strength and weakness, as shown in Figure 13-6, relative to a set of fast-moving external opportunities and threats. As a result, they have to examine their strategy regularly and decide on a course of action to renew flagging weaknesses and turn them into needed strengths so long as they can realize the implementation of the required change.

Many organizations are now reaching out to business architects to formulate a suitable response. For example, it is not unusual to see organizations implement a new technology to help them. Some have decided to acquire capability through partnerships, acquisition, or corporate consolidation. Some have realized that they must scale the business to be competitive or more cost-effective. Some need to comply with new regulations or suffer reputational risks and significant penalties. Some realize they must adapt to a competitor's actions or new market opportunity or lose it forever. Some are caught in a sweeping industry-wide disruption and must act just to survive against new entrants. The strategic choice can be proactive or reactive, but the pressures of threat and opportunity are real for everyone.

> *A Business Architecture is needed to turn a strategic change decision into a solution effectively, but the approach of method and style must fit the challenge. One way is not right for all.*

Organizational strategic response examples

Every situation is different, and you have to find the right approach for your situation. It always depends. Additional considerations may be determined by where you are on your architectural journey. You may have been at this for a while and already have some aspects well covered and an inventory of robust models. If you are more mature with well-established and modeled processes, perhaps moving to reusable capabilities may be in order or vice versa. Also, do not ignore the politics of the organization. Some powerful players may have strong opinions—well justified or not—which may dictate what is achievable.

The following will illustrate several examples of how some organizations chose to attack the business architecture. I hid the names to protect specific identities.

Regulatory agency—Business renewal and IT replacement

Ecosystem

- Operates to monitor and assure compliance with regulated products and safety practices based on regulations legislated by government and industry standards bodies

Situation

- Over the years, mandated to regulate more and more types of professional coverage
- Each area of coverage has unique rules derived from different legislation, has historically exercised different approaches to meet its mandate, and each has evolved inside its own organizational silo
- Many areas of coverage had very similar services but each developed their processes differently
- Disparate IT solutions have used different terminology for similar ideas and ran isolated software solutions despite a common flow of logic
- Some baseline IT technology in place was about to go out of vendor support

Architecture method and style

- Initial focus was on a shared strategic intention and enterprise KPIs
- A process architecture was developed to provide a management framework to assure similar work across mandated professional areas
- An information concept model was built to obtain common meaning and normalization of terminology needs
- Process prioritization was derived based on architecture, strategy, and a roadmap developed to rollout changes
- A deep dive was made into user-centric process design and IT requirements for capabilities to be shared

Financial asset investment company—Audit and compliance rethink

Ecosystem

- Deals with pension funds invested on behalf of national government and institutional stakeholders

Situation

- Strong enterprise architecture heritage for IT solutions with strong software applications perspective

- Business processes previously developed but only for usage within functional departments for controls and audit purposes not aligned to clients of the business
- Unmaintainable, out-of-date, detailed business functional descriptions in text documents
- Essential to show financial and operational risk compliance with auditors and avoid reputational risk to investors and clients

Architecture method and style

- Initial focus on doing an end-to-end process architecture in stealth (behind the scenes) mode
- Revisited enterprise architecture to incorporate process architecture and establish a governance framework for IT work
- Function by function, incrementally gained acceptance for a cross-functional model of processes with alignment to data lineage across functions due to changing audit needs
- Gained acceptance by working with the financial governance and risk group and work the processes down to auditable workflows
- Replaced functional text descriptions with process models, accepted by auditors and established process owners

Government ministry—Digitalization for new citizen service offering

Ecosystem

- Judicial Services for civil disputes for citizens of a Canadian province

Situation

- Civil justice cases were following the same rigorous court-based approach as criminal ones resulting in overwhelming backlog, delays, and cancellations of cases due to the expiry of statutes of limitations
- Need was recognized to reduce court bottlenecks (delays and resource constraints) due to small civil cases that were the majority in volume but came with significant judicial administrative overhead
- Decision was made to handle civil cases through a peer-to-peer digital platform to avoid low value-added adjudication and unclog the judicial system
- Rewrote legislation to allow a new technology platform to enable self-service management of disputes asynchronously and virtually

Architecture method and style

- Initially identified the data needed to guide cases through to resolution
- Established a visionary process architecture and optimized the workflow model satisfying various

scenarios tied to data, and legal evidence creation and usage
- Role-played scenarios based on various personas and user journeys to validate data structure and self-service digitalized process viability
- Built wireframes and ran prototypes with numerous justice stakeholders to validate feasibility of new automated services
- Developed a complete business model for a new government agency to administer the business solution in market

Insurance company—Redesign operations

Ecosystem
- Re-Insurance services for life and health insurance companies globally

Situation
- Company strategy featured significant growth aspirations—expand global reach and outgrow the market
- Company acquired another player in the industry in a different global region with different processes, data types and structure, and regulations, as well as totally different technology platforms

- To gain efficiencies and to scale globally, decided to integrate company operations and design for additional acquisitions to join in as they happen
- Concurrently, significant industry regulatory changes were announced with massively different data structures needed and huge penalties for non-compliance in new reporting structures

Architecture method and style

- Evaluated upcoming data content and structure needs and access to historical records challenge of unavailability of required data
- Developed a concept model to assure semantic consistency across all regions
- Established the process architecture and developed compliant process workflow models in detail for all regions involving a global team of business experts
- Identified required common IT capabilities and roadmap for tackling them
- Developed requirements for each capability group and conducted software assessment for global usage
- Re-examined roles, processes, data actioned, and relevant decision rules

Business architecture can provide a rich knowledge set to enable transformation and sustain a business's ability to remain relevant and agile. However, it must not be seen as or treated like a cookbook. It is not an invariant methodology. The arguments over practices are a waste of effort and are unprofessional. There is no right one approach that will always work. I guarantee you that it will always be different, so you must be ready for that. A mature business architect will know this and find the way through the minefield of methodological opinions and prejudices that undoubtedly will come up. She, despite personal preference, will listen, propose, adjust, and ultimately gain agreement for what makes sense given the situation. He will gain consensus of what to include, where to start, how broad and deep to go, how iterative to be, what resources should be marshaled, what is sufficient for the purpose, and how to retain the knowledge gained for later leverage as other efforts need to call upon the knowledge base.

The development of a comprehensive set of architectural domains is unlikely to come in one go. Business architecture will require diligence, patience, common sense, and a whole lot of judgement and passion. I wish you all the best. It may be a rocky ride, but it will not be boring.

Index

www.ingramcontent.com/pod-product-compliance
Lightning Source LLC
Chambersburg PA
CBHW071539210326
41597CB00019B/3050